T0408341

RESEARCH IN ECONOMIC HISTORY

RESEARCH IN ECONOMIC HISTORY

EDITED BY

SHAWN KANTOR

Florida State University, USA
National Bureau of Economic Research, USA

AND

CARL T. KITCHENS

Florida State University, USA
National Bureau of Economic Research, USA

United Kingdom – North America – Japan
India – Malaysia – China

Emerald Publishing Limited
Emerald Publishing, Floor 5, Northspring, 21-23 Wellington Street, Leeds LS1 4DL

First edition 2025

Reprints and permissions service
Contact: www.copyright.com

British Library Cataloguing in Publication Data
A catalogue record for this book is available from the British Library

ISBN: 978-1-83608-929-2 (Print)
ISBN: 978-1-83608-928-5 (Online)
ISBN: 978-1-83608-930-8 (Epub)

ISSN: 0363-3268 (Series)

INVESTOR IN PEOPLE

CONTENTS

List of Contributors   *vii*

Provincial Health Inequalities in Spain Since 1860   *1*
Gregori Galofré-Vilà and María Gómez León

The Geography of Infectious Disease and the European Marriage Pattern   *27*
Kirsten de Beurs, Kyle Harper and Le Wang

Economic Bonanza and Wealth Inequality: Evidence From Tax Records for Lima, Peru   *53*
Luis Felipe Zegarra

Can Land Inequality Negatively Affect Human Capital? The American Case, 1950–1970   *77*
Bárbara Tundidor

Federal Preemption of Local Government Telegraph Franchise Entry Barriers   *127*
Aaron M. Honsowetz

The Anatomy of a Policy Failure: Nixon's Attempt to Control Inflation   *157*
Burton A. Abrams and James L. Butkiewicz

LIST OF CONTRIBUTORS

Burton A. Abrams	University of Delaware, USA
Kirsten de Beurs	Wageningen University & Research, The Netherlands
James L. Butkiewicz	University of Delaware, USA
Gregori Galofré-Vilà	Universitat de València, Spain
María Gómez León	Universitat de València, Spain
Kyle Harper	University of Oklahoma, USA
Aaron M. Honsowetz	Bethany College, USA
Bárbara Tundidor	University Carlos III of Madrid, Spain
Le Wang	Virginia Tech, USA
Luis Felipe Zegarra	Pontificia Universidad Católica del Perú, Lima, Peru; CENTRUM Católica Graduate Business School, Lima, Peru

PROVINCIAL HEALTH INEQUALITIES IN SPAIN SINCE 1860

Gregori Galofré-Vilà and María Gómez León

Universitat de València, Spain

ABSTRACT

Using annual mortality rates at the provincial level for men and women, we construct a Gini index to estimate changes in regional health inequalities since 1860 in Spain. We find a long steady decline in health inequality across provinces from 1860 until today, interrupted by World War I and the Spanish Civil War. Over the 40 years of Franco's rule, health inequality stopped its downward trend and rose. Today, regional differences across provinces are at their lowest historical levels.

Keywords: Health; mortality; regional; Gini; inequality; Spain

JEL codes: J11; N23; N24; N93; N94

1. INTRODUCTION

Before the COVID-19 pandemic, Spain ranked among the healthiest places to live. Around 1880, the average life expectancy of a newborn boy in Spain was 30 years, compared to 33 years in Italy, 39 in the United States, and 43 in France. Yet, by 1980, Spain had caught up with Italy, France, and the United States, and in 2019, it only trails Japan globally (Riley, 2005). However, a close look at Spanish life expectancy in recent decades also shows heterogeneity across provinces with some places falling behind (Fig. 1). For instance, in 2019, the average life expectancy at birth in Alava, Guadalajara, Navarra, Salamanca, Segovia, Soria, and Valladolid was above 84.5 years and exceeding 85 years in the case of Madrid. By contrast, a newborn in Almería, Cádiz, Huelva, and Sevilla could expect to live less than 82 years, reaching only 81 in the case of Ceuta and Melilla. These patterns draw a north/south divide, with higher values in the center and northern areas and lower in the south and southwestern regions.

Research in Economic History, Volume 38, 1–25
Copyright © 2025 Gregori Galofré-Vilà and María Gómez León
Published under exclusive licence by Emerald Publishing Limited
ISSN: 0363-3268/doi:10.1108/S0363-326820250000038001

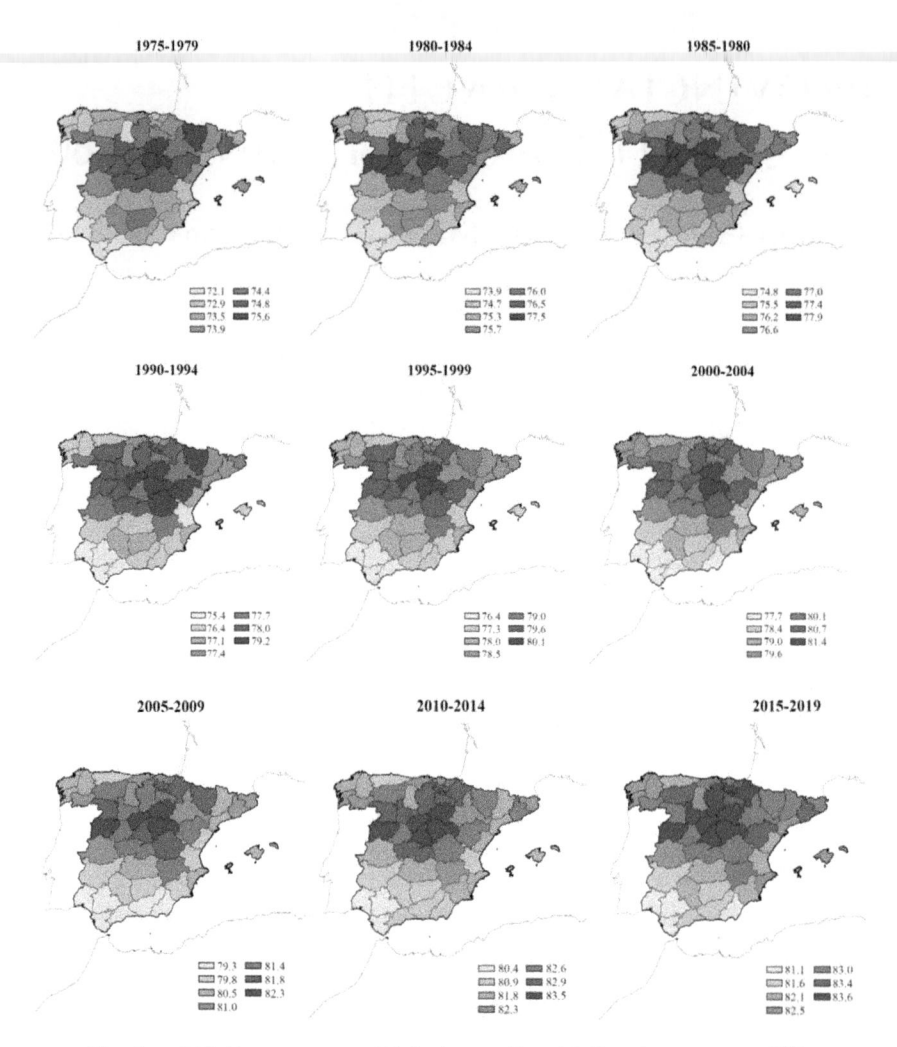

Fig. 1. Life Expectancy at Birth Across Spanish Provinces. *Notes:* Life expectancy at birth is defined as the average number of years that a newborn could expect to live if they were to pass through life subject to the age-specific mortality rates of a given period. As explained in Section 2, we are not showing data from Ceuta, Melilla, Santa Cruz de Tenerife, and Las Palmas. To display the life expectancy data across space, we use seven breaks in the data by the different Jenks. Jenk classes are based on natural groupings inherent in the data, whose boundaries are set where there are relatively big differences in the data values. *Sources:* Instituto Nacional de Estadística.

Given these gaps in recent decades, in this chapter, we document, for the first time, how health has varied across Spanish provinces in the last 150 years. Using official sources of death registers, we created a new data set with the number of yearly deaths per 1,000 population at the provincial level by sex. We focus on crude death rates, as historical age-adjusted population data to estimate life expectancies at birth are only available at census years (about every 10 years). While, in essence, our work is highly descriptive, we compute a Gini index and compare it with additional inequality indicators such as the Theil index and sigma- or beta-convergence.

By exploring these indices, we find that since 1860, there has been a process of health inequality reduction (i.e., a process of convergence) between Spanish provinces, which was interrupted in time during the Spanish Civil War and Franco's dictatorship (1936–1975) and resumed from 1980 onward. Using cause-specific mortality, we find that this last period of convergence is likely to be driven by advances in preventive mortality (i.e., deaths from cancer) and communicable and infectious diseases such as influenza and pneumonia. We also find divergence in recent decades in deaths from coronary and cardiovascular diseases. Finally, throughout, we also highlight some historical junctures and policies that can be behind periods of convergence or divergence.

While there is a wealth of research on health inequalities driven by socio-economic and educational groups (Case & Deaton, 2015; Currie & Schwandt, 2016), our paper is among the few exploring adult health inequalities historically. One notable exception is the recent work of Bonnet and D'Albis (2020), which explore convergence and divergence in life expectancy across French departments since the beginning of the 19th century. Between 1800 and 1880, they find zigzagged periods of convergence and divergence, followed by a century-long period of convergence. Another related paper is the work from Feigenbaum et al. (2019), showing that in the first half of the 20th century, not only were deaths from infectious diseases higher in the US South, but they also started to decline later than elsewhere in the country.

For the Spanish case, Pérez Moreda et al. (2015) also explored changes in mortality spatially, but their work is limited to urban regional differences during the first third of the 20th century. The work from Cussó Segura and Nicolau (2000), Gómez Redondo (1992), and Sanz Gimeno and Ramiro Fariñas (1999a, 1999b) is also very relevant here, but these studies aimed to explore infant and child mortality at some benchmark years. Our work directly connects with González and Rodríguez-González (2018), but while they begin to document regional health differences in 1990, we can go back to 1860.

There is also a broad and rich body of economic history literature looking at regional income inequality in Spain using gross domestic product (GDP) data (Díez Minguela et al., 2018; Martínez-Galarraga et al., 2018; Rosés et al., 2010; Rosés & Wolf, 2018), real wages (Rosés & Sánchez-Alonso, 2004) with some papers examining regional inequality and education (Beltrán Tapia et al., 2021; Beltrán Tapia & Martinez-Galarraga, 2018), and economic growth (Beltrán Tapia & Martinez-Galarraga, 2020; Martínez-Galarraga et al., 2015). Ultimately, our work directly contributes to this strand of scholarship, looking at the regional differences in health in the long run.

The paper continues as follows. We next present our data and methodology (Sections 2 and 3) to compute the mortality Gini index. Sections 4 and 5 describe the patterns of inequality in mortality over time and put them into an historical narrative. Section 6 concludes.

2. MORTALITY DATA: PATTERNS ACROSS PROVINCES AND ACROSS TIME

In this section, we will discuss data sources and limitations. We will also illustrate the heterogeneity across provinces and trends across time. Using a previously untapped data source to explore regional health inequalities, the *Movimiento Nacional de la Población*, edited by the *Instituto Geográfico y Estadístico*, we have manually transcribed the annual number of deaths for each of the 48 Spanish provinces since 1860 for men and women. For geographical reasons, we did not transcribe data from the provinces of Ceuta and Melilla (located in Africa) and Santa Cruz de Tenerife and Las Palmas, lying far away from the Spanish peninsula.

Because annual population figures at the provincial level are only available in census years (i.e., every 10 years), our outcome measure is simply the crude death rate (i.e., the number of deaths within a population). We computed it by dividing the annual deaths in the province i and year t by the population in the same province i and year t, where the annual population is interpolated between census years. To control for the process of ageing, after 1975, we use the official age-adjusted mortality statistics available from the *Instituto Nacional de Estadística*. Unfortunately, we have a gap in the data, as the *Movimiento Nacional de la Población* was not printed between 1871 and 1885, and mortality data by sex were also unreported between 1886 and 1899 (registering only total mortality). When we compute crude death rates for men and women, in the denominator, we use the male or female population in the province i and year t.

Fig. 2 displays the evolution of the crude death rates in each of the Spanish provinces from 1860 onward and compares it with the Spanish mean. Though each province follows a unique path, there are some general patterns. Mortality reached its peak in the 1870s and then started a long fall, reaching a plateau already in the 1960s until today. The demographic transition likely accounted for this decline (Omran, 1971). Starting from a regime of high birth and death rates and slow population growth, from 1880 onward, the death rate began to fall, accelerating the population increase. Then mortality and population were stabilized in the first half of the 20th century, when birth rates also fell, and the demographic transition was completed by 1960. It is also possible to see a short-lived peak of mortality in 1918, due to the 1918 influenza pandemic, and another increase of mortality during the second half of the 1930s, due to the Spanish Civil War.[1]

We also use the age-adjusted mortality data in 1975 and 2017 to show the distribution of the provincial mortality across space (Fig. 3). As with life expectancy, the mortality data also display a north south divide, with the provinces that registered higher mortality rates located in the South and Levante, including Almería, Cáceres, Granada, Málaga and València, and places with

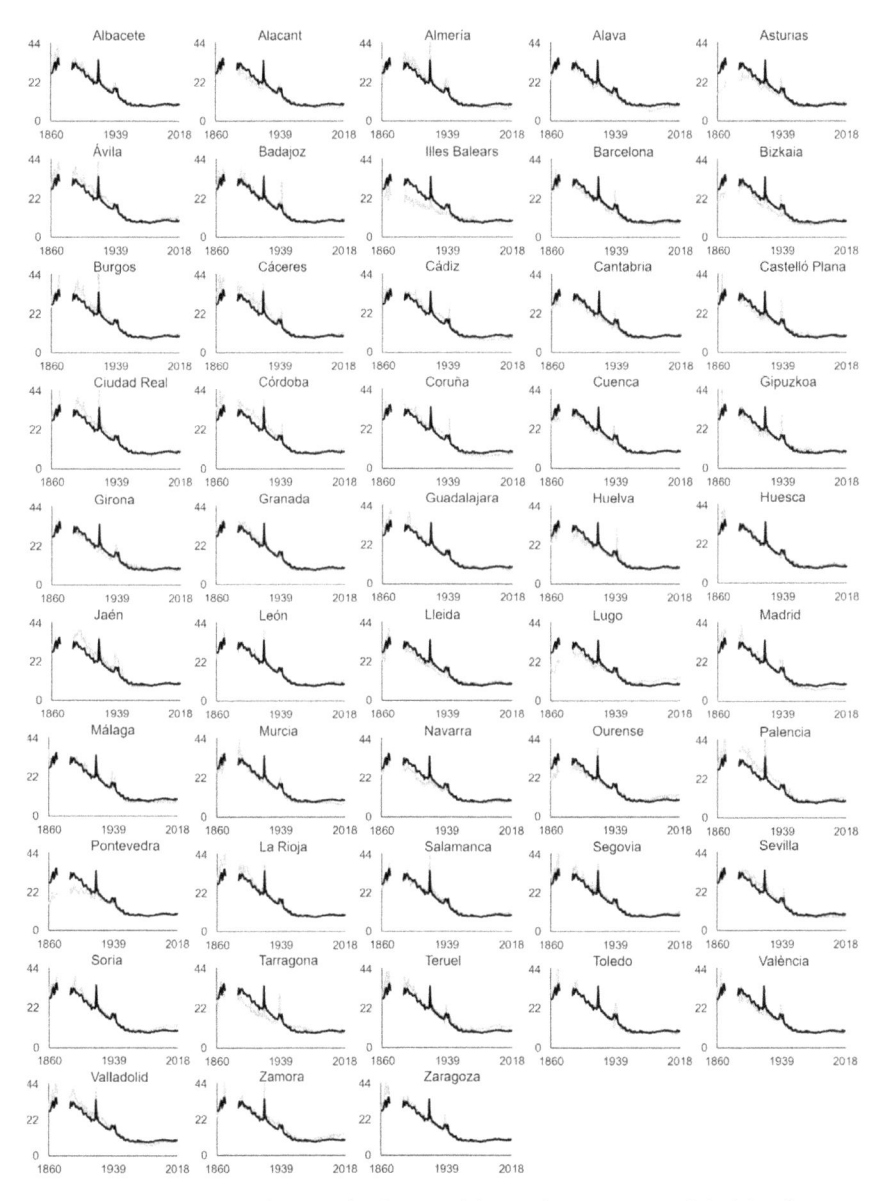

Fig. 2. Crude Death Rates in the Spanish Provinces. *Notes:* Light blue lines show annual average crude death rates in particular provinces. Dark black lines show annual average crude death rates in Spain. As explained in Section 2, we are not showing data from Ceuta, Melilla, Santa Cruz de Tenerife, and Las Palmas. *Sources:* Mortality data are from *Movimiento Nacional de la Población* and population data from census years; for more details, see Section 2.

1975   2017

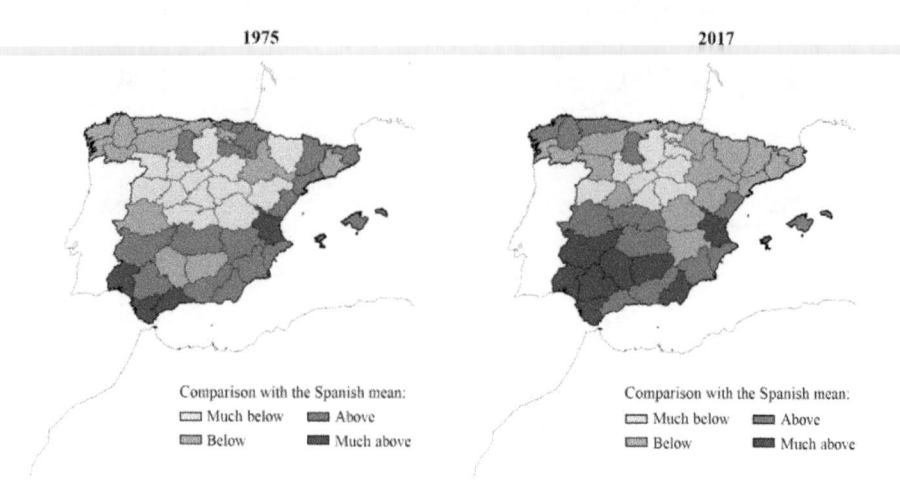

Fig. 3.   Age-Adjusted Mortality Rates Across Spanish Provinces. *Notes:* As
explained in Section 2, we are not showing data from Ceuta, Melilla, Santa Cruz de
Tenerife, and Las Palmas. To display the age-adjusted mortality data across space, we
use four breaks in the data by the different Jenks. Jenk classes are based on natural
groupings inherent in the data, whose boundaries are set where there are relatively big
differences in the data values. The categories of much below, below, above, and much
above are calculated in relation to the Spanish average. *Sources:* Instituto Nacional de
Estadística.

lower mortality rates clustered in the North, including Asturias, Bizkaia,
Gipuzkoa, A Coruña, Lugo, and Pontevedra.[2] Using crude death rates, the north/
south divide was already visible back in the 19th century.

Beyond differences in total mortality, we also computed sex mortality ratios
(the ratio of male to female death rates per 100) across time in the different
provinces (Fig. 4). Broadly speaking, women, due to biological factors, lifestyles,
and risk behaviors, had nearly always achieved lower mortality rates than men
(Goldin & Lleras-Muney, 2019). Nevertheless, in the last 50 years, there has been
wide heterogeneity in the male to female mortality ratio across the different
provinces, with some provinces registering low sex mortality ratios (such as
Cáceres, Ciudad Real, and Jaén) when compared to others (Alava, Baleares,
Burgos, and Gipuzkoa). Differences here are likely due to cause-specific mortalities (Pérez Moreda et al., 2015). Over time, the sex mortality ratios also show
how during the Civil War, men who were sent to the front died prematurely.
However, there is less evidence of gender discrimination in mortality during the
1918 influenza pandemic.

To control for unobservables in the crude death rates, such as the age distribution and the environmental and social characteristics of the provinces, we next
examine the timing of the decline in mortality with a simple ordinary least
squares (OLS) regression model, with the crude death rates as outcome and
regressing the mortality on region and year dummies. Specifically, we organize

Fig. 4. Sex Mortality Ratios in the Spanish Provinces. *Notes:* Light blue lines show annual sex mortality ratios, and dark black lines show annual average sex mortality ratios in Spain. As explained in Section 2, we are not showing data from Ceuta, Melilla, Santa Cruz de Tenerife, and Las Palmas. *Sources:* Mortality data are from *Movimiento Nacional de la Población* and population data from census years; for more details, see Section 2.

the annual provincial crude death rates into groups of 20 years (1900–1919, 1920–1939, etc.) and use the following equation:

$$\text{CDR}_{p_t} = \alpha + \gamma_r + \delta_t + \epsilon_{p_t} \tag{1}$$

where p denotes provinces ($p = 1, \ldots, 48$), t years (for instance, the group 1900/19 will include the years 1900, 1901, ..., 1919, the group 1920/1939 the years 1920, 1921, ..., 1939, and so on), *CDR* denotes our outcome variable (crude death rates), γ_r are region fixed effects (for region here, we deploy the *Comunidad Autónoma* distinction, one of the highest levels of aggregation and above provinces, $r = 1, \ldots, 16$), δ_t are year fixed effects within the years of the different time groups (for instance, the group 1900/1919 adds dummies for the years 1900,...,1919, the group for 1920/1939 adds dummies for the years 1920,...,1929, etc.), and ϵ_{p_t} is the error term, clustering the standard errors at the provincial level.[3]

Point estimates in Fig. 5 represent the slope coefficients of the different time periods, measuring the pace of the mortality decline. Grey areas plot 95% confidence intervals. For comparison, in the first place, we present the slopes without region or time fixed effects (unconditional models). Looking down the figure, the means declined gradually, showing that mortality declined over time. This pattern appears to hold for men and women, but means are nearly always higher for men and, in the period 1940–1959, differences in sex mortality get bigger, despite being statistically significant only when adding the regional and year fixed effects. We next investigate how these trends evolved across time and between Spanish regions with a range of inequality measures.

3. GINI AND OTHER MEASURES OF INEQUALITY

Using the annual provincial crude death rates, we next compute the Gini index to measure health inequality. The Gini index is a measure of inequality, which measures the extent to which a variable "y" (usually income or wealth) is equally or unequally distributed among individuals. The Gini (expressed in percentages) ranges from 0 to 100, where 0 would denote a perfect egalitarian distribution of "y" among individuals and 100 would indicate that "y" is fully concentrated by one individual. While the Gini index is generally used to study income and wealth concentration, it has also proved to be useful to assess inequalities in other dimensions, such as life expectancy and mortality (Peltzman, 2009). For its computation, we use the following equation:

$$\text{Gini} = \frac{1}{2n^2 \bar{y}} \sum_{i=1}^{n} \sum_{j=1}^{n} |y_i - y_j| \tag{2}$$

where n is the number of provinces, $\bar{y}$ is the overall mean crude death rate in all provinces, and y_i is the mean crude death rate of people belonging to the i-th province, with provinces ranked in ascending order ($y_j > y_i$). As Peltzman (2009)

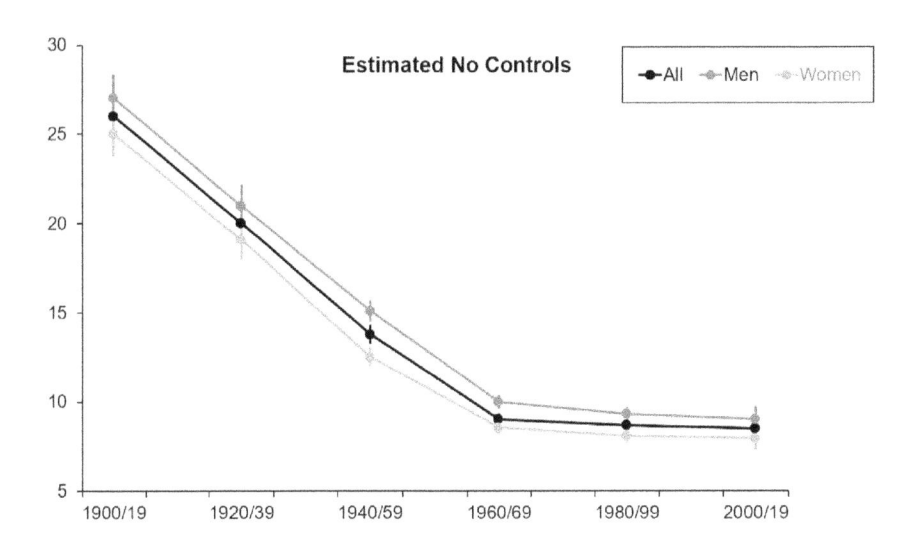

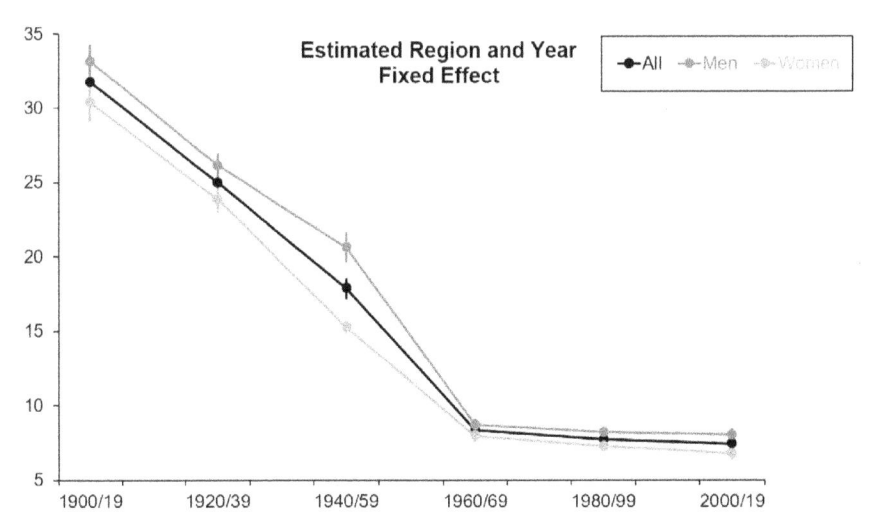

Fig. 5. Estimated Region Fixed-Effect and Year-Effect Coefficients. *Notes:* The outcome variable is the crude death rate in the province i and year t. In the bottom figure, we employ region fixed effect (based on the distinction of *Comunidad Autónoma*, which is above provinces) and year effect. We plot 95% confidence intervals from the regressions around each coefficient, clustering standard errors at the provincial level. *Sources:* Mortality data are from *Movimiento Nacional de la Población* and population data from census years; for more details, see Section 2.

notes, the interpretation of the Gini index for mortality is also analogous to that for income. The Gini coefficients will grow with the degree to which Spain's mortality is concentrated in a few provinces. In a perfect egalitarian situation (a Gini coefficient equal to 0), each province would have the same crude death rate. Oppositely, in a situation of maximum inequality (with a Gini coefficient of 100), one province will concentrate all the national mortality.

Beyond these two situations at the extremes, in practice, it is important to consider that, as we showed in Figs. 2 and 3, the crude death rate of each province is bounded by the nature of death (nowadays, life expectancy at birth in Spain is about 82 years), where the Gini coefficients will be affected by the absolute variability of the crude death rates over space and time. Thus, our mortality Gini based on provincial data would range from about 4 to 13. When we look at cause-specific mortality (in Section 5), the mortality Gini ranges from 15 to 35, since there is more variation across provinces in some causes of death, such as influenza. Unfortunately, for comparison, we are only aware of the Gini index using regional French data in life expectancy, which, similarly to our levels, shows a maximum Gini value of around 15 (Bonnet & D'Albis, 2020, Fig. 2). For robustness, we computed a Gini using the provincial Spanish GDP per capita data (Díez Minguela et al., 2018), and they range from 11 to 21. Finally, income Gini indices typically range from 20 to 70 (Ferreira & Ravallion, 2009). But this is based on national income data (not exploiting regional variation), where the income of a given population can range from 0 to extremely high values (i.e., very rich people).

Fig. 6 displays the evolution of the total mortality Gini between 1860 and 2017. While we discuss the details of the mortality Gini for the different historical

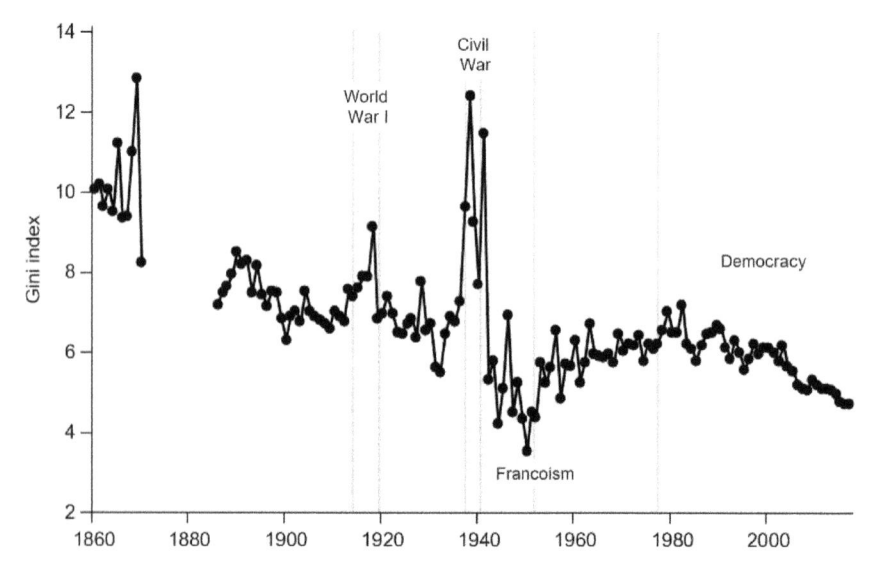

Fig. 6.   Gini Mortality in Spain. *Notes:* Gini coefficients are expressed as percentages and range from 0 to 100. *Sources:* Mortality data are from *Movimiento Nacional de la Población* and population data from census years; for more details, see Section 2. We also add grey light vertical lines indicating major events superimposed on the Gini timeline.

periods in the next sections, briefly, during the second half of the 19th century, there was a stable decline in regional health inequalities, with Gini moving from 10 (in 1860) to 6.3 (in 1900). This decline was somewhat disrupted during the early 20th century and in particular during World War I and the 1918 influenza pandemic, with regional inequalities reaching a Gini value of 9.2 in 1918. From the end of World War I to the arrival of the Second Republic (1931), Spain registered a new drop in health inequalities across provinces (with Gini values falling to 5.5 in 1931). Regional health inequalities skyrocketed during the Spanish Civil War (1936–1939), reaching a peak in 1938 (with a Gini of 12.4), to rapidly fall again during the postwar years, with the Gini index reaching its minimum (3.6) in 1950. A reversal occurred coinciding with Franco's seizure to power, and regional health inequalities increased by three Gini points between 1950 and 1978.[4] However, during the 1980s, under democracy, regional health inequalities resumed the downward trajectory initiated in the mid-19th century. Therefore, it is possible to identify two periods of health convergence between provinces (1860s–1950s, 1980s–2017) interrupted by three periods of increasing health inequalities (1910s–1920s, 1936–1939, and 1950–1980s).

Given the sex mortality ratios shown in Fig. 4 and how they evolved over time, we computed the mortality Gini separately for men and women. Results by gender (Fig. 7) show that the mortality Gini moved roughly in tandem for men and women. Yet there are some periods of divergence, first during the Civil War and then during the first years of the transition to democracy, where mortality inequality levels were higher among men than among women. Meanwhile, levels

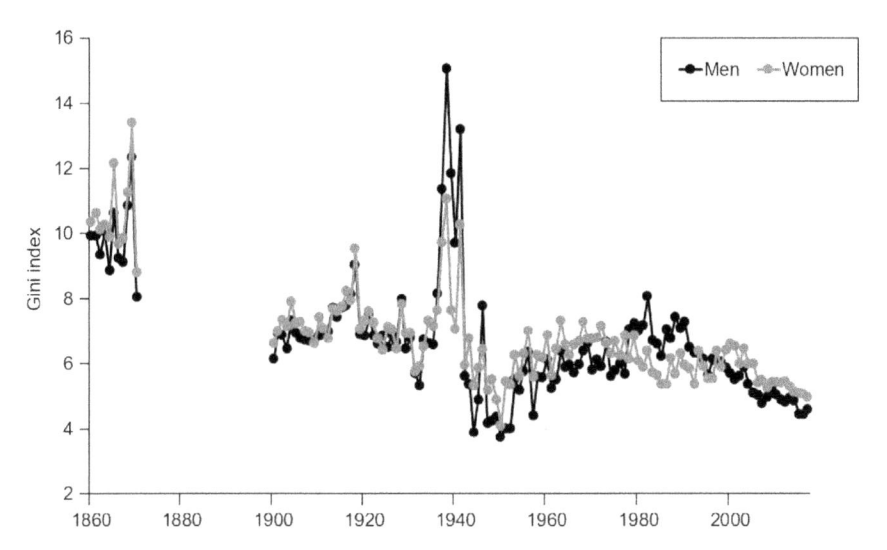

Fig. 7. Mortality Gini by Sex. *Notes:* Gini coefficients are expressed as percentages and range from 0 to 100. For details on methods, see text at Fig. 6. *Sources:* Mortality data are from *Movimiento Nacional de la Población* and population data from census years; for more details, see Section 2.1.

of inequality in mortality among women were higher than those registered between males under the dictatorship, and during the two most recent decades.

Are these trends robust to other indicators of inequality? In Fig. 8, we estimate health inequalities in Spain by applying different measures of inequality to data from crude death rates. First, we computed the mean logarithmic deviation, the

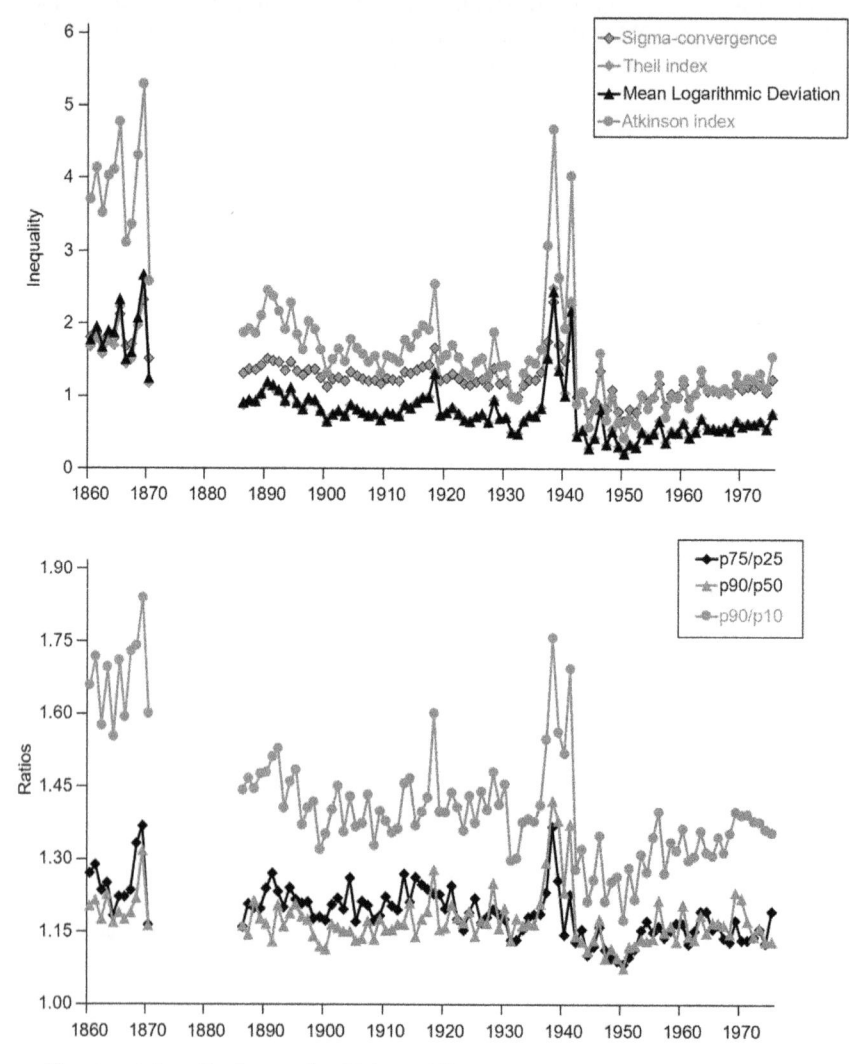

Fig. 8. Mortality Inequality Using Different Measures. *Notes:* For details on methods, see text in Section 3. We multiplied the values of sigma convergence x100 to insert them in the same scale as the other inequality measures. *Sources:* Mortality data are from *Movimiento Nacional de la Población* and population data from census years; for more details, see Section 2.

Theil index, the Atkinson index, and the so-called sigma convergence. The latter is simply the coefficient of variation, a summary measure computed as the standard deviation divided by the mean, and indicates if there was a period when the variance of average mortality levels across provinces declined.

As for the other measures, the inequality indices differ in their sensitivities to differences occurring at different parts of the distribution (Cowell, 2000). In particular, the Gini index is most sensitive to differences registered at the middle part of the distribution; meanwhile, the group of general entropy measures allows to explore inequality when assuming some sensitiveness to changes occurring either at the bottom or the top part of the distribution. Being n the number of provinces, $\bar{y}$ the overall mean crude death rate in all provinces, y_i the mean crude death rate of the i-th province, the mean logarithmic deviation, which is particularly sensitive to changes in the bottom, can be computed by:[5]

$$\text{Mean Logarithmic Deviation} = \frac{1}{n} \sum_{i=1}^{n} \log\left(\frac{\bar{y}}{y_i}\right) \qquad (3)$$

Using the same terminology, the Theil index, which is sensitive to changes occurring in the upper part, can by defined by:

$$\text{Theil index} = \frac{1}{n} \sum_{i=1}^{n} \frac{y_i}{\bar{y}} \log\left(\frac{y_i}{\bar{y}}\right) \qquad (4)$$

Finally, the Atkinson index permits to test inequality when assuming some aversion (ϵ-value) to changes occurring at a particular part of the distribution. The more positive the "inequality aversion parameter" is, the more sensitive the Atkinson index is to differences at the bottom. We take the customary maximum value of $\epsilon = 2$, using the following equation:

$$\text{Atkinson index}_\epsilon = 1 - \left[\frac{1}{n} \sum_{i=n}^{n} \left[\frac{y_i}{\bar{y}}\right]^{1-\epsilon}\right]^{\frac{1}{1-\epsilon}} \qquad (5)$$

These other indices of inequality are highly robust to the results shown by the mortality Gini. That is, a long decline in inequality interrupted briefly by WWI, strongly by the civil war, and also by the period of Franco's rule. A look at the Atkinson index – which gives more weight to mortality differences among provinces placed at the bottom part of the distribution (i.e., the healthiest provinces) – suggests even more dramatic changes occurring in the mid-19th century and during the Civil War.

We also display results with more intuitive range measures of inequality such as the evolution of the P90/P10, P90/P50, and P75/P25 ratios.[6] In order to compute range measures, provinces are ranked according to their average crude death rates (starting from the most to the least favored ones) and organized into percentiles. Here, the first decile (i.e., P0/P10) contains the 10% of provinces with the lowest average mortality rates, the second decile (P10–P20) the next 10%, and so on. In this sense, the P90/P10 is the ratio between the crude date rates registered by the 10% "less-healthy" provinces and the average crude death rates registered by the "healthiest" provinces (at the bottom 10). The P90/P50 measures the distance between the "least healthy" provinces and those placed in the middle part of the distribution, and the P75/P25 registers the distance between the upper-middle and the lower-middle parts of the distribution, avoiding potential outliers at the extremes. Our bottom line using these ratios is that these measures of inequality display the same general picture as the Gini index and suggest that most inequality changes were driven by changes at both extremes of the distribution (P90/P10).[7]

Next, in Fig. 9, we pursue an additional robustness check on the mortality Gini. To account for outliers and statistical precision in the Gini estimates, we computed bootstrapping standard errors for the Gini index using 50 repetitions in the resampled data and plot the means with the 95% confidence intervals. Our material analysis of health inequality remains unchanged.

We also use the official statistics on life expectancy data at the provincial level available since 1975 from the *Instituto Nacional de Estadística* (Fig. 10). This robustness shows that other measures of health, such as the number of years lived, display a similar picture to that obtained with the mortality Gini. Naturally, both are related as for constructing data on life expectancy one needs *Life*

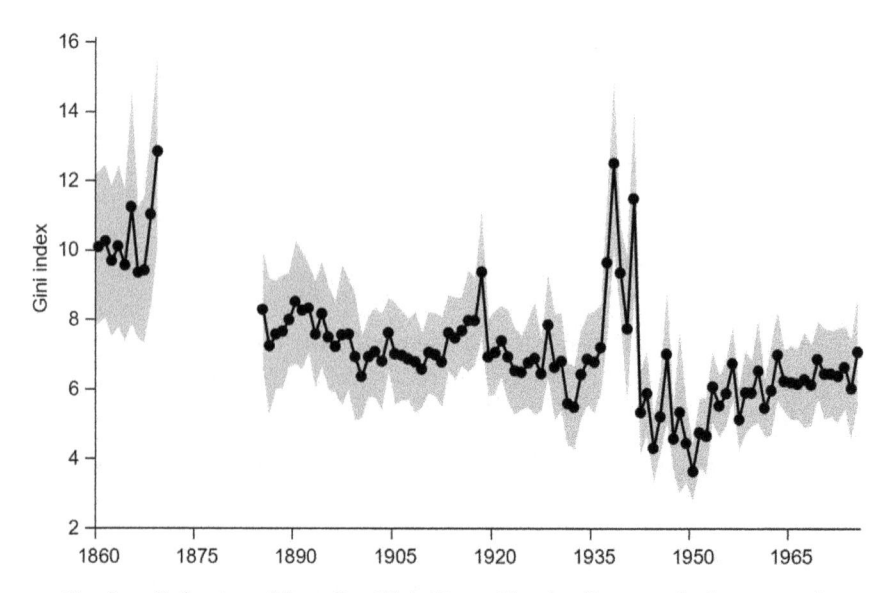

Fig. 9. Robustness Mortality Gini. *Notes:* For details on methods, see text in Section 3. *Sources:* Mortality data are from *Movimiento Nacional de la Población* and population data from census years; for more details, see Section 2.

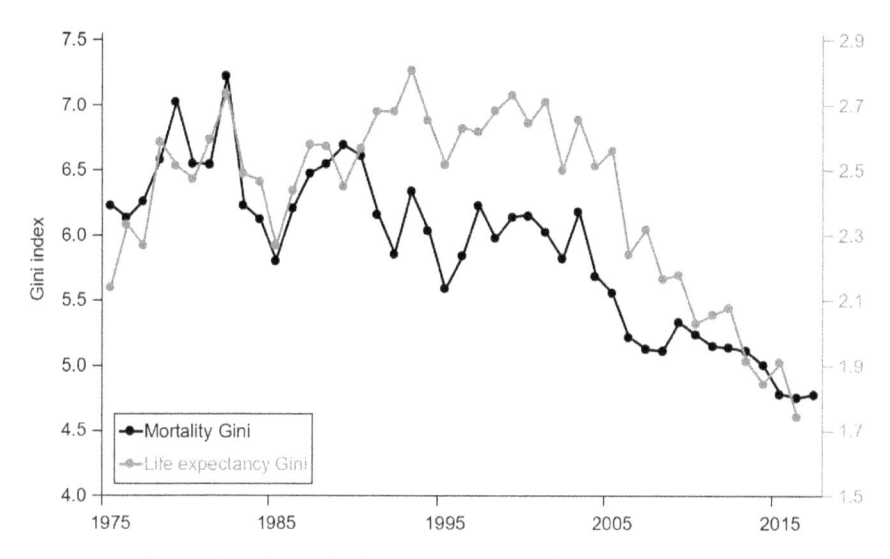

Fig. 10. Mortality and Life Expectancy Ginis. *Notes:* For details on methods, see text in Section 3. *Sources:* Mortality data are from *Movimiento Nacional de la Población* and population data from census years, and life expectancy data are from *Instituto Nacional de Estadística*; for more details, see Section 2.

Tables which are based on mortality and population statistics, but they add age and cohorts' effects.

We also formally tested for beta-convergence, allowing us to see the rate and whether provinces with higher mortality rates improved faster than provinces with lower mortality rates (Barro & Sala-i-Martin, 1992). If $g_{i,t,t+T} \equiv \log (y_{t+T}/ y_{i,t})$ (6) represents the province's annualized growth rate in the crude mortality rate between t and $t + T$, there would be absolute beta-convergence (divergence) if beta (β) is statistically significant and negative (positive) according to $g_{i,t,t+T} = \alpha + \beta (y_{i,t}) + u_{i,t}$ (7).

In Fig. 11, we split the data into decadal intervals, and following Eqs. (3) and (4), we plot the β coefficients with their associated 95% confidence intervals. As already seen with the mortality Gini and other indicators of inequality, there is absolute divergence in the period of the 1860s ($\beta > 0$), but gradually, throughout the end of the 19th century and the first three decades of the 20th century, this turned into a process of convergence, meaning that provinces with higher mortality rates improved faster in terms of health than provinces with lower mortality rates. This was, however, interrupted during the 1930s, and this process of convergence reversed in the first half of the 20th century. In the last decades of the 20th century, despite $\beta > 0$, the speed of divergence slowed down, and by the 2000s, it turned again to greater convergence.[8]

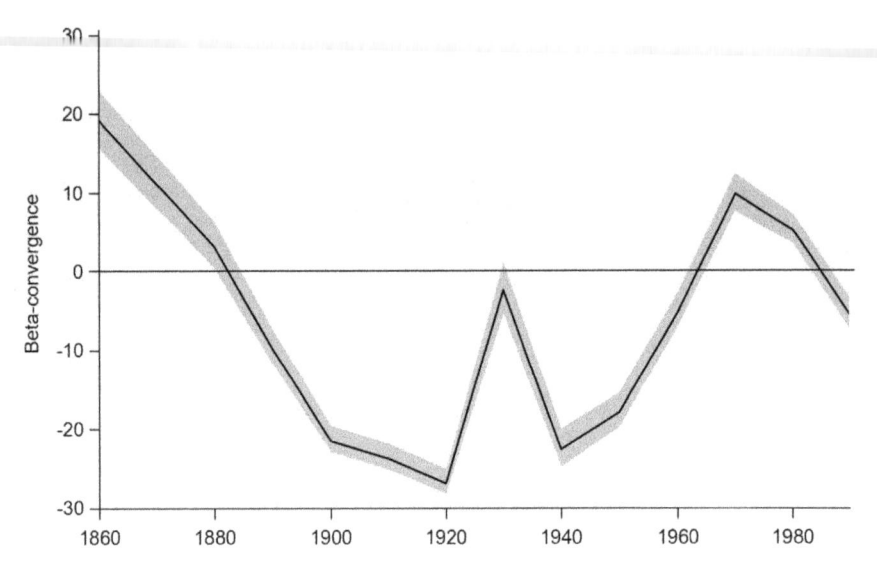

Fig. 11. Beta-Convergence in Crude Death Rates Across Spanish Provinces. *Notes:* For methods, see text in Section 3. We split the annual data into decadal intervals, and following Eqs. (3) and (4), we plot the β coefficients with their associated 95% confidence intervals in shared grey areas. *Sources:* Mortality data are from *Movimiento Nacional de la Población* and population data from census years; for more details, see Section 2.

4. PATTERNS OF MORTALITY GINIS

In this section, we present the different historical periods and patterns of the mortality Gini. Overall, as Fig. 12 shows, there is a strong positive correlation between the mortality Gini and the crude death rates over time. However, while decreasing inequalities lead to a falling death rates, there is a great deal of nuance in the pattern, and there are some decades of the late-19th century in which the Gini fell quickly (i.e., from 1860 to 1890) but mortality levels remained high. The decades from 1900 to 1930 show similar Gini values, but mortality started to fall quickly. Finally, after the 1940, both the Gini and mortality move at a similar rate with a general decline in both indicators, despite an increase of the Gini from 1960 to 1980. While in this paper we do not account for potential causal chains and the direction of causality, these movements and speeds highlight the importance of history, policy, and medical improvements.

The first long, if interrupted, period of health convergence across provinces between the 1860s and 1950s coincided with the epidemiological transition that started in 1880, when, as in other Western nations, birth rates remained stable, death rates began to fall, and population growth accelerated due to the end of epidemics and decline of infant mortality (Omran, 1971).[9] The literature suggests urbanization in the 1920 could be another potential contributing factor for convergence in the early period (Galofré-Vilà, 2021a; Martínez-Carrión & Pérez

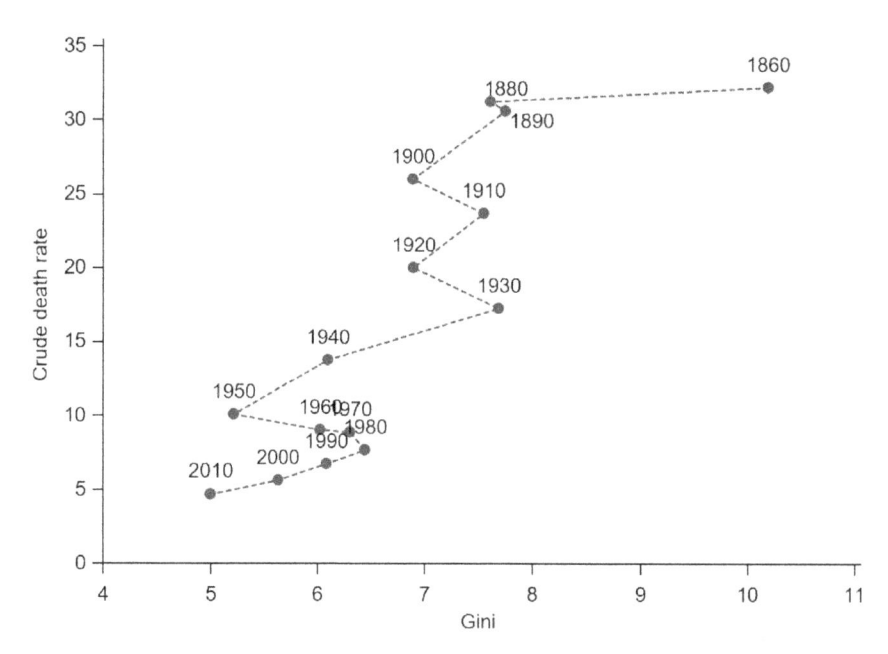

Fig. 12.   The Decadal Relationship Between Crude Death Rates and the
Mortality Gini. *Notes:* Each dot summarizes the mean decadal values of crude death
rates and the mortality Gini. As explained in Section 2, data for 1870 were missing
and data for the 1880 related to the second half of the 1880s. The dashed line of
tendency connects the dots in chronological order. *Sources:* Mortality data are from
Movimiento Nacional de la Población and population data from census years; for
more details, see Section 2.

Castejón, 1998; Pérez Moreda et al., 2015). While we cannot test this hypothesis
with our current data (each province involves cities of different sizes), when urban
centers began the fight against mortality with public health movements and
sanitary reforms, the urban penalty fell, and living in a rural area was no longer a
better option in terms of longevity. For instance, if by 1900, a person living in an
urban area (the capital of a province) could expect to live 5–6 years shorter than
those living in rural areas, by 1930, a reversal had occurred.

A first interruption in the decline of regional inequalities in Spain during the
1910s was likely due to the economic disruption associated with World War I,
whose effects were unevenly distributed across regions (Rosés & Sánchez-Alonso,
2004). Despite the fact that Spain was a neutral country and did not send men to
war, early in the war, its economy enjoyed a short-lived export boom, which
fostered industries located in the northern regions (the main producers of textiles,
machinery, and chemical products), and penalized traditional Spanish exports of
vegetables and Mediterranean citrus. Yet the war also brought inflation, and
northern and more economically developed regions open to trade were hit hardest
when the international markets were closed and prices started to rise

(Díez-Minguela et al., 2018).[10] These events not only affected the economic and labor outcomes of men, but also, as recently shown by Galofré-Vilà and Harris (2021) for the city of Barcelona, there was a decline in the health of women in these industrial centers.

These findings align with the work from Rosés and Sánchez-Alonso (2004, p. 405) when looking at other indicators of living standards. According to them, "we show that substantial [real] wage convergence across regions took place prior to World War I [between 1850 and 1913, however]... the process of wage convergence was interrupted by World War I, which produced a sharp increase in regional wage differentials. These increases proved to be temporary, however; wage convergence re-emerged in the 1920s." Later on, with the 1918 influenza pandemic, Chowell et al. (2014, p. 1) also "revealed high geographic heterogeneity in pandemic mortality impact... with the North experiencing highest excess mortality rates."[11]

A more intense interruption of the reduction of regional health inequalities occurred during the Civil War (1936–1939) and the immediate postwar years, when Gini coefficients climbed from 7.3 in 1936 to 11.5 in 1941. Following the reforms implemented by the Republican governments (in office from 1931 to 1936) and increasing tensions between conservative factions and leftist organizations, a military coup initiated the confrontation in 1936.[12] In terms of deaths, the Civil War was a demographic catastrophe. It is estimated that up to 800,000 people died during the war, out of a total population of 23.6 million in 1930 (Preston, 2011). As noted by Ortega and Silvestre (2006, p. 55), "during most of the war, the population was distributed in two zones of about the same size. However, ... the demographic consequences of the war were different in one side and another."

During the first decade that followed the defeat of the Republic in 1939, the mortality Gini resembled its prewar downward trend. However, an inflection point occurred through the second decade of the early Francoism, when mortality Ginis increased from 3.6 in 1950 to 6.3 in 1960.[13] In terms of social policy and healthcare programs, Franco's regime made few changes with respect to the prewar period (Pérez Moreda et al., 2015), while some of the initiatives implemented implied an unequal distribution of resources that did not equally match the emergent needs (Bernabeu-Mestre et al., 2006). For instance, Pérez Moreda et al. (2015) pointed out that the *Ley de Bases de Sanidad* of 1944, which aimed to reform sanitary conditions, was just a continuation of the prewar model, and Pons-Pons y Vilar-Rodríguez (2015) found the share of money devoted to health and healthcare (*Dirección General de Sanidad*) was about the same between 1943 and 1958 (1.05% compared to 1.02% from the total Spanish budget).[14]

Likewise, the health insurance law of 1942 was very similar to the one passed in July 1936, under the government of the Republic, and it still left out the majority of farmworkers and jobless people. The regime started some health and educational campaigns aimed at mothers and infants (for instance, the *Ley de Sanidad Maternal e Infantil* of 1941), which, while successful in continuing to combat infant mortality, actually increased health inequalities. For instance, Bernabeu-Mestre et al. (2006, p. 193) denounced the fact that "one of the characteristics that defined those initiatives was the unequal distribution of resources in the provinces most affected by infant mortality where, paradoxically, certain resources were less developed." In this regard, Barciela (2001) and Bernabeu-Mestre et al. (2006) pointed out the absence of equitable economic criteria in the provision of healthcare, the implementation of which responded to ideology and sociopolitical control.[15]

During the 1950s and 1960s, there were important epidemiological changes that likely affected provinces differently. For instance, the antibiotic revolution was successful in reducing some poverty-related causes of death, such as communicable and infectious diseases that mostly hit rural areas. At the same time, the decline of infectious and communicable diseases meant the rise of degenerative diseases, such as cancers and diabetes in richer and more developed provinces. According to Cussó Segura and Garrabou Segura (2007), the nutritional transition was also manifested more in urban and more economically developed urban areas, and in the 1950s, migration between rural and urban settings increased to a new height – being the first time that people from provinces in the south (Andalucía, Extremadura, and Castilla La Mancha) migrated massively to Barcelona and Madrid (Sánchez-Alonso, 1995; Silvestre, 2010).[16] All these factors likely helped to create a complex epidemiological framework that contributed to increasing regional health inequalities, but this time with rural provinces in Andalucía and economic hubs in the Basque Country and especially Madrid performing better than the rest.

During the second stage of the Francoist regime (1960–1975), the mortality Gini remained fairly stable at around six. Importantly, Franco's government limited increases in wages and set them at a national level, easing any regional difference across provinces (Vilar Rodríguez, 2004). Yet by the end of the 1950s, Spain's economic and political situation was also very fragile, and reforms under the *Plan de Estabilización y Liberalización Económicas* of 1959 ended with autarky and opened up the Spanish economy to the European market. In principle, these reforms have been seen as highly successful, starting a Golden Age of economic prosperity where GDP per capita rose seven times faster between 1950 and 1974 than in the previous 100 years (Prados de la Escosura, 2017; Prados de la Escosura & Rosés, 2009). New reforms were also implemented to narrow some existing social tensions between regions. For instance, although the efforts were modest, compulsory health insurance was expanded, and in 1953, farmworkers were added to the social scheme. Later on, the *Ley de Bases de la Seguridad Social* of 1963 sought to unify and integrate the various social insurances. However, this act continued to marginalize those without stable ties to the labor market, and funding relied on employers' and workers' compulsory contributions.

Once Franco died, and through to the first years of the transition to democracy, mortality Ginis for men continued to increase, reaching a Gini coefficient of eight in 1982. Notably, provincial health inequalities for women started to decline in the 1970s, while, for males, the decline began more than a decade later. Although the right to social security was enshrined in Article 41 of the Spanish Constitution of 1978, it was not until the elections of 1982, when the socialist party achieved the majority, that modern democracy and social policy started. With the rollout of hospitals in each provincial center that began in the 1970s, a significant number of programs were devoted to mothers, including, but not limited to, the supply of primary and open care and family planning.

In the 1980s, health care also became universal, the system of pensions for senior citizens was further developed, and unemployment benefits were expanded. This has the potential to further explain the decline of regional differences in mortalities for both men and women. As noted by González and Rodríguez-González (2018, p. 104), with the "universal health insurance system, … most health care is provided free of charge by public hospitals and primary care centres. These features might mitigate the impact of income inequality on health and mortality." Moreover, in the late 1990s (following the *Pacto de Toledo* of 1995), regions gradually launched programs for low-income families. The last step of this transition came with the *Ley General de Sanidad* of 1986 and *Ley de Sanidad* of 2003, which allowed for the healthcare systems (along with education) to be decentralized among Spanish regions.

5. COMPARISONS BY CAUSE OF DEATH

On the potential causes for health to converge, Fig. 13 presents cause-specific mortality Ginis for communicable and infectious diseases. From the *Movimiento Nacional de la Población*, we collected new data from the number of deaths of influenza and pneumonia. We decided not to collect data for other causes, due to coding transfers in the different causes of death overtime and because it is

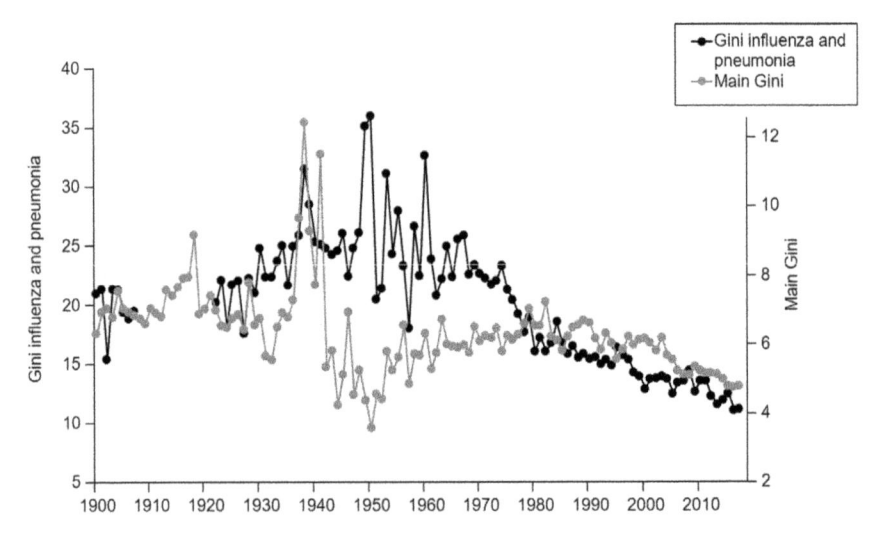

Fig. 13. Mortality Gini From Influenza and Pneumonia. *Notes:* Gini coefficients are expressed as percentages and range from 0 to 100. *Sources:* Mortality data are from *Movimiento Nacional de la Población* and population data from census years; for more details, see Section 2.

unknown how well deaths from cancers or cardiovascular problems were recorded in the past. Other causes of death such as tuberculosis also virtually disappeared in the 20th century. Hence, to calculate the mortality Gini, we simply combined deaths from influenza and pneumonia to proxy communicable and infectious diseases (expressed in per 1,000 population).

We find a process of divergence in the regional deaths from infectious and communicable diseases, starting to increase during the Civil War and reaching a plateau during Franco's 40-year dictatorship but clearly converging thereafter. Nowadays, these are causes that can be cured with relatively inexpensive treatment and highly avoided with better nutrition, but sulfa drugs, providing the first effective treatment to combat infectious and communicable diseases, were not discovered until 1930, (Jayachandran et al., 2010). Moreover, in Spain, it was not until 1944 that penicillin was first used (*La Vanguardia* September 21, 1944), and it was not until 1965 that the government assumed its costs, being unevenly used across regions in the 1940s and 1950s given its cost and availability (Santesmases, 2018). When compared to the overall mortality Gini, the main period of divergence occurred between 1940 and the late-1970s.

For the last 45 years, we also use age-adjusted mortality rates from cancer and cardiovascular problems calculated by the *Instituto Nacional de Estadística*. Despite the fact that Fig. 14 only displays data since 1975, it concerns to two leading causes of death in Spain, accounting for more than 60% of all deaths in 2019.[17] Overall, there has been a solid process of convergence across Spanish regions in deaths from cancer, which can be linked to preventive measures and

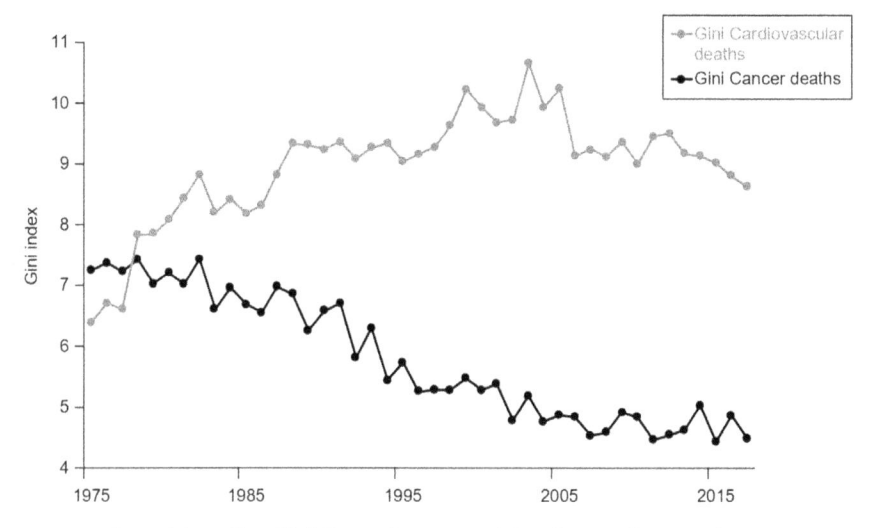

Fig. 14. Mortality Gini From Cancer and Cardiovascular Deaths. *Notes:* Gini coefficients are expressed as percentages and range from 0 to 100. *Sources:* Mortality data are from *Instituto Nacional de Estadística*; for more details, see Sections 2 and 3.

universal treatment financed by the national system of social security. By contrast, regional differences in cardiovascular deaths increased among provinces that respond to different patterns of lifestyle and the consumption of red meat and alcohol.

6. DISCUSSION

This chapter describes how health inequalities evolved across Spanish provinces since 1860. We find a process of convergence from 1860 to 2017, interrupted by World War I and the Civil War. The legacy left by Franco's 40-year dictatorial regime is also one of divergence, increasing health disparities across regions between the 1950s and 1980s.

In the course of the 20th century, Spain, like other countries such as Italy, France, Taiwan, and Japan, improved longevity into new and uncharted territories, moving from a regime of pestilence and high mortality levels into places where people enjoy the healthiest and longest lives. Of course, this dynamic, as part of the demographic transition, encompasses new challenges associated with longevity, such as an inclusive health system to cover all citizens. In this sense, Spain seems to have fared well in the most recent decades, creating a good environment for health to converge across different provinces and Spanish vicissitudes. Yet, the COVID-19 pandemic has magnified the vulnerabilities of the Spanish public health system and interacted with political goals, making it likely that differences can grow again.

ACKNOWLEDGMENTS

We would like to thank Miguel Artola Blanco, Albert Carreras, Alfonso Díez-Minguela, Libertad González, Leandro Prados de la Escosura, Beatriz Rodríguez Sánchez, Susan Wolcott (the editor), and an anonymous referee for helpful comments on an early draft.

NOTES

1. What is not shown in Fig. 2 (due to lack of data) is the cholera epidemic of 1885 (believed to have killed 120,000 people) and representing another peak in the Spanish trend.

2. The case of Madrid is of special importance, as while historically, it was above the Spanish mean, after the Civil War and, for political reasons, given its interest as the capital of Spain, it turned to be one of the healthiest places.

3. In Spain, a *Comunidad Autónoma* (autonomous community or region) is a first-level political and administrative division. There are in total 17 divisions: Andalusia, Aragó, Asturias, Illes Balears, Basque Country, Canary Islands, Cantabria, Castilla-La Mancha, Castile and León, Catalunya, Extremadura, Galicia, La Rioja, Madrid, Murcia, Navarra, and València.

4. While Franco died in 1975, the first free elections following the dictatorship were celebrated in 1977, and a constitution was approved by referendum in 1978.

5. For further detail on different inequality measures, see Cowell (2000) and Jenkins (1991).

6. Here *P* stands for the different percentiles of the distribution.

7. As Fig. 8 shows, the P90/P10 ratio indicates that the least-favored provinces registered mortality rates between 20% and 80% above the most-favored ones.

8. Note that we lack data for the years 1871–1885, so we left two empty spaces to illustrate missing data. For the growth rate of 1860, we employed 1860 and 1890, as we lacked data for 1870 and 1880.

9. That means a transition from a regime of low population growth associated with high birth rates and high death rates to one of population growth given a context of falling death rates, along with remaining high birth rates. The beginning of the epidemiological transition in Spain has been placed at 1880, when the death rate began to fall, accelerating the population increase. Mortality and population were stabilized in the first half of the 20th century, when birth rates also fell, with the transition being completed by 1960. See Pérez Moreda et al. (2015) for a review of these demographic issues in historical Spain.

10. For a study of the German hyperinflation and health, see Galofré-Vilà (2021b).

11. For a study of the 1918 influenza pandemic in Italy, see Galofré-Vilà et al. (2021).

12. More controversial reforms dealt with land distribution, worker protections, female suffrage, and the separation of church and state.

13. The Francoist dictatorship lasted until Franco died in 1975, and it is possible to identify two political stages of the dictatorship. The first stage, called the early Franco regime, spans from the end of the Civil War in 1939 until the end of the autarkic policies with the Stabilization Plan of 1959. The late Francoist regime, characterized by openness and economic success, spans from 1960 to Franco's death in 1975 and the transition to democracy.

14. Specifically, they argue that "after the Civil War, there was the *Ley de Bases de Sanidad* of 1944, which aimed to reform sanitary conditions, but it just continued the essential characteristics of the prewar model" (Pérez Moreda et al., 2015).

15. Other developments in terms of health included a rudimentary system of pensions for senior citizens in 1947 (*Seguro Obligatorio de Vejez e Invalidez*) and coverage for labor accidents (*Ley de Accidentes de Trabajo*). However, these were poorly funded.

16. The nutritional transition involved the transformation of basic diets – based on bread, potatoes, and legumes – through the incorporation of highly nutritional products, such as meat, milk, sugars, and vegetables.

17. Data on cause-specific mortality are from *Instituto Nacional De Estadística*.

REFERENCES

Barciela, C. (2001). *La España de Franco (1939–1975)*. Síntesis.

Barro, R., & Sala-i-Martin, X. (1992). Convergence. *Journal of Political Economy*, *100*(2), 223–251.

Beltrán Tapia, F. J., Díez-Minguela, A., Martinez-Galarraga, J., & Tirado-Fabregat, D. A. (2021). Two stories, one fate: Age-heaping and literacy in Spain, 1877–1930. *Journal of Iberian and Latin American Economic History*. https://doi.org/10.1017/S0212610921000033

Beltrán Tapia, F. J., & Martinez-Galarraga, J. (2018). Inequality and education in pre-industrial economies: Evidence from Spain. *Explorations in Economic History*, *69*, 81–101.

Beltrán Tapia, F. J., & Martinez-Galarraga, J. (2020). Inequality and growth in a developing economy: Evidence from regional data (Spain, 1860–1930). *Social Science History*, *44*(1), 169–192.

Bernabeu-Mestre, J., Caballero Pérez, P., Galiana Sánchez, M. E., & Nolasco Bonmatí, A. (2006). Niveles de Vida y Salud en la España del Primer Franquismo: Las Desigualdades en la Mortalidad Infantil. *Revista de Demografía Histórica*, *24*(1), 181–201.

Bonnet, F., & D'Albis, H. (2020). Spatial inequality in mortality in France over the past two centuries. *Population and Development Review*, *46*(1), 145–168.

Case, A., & Deaton, A. (2015). Rising morbidity and mortality in midlife among white non-Hispanic Americans in the 21st century. *PNAS*, *112*(49), 15078–15083.

Chowell, G., Erkoreka, A., Viboud, C., & Echeverri-Davila, B. (2014). Spatial-temporal excess mortality patterns of the 1918–1919 influenza pandemic in Spain. *BMC Infectious Diseases*, *1*(371), 1–12.

Cowell, F. A. (2000). Measurement of inequality. In A. B. Atkinson & F. Bourguignon (Eds.), *Handbook of income distribution* (pp. 59–85). Elsevier Science.

Currie, J., & Schwandt, H. (2016). Mortality inequality: The good news from a county-level approach. *The Journal of Economic Perspectives*, *30*(2), 29–52.

Cussó Segura, X., & Garrabou Segura, R. (2007). La Transición Nutricional en la España Contemporánea: Las Variaciones en el Consumo de Pan, Patatas y Legumbres (1850–2000). *Investigaciones de Historia Económica*, *7*, 69–100.

Cussó Segura, X., & Nicolau, R. (2000). La Mortalidad antes de Entrar en la Vida Activa en España. Comparaciones Regionales e Internacionales, 1860–1960. *Revista de Historia Económica*, *18*(3), 525–551.

Díez-Minguela, A., Martinez-Galarraga, J., & Tirado-Fabregat, D. A. (2018). *Regional inequality in Spain, 1860–2015*. Palgrave Studies in Economic History.

Feigenbaum, J. J., Muller, C., & Wrigley-Field, E. (2019). Regional and racial inequality in infectious disease mortality in U.S. cities, 1900–1948. *Demography*, *56*, 1371–1388.

Ferreira, F. H., & Ravallion, M. (2009). Poverty and inequality: The global context. In W. Salverda, B. Nolan, & T. Smeeding (Eds.), *The Oxford handbook of economic inequality* (pp. 599–638). Oxford University Press.

Galofré-Vilà, G. (2021a). Height, chest size and household composition in late-nineteenth century Catalonia. *Social Science History*, *45*, 111–129.

Galofré-Vilà, G. (2021b). *The costs of hyperinflation: Germany 1923*. UPNA Working Paper D.T. 2101. https://www.sciencedirect.com/science/article/pii/S0014498322000572

Galofré-Vilà, G., & Harris, B. (2021). Growth before birth: The relationship between placental weights and infant and maternal health in early-twentieth century Barcelona. *The Economic History Review*, *74*(2), 400–423.

Galofré-Vilà, G., McKee, M., Gómez León, M., & Stuckler, D. (2021). A lesson from history? The 1918 influenza pandemic and the rise of Italian fascism: A cross-city quantitative and historical text qualitative analysis. *American Journal of Public Health*. Forthcoming. https://ajph.aphapublications.org/doi/10.2105/AJPH.2021.306574?url_ver=Z39.88-2003&rfr_id=ori%3Arid%3Acrossref.org&rfr_dat=cr_pub++0pubmed

Goldin, C., & Lleras-Muney, A. (2019). XX>XY? The changing female advantage in life expectancy. *Journal of Health Economics*, *67*, 1–14.

Gómez Redondo, R. (1992). *La Mortalidad Infantil Española en el siglo XX*. España Editores.

González, L., & Rodríguez-González, A. (2018). Inequality in mortality in Spain. *Fiscal Studies*, *42*(1), 103–121.

Jayachandran, S., Lleras-Muney, A., & Smith, K. V. (2010). Modern medicine and the twentieth century decline in mortality: Evidence on the impact of sulfa drugs. *American Economic Journal: Applied Economics*, *2*(2), 118–146.

Jenkins, S. P. (1991). The measurement of income inequality. In L. Osberg (Ed.), *Economic inequality and poverty: International perspectives* (pp. 19913–19938). M. E. Sharpe.

Martínez-Carrión, J. M., & Pérez Castejón, J. J. (1998). Height and standards of living during the industrialisation of Spain: The case of Elche. *European Review of Economic History*, *2*, 201–230.

Martínez-Galarraga, J., Rosés, J. R., & Tirado, D. A. (2018). The evolution of regional income inequality in Spain, 1860–2010. In J. R. Rosés & N. Wolf (Eds.), The economic development of Europe's regions. A quantitative history since 1900 (pp. 269–290). Routledge Explorations in Economic History.

Martínez-Galarraga, J., Tirado, D. A., & González-Val, R. (2015). Market potential and regional economic growth in Spain (1860–1930). *European Review of Economic History*, *19*(4), 335–358.

Omran, A. R. (1971). The epidemiologic transition: A theory of the epidemiology of population change. *Milbank Memorial Fund Quarterly*, *49*, 509–538.

Ortega, A., & Silvestre, J. (2006). Las Consecuencias Demográficas. In P. Martín Aceña & E. Martínez Ruiz (Eds.), *La Economía de la Guerra Civil* (pp. 53–106). Marcial Pons Historia.

Peltzman, S. (2009). Mortality inequality. *The Journal of Economic Perspectives*, *23*(4), 175–190.

Pérez Moreda, V., Reher, D. S., & Sanz Gimeno, A. (2015). *La Conquista de la Salud: Mortalidad y Modernización en la España Contemporánea*. Marcial Pons Historia.

Pons-Pons, J., & Vilar-Rodríguez, M. (2015). *El Seguro de Salud Privado y Público en España: Su Análisis en perspectiva Histórica*. Prensas Universitarias de Zaragoza.

Prados de la Escosura, L. (2017). *Spanish economic growth, 1850–2015*. Palgrave MacMillan.

Prados de la Escosura, L., & Rosés, J. R. (2009). The sources of long-run growth in Spain, 1850–2000. *The Journal of Economic History*, *69*(4), 1063–1091.

Preston, P. (2011). *El Holocausto Español*. Debate.

Riley, J. C. (2005). Estimates of regional and global life expectancy, 1800–2001. *Population and Development Review*, *31*(3), 537–543.

Rosés, J. R., Martínez-Galarraga, J., & Tirado, D. A. (2010). The upswing of regional income inequality in Spain (1860–1930). *Explorations in Economic History*, *47*(2), 244–257.

Rosés, J. R., & Sánchez-Alonso, B. (2004). Regional wage convergence in Spain 1850–1930. *Explorations in Economic History*, *41*, 404–425.

Rosés, J. R., & Wolf, N. (2018). *The economic development of Europe's regions: A quantitative history since 1900*. Routledge Explorations in Economic History.

Sánchez-Alonso, B. (1995). *Las Causas de la Emigración Española, 1880–1930*. Alianza Editorial.

Santesmases, M. J. (2018). *The circulation of penicillin in Spain. Health, wealth and authority*. Palgrave Macmillan.

Sanz Gimeno, A., & Ramiro Fariñas, D. (1999a). Cambios Estructurales en la Mortalidad Infantil y Juvenil Española, 1860–1990. *Boletin de la Asociacion de Demografia Historica*, *17*(1), 49–87.

Sanz Gimeno, A., & Ramiro Fariñas, D. (1999b). Estructuras Internas de la Mortalidad de la Infancia (0–4 años) en la España del siglo XX. *Historia Contemporanea*, *18*, 129–191.

Silvestre, J. (2010). Las Emigraciones Interiores en España, 1860–2007. *Historia y Política*, *23*, 113–134.

Vilar Rodríguez, M. (2004). La Ruptura Posbélica a Través del Comportamiento de los Salarios Industriales. Nueva Evidencia Cuantitativa (1908–1963). *Revista de Historia Industrial*, *25*, 81–126.

THE GEOGRAPHY OF INFECTIOUS DISEASE AND THE EUROPEAN MARRIAGE PATTERN*

Kirsten de Beurs[a], Kyle Harper[b] and Le Wang[c]

[a]*Wageningen University & Research, The Netherlands*
[b]*University of Oklahoma, USA*
[c]*Virginia Tech, USA*

ABSTRACT

The European Marriage Pattern (EMP) was characteristic of preindustrial northwestern Europe and, in recent years, has been proposed as an important factor in the rise of the West. Yet, the origins and ultimate causes of the EMP remain obscure. We examine a novel hypothesis that the EMP can emerge in geographic environments with a lighter infectious disease burden. We overcome significant challenges facing empirical analysis of premodern societies. Using a large, individual-level database of marriages from the county of Kent, England, as well as a spatial regression discontinuity approach, we demonstrate a robust association between physical ecology and female age at first marriage (FAFM). We also find that the two potential channels proposed in the literature play starkly different roles in explaining our finding. Specifically, we fail to find that pastoralism plays any significant role in explaining the

---

This work is based on data provided through www.VisionofBritain.org.uk and uses historical material which is copyright of the Great Britain Historical GIS Project and the University of Portsmouth. This research was partially supported by the NASA: Land-Cover/Land-Use Change project entitled "Land use patterns and political instability as predictors for the re-emergence of malaria in the Caucasus" to KdB. Project number: 16-LCLUC16-2-0017. We are grateful for the kind assistance of Jean Skilling of the Kent Family History Society and for comments from audiences at Northwestern University, George Mason University, and Yale University. We thank Peter Temin for suggestions on an earlier draft and Katrin Gaardbo Kuhn for sharing data on the ague index, and we thank our research assistants Elizabeth Anderson and Sam Quick. The authors are listed in alphabetical order.

Research in Economic History, Volume 38, 27–51
Copyright © 2025 Kirsten de Beurs, Kyle Harper and Le Wang
Published under exclusive licence by Emerald Publishing Limited
ISSN: 0363-3268/doi:10.1108/S0363-326820250000038002

EMP, while the mortality rate channel accounts for a significant portion of the
observed relationship between the disease environment and FAFM.

Keywords: Historical demography; infectious disease; European marriage
pattern; origins of divergences; European agricultural history

JEL codes: N33; N53; J13

1. INTRODUCTION

The "European Marriage Pattern" (EMP) is a central observation in historical
demography, defined by a contrast between the marriage patterns of preindustrial
northwestern Europe and the rest of the world (Hajnal, 1965, 1982; Lundh &
Kurosu, 2014). The EMP was characterized by relatively late female age at first
marriage (FAFM) and a high proportion of persons never marrying. The kernel
of this idea was present already in Malthus (as early as 1798), who associated the
"preventative check" of late marriage with western European societies; formal-
ized by John Hajnal in 1965, the construct has proven durable. In recent years,
the EMP has become an important theme in debates about the origins of
comparative development. The EMP is associated with measures of female
empowerment, human capital formation, and long-run economic development,
and societies with the EMP were in the vanguard of early economic growth (De
Moor & Van Zanden, 2010; Zanden et al., 2019, and for a critique, Dennison &
Ogilvie, 2014).

Despite its obvious importance, the origins of the EMP remain obscure. There
are two prominent hypotheses proposed in the recent literature. In the first
hypothesis, Voigtländer and Voth (2013) (hereafter VV) propose that the EMP
emerged in societies which had a relatively high component of pastoral agriculture as a result of land abundance due to the Black Death. Specifically, women
had a comparative advantage in pastoral agriculture relative to arable agriculture. Labor-market opportunities gave women the ability to substitute fertility for
income, thus delaying marriage since FAFM was the principal fertility control in
premodern times. The second hypothesis, Foreman-Peck (2011), highlights the
role of low child mortality rates in parts of Europe; this model outlines how lower
child mortality rates could lead to lower demand for births and incentivize later
marriage, on the assumption that families aimed at a target completed fertility
rate. In the VV paper, the effect is identified via exogenous variations in certain
geographic features (such as land suitability) and weather. In the second
hypothesis, the exogenous source of the low mortality rates is unspecified. These
considerations leave open questions as to whether there could be deeper roots
behind agricultural structure and mortality rates that could lead to the EMP.

We propose a new hypothesis to help explain the origins of the EMP, arguing
that the geography of infectious disease was a significant yet neglected factor in
historical marriage patterns. Already in 1988, Wrigley suggested that "the
European marriage system is a 'luxury' that populations through much of the
traditional world may have been unable to afford. Where endemic diseases were

many and fatal, where epidemic diseases were frequent and devastating, where food supplies were subject to violent and unpredictable fluctuations, or where some combination of these dangers prevailed, early and universal marriages may have been mandatory" Wrigley (2018). We find this intuition compelling and support empirically here. It is important to underscore at the beginning, however, that marriage patterns are complex phenomena, likely to be shaped by many variables. We believe the health environment was only one factor among others, albeit important, heretofore neglected, and significantly exogenous.

The EMP could emerge in areas with a lower disease burden for at least the two reasons suggested by the hypotheses described above. Geographic areas with higher disease burdens had higher mortality rates that could incentivize households' desires to marry younger in order to have more births. Or, similar to VV, a more disease-burdened environment with higher mortality rates could lead to relative land abundance, which would also favor the development of the pastoral sector and in turn lead to differences in FAFM across areas.

This chapter provides what we believe to be the first rigorous empirical demonstration of Wrigley's intuition that the EMP was a "luxury" afforded to societies located in regions with an exogenously lower disease burden. To test the relationship between the disease environment and marriage patterns, we overcome two significant challenges in the premodern (as opposed to modern) historical context. The first is concerned with data availability. The importance of health in economic history (Deaton, 2013; Gallup & Sachs, 2001) is increasingly recognized, but the lack of data has made it difficult to extend analysis of the relationship between health and economic development into the deep past. Furthermore, the aggregated data typically used for FAFM are derived from English parish registers in which migrants are invisible, a problem well-known to historical demographers (Ruggles, 1992); correcting for systemic "migration censoring" can potentially impact the previous studies of the determinants of the EMP and calls for an analysis of individual-level data. To this end, we first assemble a novel dataset from the county of Kent, England, covering the 17th and 18th centuries. The Kent data possess rich historical documentation, allowing us to construct one of the oldest individual-level marriage datasets yet assembled and to combine it with information on the disease environment at high geographic resolution. Moreover, our data include information on place of origins and also avoid any sorting in marriage behavior based on geographic environment, which typically leads to biased estimation.

The second challenge is whether and how we can isolate the causal relationship between disease and the marriage pattern. This is by no means a trivial task, especially when disease is often measured with observed death rates, which can themselves be an outcome of marital and reproductive behavior. For example, later marriages and a reduction in fertility can have a direct impact on child mortality rates (Ronsmans, 1996). Also, the relationship between the observed health outcomes and the marriage pattern may be driven by other factors such as cultural norms and institutions. This presents an even bigger challenge in a premodern context like ours. Given the paucity of information and data, typical solutions such as controlling for more variables and using an instrumental variable (IV) are usually not feasible. For example, in the VV paper, they can control only for population density at the county level and regional fixed effects, and their IV is also measured at the county level and can potentially be correlated with or affect economic development via other institutional determinants of marriage behavior at the county level.

We address the challenge of isolating the causal relationship with three strategies: careful choice of measurement, data, and econometric method. Our focus here is on malaria burden. Malaria was one of the leading causes of the historical variation in mortality, especially in Kent, and continues to be the "one of the world's greatest public health challenges" (Yamana, 2015). This disease also places significantly higher burden on children than adults. We first construct an exogenous measure of malaria burden developed in the medical literature known as the topographic wetness index (TWI); because malaria was a vector-borne disease, transmitted by specific mosquito vectors with often highly particular ecological requirements, the transmission patterns and disease burden were largely exogenous to social factors and human behavior before modern malaria control. We focus on data about individuals in the parishes of Kent, a single county of England that was institutionally, technologically, and culturally homogenous, which provides a natural control on many potentially important variables (See the left side of Fig. 1 for the location of Kent in England). This focus effectively controls for county-fixed effects and hence any determinants of marriage behavior at the county level, be it observable or unobservable. One concern for analysis at such a refined scale is usually lack of variation in the variables of interest, especially regarding infectious disease. This is not the case for Kent. The county was notorious for its sharp health gradients determined by exogenous geographic factors (Dobson, 2003). Some parishes in Kent were low-lying marshes, while others nearby were upland meadow or forest. Consequently, there was remarkable small-scale variation in the mortality rate, such that nearly adjacent parishes experienced radically different health environments (The right side of Fig. 1 illustrates the variations of TWI in the county).

We further our analysis by introducing regression discontinuity, a novel method by which we test differences only between parishes physically bordering each other, further reducing the possibility that unobserved variables might explain variation.

Use of an exogenous measure of the disease burden, as well as within-county and even neighboring parishes analyses, all aid in identifying a more credible relationship between disease environment and FAFM. Using our novel individual-level dataset created from original sources, we indeed find a highly significant association between malaria burden, measured by the TWI, and female age at first marriage, confirming that marshy parishes experienced lower FAFM. Our regression discontinuity results lend further support to our hypothesis. We investigate two possible mechanisms through which malaria burden may affect age at first marriage: mortality rates and agricultural structure. We collect historical tithing records that preserve parish-level data on land-use to examine whether pastoral agriculture was associated with lower FAFM in Kent. In stark contrast to VV, we fail to find that there was any significant relationship between pastoralism and FAFM, or that pastoralism plays any significant role in explaining our finding. Instead, using another historical dataset on parish-level crude death rates that we compile, we find that the mortality channel can account for a significant portion of the relationship between malaria burden and marriage behavior. Our results confirm Wrigley's intuition that the EMP is a "luxury" – that lower mortality rates may have lowered pressure on female fertility, permitting women to marry later. Perhaps some societies were simply ecologically lucky, blessed with a light disease burden that permitted a low pressure demographic regime conducive to human capital formation, female empowerment, and economic growth. Our findings link to current debates about the role of geography in shaping institutions and economic performance (Acemoglu & Robinson, 2012; Sachs, 2012), and to the extent that the EMP was linked to other determinants of interest such as human capital formation (Zanden et al., 2019), they suggest an important new channel through which the geography of infectious disease might have influenced long-run economic development.

2. MALARIA BURDEN AND ITS EXOGENOUS MEASURE

In premodern England, vivax malaria was a significant burden in the marshlands and fens, a pattern that endured from at least Anglo-Saxon times through the 19th century (Gowland & Western, 2012; Kuhn et al., 2003). It is worth noting that the measures we use for variations in the environment (TWI) and mortality (CDR) in Kent were reflected in the common qualitative understanding among contemporaries that marshy regions of the county were disproportionately afflicted by the "agues" (a term for intermittent fever characteristic of malaria). Consider the description of one marsh parish by a highly informed local antiquarian: "the greatest part lying so exceeding low and watry, enveloped by creeks, marshes and salts, [that] the air is very gross, and much subject to fogs, which smell very offensive, and in winter it is scarce ever free from them, and when most so, they yet remain hovering over the lands for three or four feet or more in height, which, with the badness of the water, occasions severe agues, which the inhabitants are very rarely without, whose complexions from those distempers become of a dingy yellow colour, and if they survive, are generally afflicted with them till summer, and often for several years, so that it is not unusual to see a poor man, his wife, and whole family of five or six children, hovering over their fire in their hovel, shaking with an ague all at the same time; and Dr. Plot remarks, that seldom any, though born here, continuing in it, have lived to the age of twenty-one years." (Hasted, 1798, 6.144). The main cause of the variation in malaria burden and health outcomes was the prevalence of a single pathogen, Plasmodium vivax. P. vivax is a parasite that causes the vector-borne disease malaria; along with P. falciparum, it is one of the two most important malaria parasites and a major burden on human health (Baird, 2013). Because the parasite can only be transmitted by particular mosquito vectors (in this case, Anopheles atroparvus), its geographic distribution is heavily controlled by factors affecting mosquito habitats. Specifically, vivax malaria thrived in the wet, marshy parishes where the mosquito vector reproduced in abundance. Such ecological factors were historically exogenous to social dynamics and human behavior.

We employ an exogenous measure developed in the medical literature known as the TWI to capture malaria burden. The TWI was developed as a physically based variable that can be used to quantify spatially explicit potential water accumulation (Beven & Kirkby, 1979). Specifically, the TWI is "calculated as the ratio of the area upslope from any given point on the landscape to the local slope at that point, and thus represents the amount of water that should enter a given spatial unit divided by the rate at which the water should flow out of that unit" (Cohen et al., 2008, 2010). The TWI provides a "simple, biologically meaningful description" of the malaria environment, and it is only determined by the local shape of the land and completely exogenous to other variables that may confound our analysis. Cohen et al. (2010) found that in the western Kenyan highlands, people living in areas with high TWI appeared to be exposed to a greater risk of malaria then those in areas with low TWI. They also report that the effect of TWI appears stronger than that of land use.

Our TWI measure follows the long-standing tradition in the literature, especially modern macroeconomics on economic growth and development, that treats geographic features as exogenous. As noted in Nordhaus (2006), these geographic variables "may be nonstochastic on the relevant time scale (such as latitude, distance from coastlines, or elevation) or they may be stochastic with slowly moving means and variability (such as climate or soils)..... [they] are statistically exogenous in the sense that they cause, but to a first approximation are not caused by, economic and other social variables." In this context of historical demography (marriages), the VV paper argues for the assumption that variations in certain geographic features (such as land suitability) are exogenous. The literature has also used similar measures of malaria risks and argues for their exogeneity. For instance, like our measure, McCord et al. (2017) is based only on the geographic landscape in the area and does not use any information on human population and behavior (such as population density), which can affect malaria outcomes but are endogenous to marriage and fertility behavior. Effectively, such identification comes from a very specific interaction between the Anopheles vector and the geographic features of the landscape. Our measure is intuitively similar to the one used in McCord et al. (2017) in that we both use exogenous ecological conditions to capture the malaria burden, but we use geographic information that is more readily available and hence more suitable in the historical context. Mitton (2016) and Kiszewski et al. (2004) create a global grid of malaria risk based on climatic factors that are tied to specific locations (temperature and precipitation). They also argue that "as the measure is based on predetermined factors, it is arguably exogenous to income levels (see Sachs, 2003)." Furthermore, in our analysis, we also control for many refined fixed effects in our estimations that would at least make the conditional exogeneity assumption of TWI plausible. That our results are robust to addressing these issues lends further credibility to the exogeneity assumption.

It is also useful to note that arguing the TWI is exogenous does not preclude the possibility that it is correlated with other determinants of marriage timing. The geographic factors could affect marriage timing indirectly via other determinants of marriage timing such as pastoralism and mortality rates (see below), and such mechanisms by definition imply correlations between the TWI and these variables. However, such correlation is not to be confused with omitted variable bias, but simply the estimated effects should be interpreted as the total effects of the disease burden on marriage timing, including the indirect effects. In the premodern historical context, for instance, it is difficult to measure economic development, such as income and wealth, and culture at the parish level. These unobservables, as alluded above, are important channels through which geography affects marriages rates since they are shaped by geographic variables but are also determinants of marriage rates. When such unobservables are excluded in estimations, our estimated coefficients capture such indirect effects.

3. DATA

Kent Female Age at First Marriage. The outcome variable of interest. Prior to civil marriage in 1836, legal marriages in England were administered by the church, and the vast majority of marriages were conducted by the Church of England. In part to prevent consanguineous or otherwise invalid marriages, a couple wishing to be married had to acquire permission via a license from the bishop or via the "bann" (a waiting period of 3 weeks during which the impending nuptials were publicly announced). Licenses were a popular method of obtaining formal permission from the church to marry; it has been estimated that one-fifth to one-third of marriages were approved via license rather than bann (Outhwaite, 1973). In 1694, a small fee of 5s. was required for a license, but this falls at the very end of our study period; marriage licenses are often used as a source for historical demography (Laslett, 1965, p. 112, used precisely the same archive we use for a county-level reconstruction), and since we are interested in cross-parish comparisons, any sample biases that did arise from the choice of licenses as a data-source should not affect our analysis: there is no particular reason why the choice to obtain authorization via license rather than bann would systematically vary according to the health environment of the parish. The ecclesiastical authorities in Canterbury (the episcopal seat of Kent) kept records of the marriage licenses issued from the 16th century onward. Marriage licenses are a major source of genealogical reconstruction, preserved in church archives across England.

By a stroke of good fortune, the marriage licenses preserved in the Archives of Canterbury have been published in full (spanning nine volumes) because of their genealogical interest. Each marriage recorded follows a standard format, providing necessary information for our analysis, albeit limited, such as the name of the bride and groom, their home parish, and date of marriage. We include only records in which the woman is marrying for the first time, confirmed by her explicit identification as virgin or spinster. It is worth noting that the use of license records as the source of data avoids some of the pitfalls of family reconstitution data, since a bride did not have to marry in her parish of birth in order to be included. Our empirical analysis includes 4,843 individuals from 261 parishes during the period of 1600–1700.

TWI Wetness index, our measure to capture disease environment. To calculate the TWI for Kent, we first projected the Digital Elevation Model (DEM) data from the Shuttle Radar Topography Mission to a projected coordinate system (British National Grid). We then calculated the slope, flow direction, and flow accumulation based on the elevation data for each grid cell in a parish. The TWI was calculated as follows:

$$\text{TWI} = \ln(a/\tan b)$$

where a is the local upslope area that drains through a certain grid cell and b is the local slope in radians. As we can see in Fig. 1, there exists substantial variation in TWI in Kent. We also plot the distribution of average parish-level TWI in Fig. 2. The mean level of TWI in our full-sample is 12.280, with the standard deviation of 1.064. The maximum level is 17.028 and the minimum is 10.168. In addition to cross-parish variations in TWI, there also exist substantial variations in TWI between neighboring parishes. Fig. 1 illustrates the pattern: parishes Headcorn (labelled as A) and Ulcombe (labelled as B) are neighboring parishes sharing a border but have starkly different disease environments. As we will see, such variations will provide enough source of identification power for our regression discontinuity approach below. Specifically, it ensures a sharp discontinuity in TWI exposure and geocoded marriage data at the parish borders so that we can zero in on marriages occurring within a narrow bandwidth (distance to border) of that discontinuity.

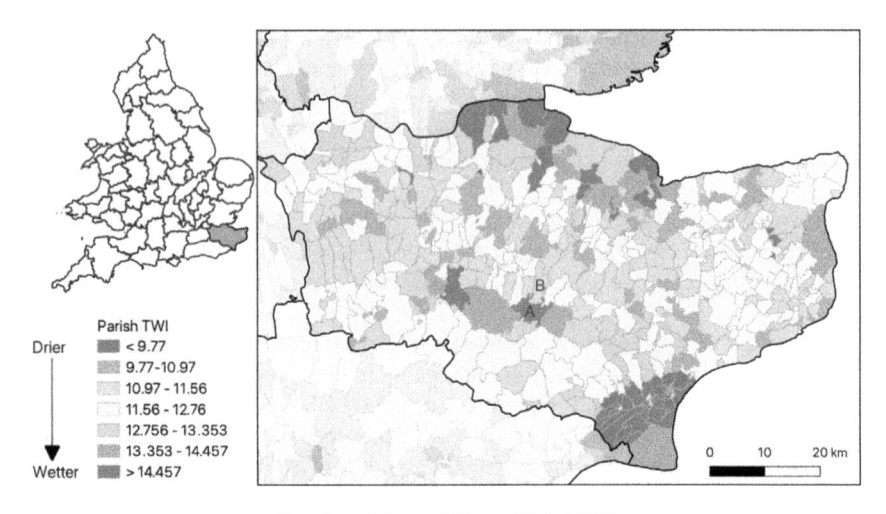

Fig. 1.   Map of Kent With TWI.

For our analysis of potential mechanisms driving our results, we also construct the following variables.

Kent Crude Death Rate/Crude Birth Rate. To construct CDR/CBRs, the total number of deaths/births and the total at-risk population must be known. We have assembled a CDR and CBR for 146 parishes in Kent by averaging annual births/deaths over two 25-year periods, 1676–1700 and 1776–1800, when an approximately contemporaneous census gives a reasonable measure of the total at-risk population. The number of births and deaths are constructed from the parish registers which have been transcribed and are available for purchase from the Kent Family History Society (https://www.kfhs.org.uk). The authors have manually tabulated the number of baptisms and burials for each of these 25-year intervals. The total at-risk population for each parish in 1676 has been drawn from the Compton Census of 1676, one of the earliest counts of English population at the parish level (Whiteman, 1986). The population figures for 1801 are derived from the national census of that year, as corrected by Wrigley (Wrigley and Satchell, 2011). It should be noted that these reconstructions are far more fine-grained than most historical analyses allow, and yet they are also rough by the standards of more modern datasets. We have had to treat the populations in 1676 and 1801 as though they were the at-risk population for each of the 25 years averaged in the series of births and deaths, but such a procedure accurately captures the spatial variation without introducing systemic bias. In this chapter, the CDR is always reported as a measure of deaths per 1,000 at-risk population.

Kent Land-use. Data on the amount of each parish dedicated to pastoral agriculture has been derived from the detailed land surveys that were carried out following the Tithe Commutation Act of 1836 (Kain & Prince, 2006). Following what has been done for the county level in previous analyses Voigtländer and Voth (2013), we tabulated the amount of land categorized as pasture for each parish and divided by the sum of land categorized as pasture plus land categorized as arable, to compute the pastoralism index.

4. STATISTICAL METHOD

Our baseline specification is given by

$$\text{FAFM}_{ij} = \beta_0 + \beta_1 \cdot \text{Disease}_j + \epsilon_{i,j}$$

where FAFM_{ij} is ith female age at first marriage in jth parish; Disease_j is the TWI capturing the disease environment in parish j. The coefficient β_1 is the parameter of interest, measuring the relationship between disease environment and female age at first marriage.

In the premodern historical context, we often cannot observe individual or parish characteristics, and hence, one may be concerned that results are influenced by omitted variables. It is, however, compelling to have individual-level data from a small region with enormous heterogeneity in the health environment but otherwise homogeneous culture, technology, and institutions. Kent was dominated by Anglican Christianity, equipped by the same technologies, and governed by the same institutions throughout. By focusing on the parishes within the county of Kent, we are able to control for variation in any variables that vary only at the county or higher levels. Note that a lower-level fixed effects model includes all higher fixed effects such as region and country fixed effects. Furthermore, our measure of the disease environment is constructed based on factors independent of human behavior. Many variables that differ across parishes may simply be an outcome of the disease environment and do not bias the estimates; at most, they could simply change the interpretation of our results. For example, these parishes may differ in many dimensions such as mortality rates, agricultural structure, urban status, economic development, and population density, which themselves could be an outcome of the disease environment and the channels through which disease environment affects marriage behavior. Excluding these variables simply means that our coefficient captures the total effect of the disease environment. Below, we examine some of the most plausible channels, such as pastoralism and mortality. We also observe that historically, the marsh parishes were reputed for their unhealthiness, but not other particularly distinctive traits (Dobson, 2003).

To further eliminate possible omitted variable bias, we also employ the regression discontinuity (RD) approach. To the best of our knowledge, this chapter is among the first to use such a method in the premodern (as opposed to modern) historical context. The idea is to compare only individuals on opposite sides of parish boundaries. Conceptually, if the parishes vary smoothly across space, except their geographic landscapes, these individuals differ only by the geographic environment in which they live or grew up. By restricting the sample to only those close to the borders, we are then able to control for individual and parish differences (on average). The parish was the smallest possible unit in which people were organized. Specifically, we estimate the following model:

$$\text{FAFM}_{i,j,p} = \beta_0 + \beta_1 \cdot \text{Disease}_j + \gamma_p + \epsilon_{i,j}$$

where γ_p is a vector of bordering dummies, indicating the pth pair of neighboring parishes. These dummies also control for any unobservable characteristics shared by individuals on either side of the parish border. In practice, this is equivalent to calculating the differences in average age at first marriage on opposite sides of parish borders. To take into account the dyadic structure in our analysis, we bootstrap our standard errors based on 500 random samples drawn from these pairs of the original sample.

It is useful to comment on the RD approach employed here. First, as discussed above, there exists substantial variation in TWI in Kent, not only across parishes but also between neighboring parishes. Existence of such variations indeed provides a substantial discontinuity at the borders necessary for the RD estimation, which more importantly is corroborated by the significance level of our estimates below. Second, our approach is similar to Black (1999), one of the classic papers that pioneered the use of the RD approach in the economics literature; in her paper, Black (1999) compares houses located on attendance district boundaries within school districts to infer the parental valuation of elementary education since "houses then differ only by the elementary school the child attends." In our cases, parishes differ only by the geographic environment. Third, while estimation of the causal effects based on the RD design is achieved using the OLS, it is actually a nonparametric RD model with bandwidth (the distance to the border) essentially equal to zero. Wupper and Finger (2022) provide numerous examples on how historical events generate discontinuities at the border and RD are used. All such analyses rely on sorting on a unit's distance to a specific point in space. For example, Appau et al. (2021) estimate the effect of bombings and use of Agent Orange during the Vietnam War on current agricultural productivity in the country. In their RD design, distance to the border between North and South Vietnam is used as the running variable, while in our context, the use of only bordering parishes is the same as including only the areas with distance to the border being zero! Fourth, unlike many other contexts in which one may be concerned with manipulation of the "forcing variable," our case is less of a concern since again the geographic environment is relatively fixed and cannot be easily changed especially in the premodern era. Finally, econometric approaches for causal inference rely on assumptions that are essentially untestable, but its validity can only be argued for and its implications assessed. Our approach is preferred to the IV approach in VV because there could be many possible county-level variations that were correlated with and thus invalidate the IV. By contrast, our approach focusing on Kent county controls for all such county-level heterogeneities.

5. RESULTS

5.1 Relationship Between Disease Environment and Age at First Marriage

Panel A of Table 1 presents our baseline specifications. We find a robust association between the TWI and FAFM. Women in wetter parishes in Kent married significantly earlier. This relationship is robust to the measurement of the TWI, as well as further controlling for the variation of the TWI within the parish. In Columns (3) and (4) using the minimum wetness level, the impact continues to be sizeable and statistically significant, although slightly smaller than using the average index.

The effect is substantial. Take the coefficient in Column (1) as an example; increasing the wetness index by one unit can lead to a reduction of female age at first marriage by approximately 2 months (0.155×12 months). Note that the standard deviation of the wetness index is 1.06, so this impact is roughly the same as the impact of one-standard-deviation change in the index on age at first marriage. To put this result further in perspective, note that the minimum (maximum) wetness value is 10.1678 (17.028) and its corresponding age at first marriage 24.727 (20.5). Using our result, moving from minimum to maximum disease environment (holding everything else constant) can decrease age at first marriage by roughly 1.064 years, accounting for more than 25% of the difference in marriage age between minimum and maximum disease environments ($= 1.064/(24.727 - 20.5)$).

Next, we repeat our analysis using only pairs of neighboring parishes (Panel B). We continue to find a statistically significant, negative impact of malaria environment on female age at first marriage. This result implies that while there may be some

Table 1. Disease Environment (Wetness Index) and Age at First Marriage Among Parishes in Kent.

	Average TWI		Minimum TWI	
	(1)	(2)	(3)	(4)
Panel A: Pooled Sample				
Disease environment	−0.155**	−0.168**	−0.135*	−0.140*
(Wetness index)	(0.072)	(0.076)	(0.075)	(0.076)
Standard deviation		0.129		−0.029
Disease environment		(0.151)		(0.145)
Panel B: Neighboring Parishes Only				
Disease environment	−0.151*	−0.301***	−0.225***	−0.191**
(Wetness index)	(0.078)	(0.100)	(0.084)	(0.091)
Standard deviation		0.512***		0.230
Disease environment		(0.146)		(0.146)

Notes: 1. ***$p < 0.01$, **$p < 0.05$, *$p < 0.01$. Malaria burden is measured as wetness index discussed in the text. We first projected the Digital Elevation Model (DEM) data from the Shuttle Radar Topography Mission to a projected coordinate system (British National Grid). We then calculated the slope, flow direction, and flow accumulation based on the elevation data for each grid cell in a parish. *Average TWI* refers to average wetness index (disease environment) in a parish, while *Minimum TWI* refers to minimum wetness index (disease environment) in a parish.
2. In Panel A: the coefficient on *Disease Environment* is the coefficient on the wetness index from the regression of age at first marriage on (average or minimum) parish-level wetness index, without and with the within-parish standard deviation of wetness index as a control variable. The sample consists of 4,843 individuals from 261 parishes. Robust standard errors are reported in parentheses.
3. In Panel B: the coefficient on *Disease Environment* is the coefficient on the wetness index from the regression of age at first marriage on (average or minimum) parish-level wetness index, controlling for parish-pair fixed effects, without and with the within-parish standard deviation of wetness index as a control variable. 778 pairs of neighboring parishes are used in estimation (note that some parishes can have multiple neighboring parishes). Reported in parentheses are the bootstrapped standard errors taking into account the neighboring nature of the data based on 500 replications.

spatially varied determinants of marriage outcomes or migration patterns across parishes correlated with the disease environment, such correlation or heterogeneity (as a whole) may be too weak to impact our analysis. This is not surprising since our wetness index is considered to be a rather exogenous variable. To the extent that the RD (border sample) results are valid, the fact that our results are similar to the border sample should be considered as evidence of robustness.

5.2 Investigating Potential Channels

Our analysis above documents a strong association between disease environment and age at first marriage. We next examine two important hypotheses proposed in the literature: the pastoralism and mortality channels.

Mechanism 1: Disease Environment, Pastoralism, and Age at first Marriage. In VV, the authors consider that high mortality resulting from the Black Death could lead to land abundance, causing a shift to the pastoral sector in favor of female employment. In their paper, the tragic event was large scale, and their empirical analysis showing the link between the Black Death and pastoralism (Section III.B in their paper) is only anecdotal rather than formal. We note that their demonstration of the link between pastoralism and FAFM has been recently criticized, as has the requirement in their model (poorly substantiated in the medieval historical record) that the EMP emerged only following the Black Death (Edwards & Ogilvie, 2018). Nevertheless, it is important to examine whether the pastoralism channel holds in our context. The results are presented in Table 2.

Table 2. Investigating Channel A: *Pastoralism (Full Sample).*

	Average TWI		Minimum TWI	
	(1)	(2)	(3)	(4)
Panel A: Outcome – Share of Pastoralism				
Disease environment	0.091***	0.103***	0.098***	0.101***
(Wetness index)	(0.014)	(0.015)	(0.017)	(0.016)
Standard deviation of		−0.056*		0.054*
Disease environment		(0.032)		(0.028)
Panel B: Outcome – Female Age at First Marriage				
Share of pastoralism	0.099			
	(0.330)			
Panel C: Outcome – Female Age at First Marriage				
Disease environment	−0.294***	−0.406***	−0.378***	−0.371***
(Wetness index)	(0.081)	(0.091)	(0.093)	(0.093)
Share of pastoralism	−0.025	0.126	0.090	0.091
	(0.369)	(0.373)	(0.374)	(0.374)
Standard deviation of		0.487***		0.079
Disease environment		(0.177)		(0.159)

Notes: 1. See note 1 in Table (1).
2. In Panel A: the coefficient on *Disease Environment* is the coefficient on the wetness index from the regression of share of pastoralism on (average or minimum) parish-level wetness index, without and with the within-parish standard deviation of wetness index as a control variable. The sample consists of 232 parishes. Robust standard errors are reported in parentheses.
3. In Panel B: we examine whether or not *share of pastoralism* is a determinant of female age at first marriage and hence a potentially viable mechanism through which disease environment affects female age at first marriage. The coefficient on *Share of Pastoralism* is from the regression of age at first marriage on Share of Pastoralism. The sample consists of 4,474 individuals from 232 parishes. Robust standard errors are reported in parentheses.
4. In Panel C: the coefficient on *Disease Environment* is the coefficient on the wetness index from the regression of age at first marriage on (average or minimum) parish-level wetness index, controlling for share of pastoralism, without and with the within-parish standard deviation of wetness index as a control variable. The sample consists of 4,474 individuals from 232 parishes. Robust standard errors are reported in parentheses.

We first examine whether the disease environment is indeed related to pastoralism. Panel A presents these results. We find a statistically significant, positive association between the disease environment and the share of pastoralism in a parish, consistent with VV's hypothesis. However, we fail to find any significant relationship between pastoralism and female age at first marriage in our context (Panel B). When both disease environment and the share of pastoralism are included in the model, the disease environment continues to have a negative impact on FAFM. In contrast, the share of pastoralism plays no significant role in explaining FAFM, nor in accounting for the negative relationship between disease environment and FAFM. All the results are robust to use of different measures of disease environment, controlling for the standard deviation of disease environment in a parish, as well as using the regression discontinuity approach and only the neighboring parishes (Table 3).

Mechanism 2: Disease Environment, Mortality, and Female Age at First Marriage. Next, we examine whether or not mortality plays a role in explaining

Table 3. Investigating Channel A: *Pastoralism (Neighboring Sample).*

	Average TWI		Minimum TWI	
	(1)	(2)	(3)	(4)
Panel A: Outcome – Share of Pastoralism				
Disease environment	0.034***	0.035***	0.037***	0.042***
(Wetness index)	(0.009)	(0.011)	(0.010)	(0.010)
Standard deviation of		−0.002		0.037***
Disease environment		(0.016)		(0.014)
Panel B: Outcome – Female Age at First Marriage				
Share of pastoralism	0.344			
	(0.467)			
Panel C: Outcome – Female Age at First Marriage				
Disease environment	−0.252**	−0.446***	−0.297***	−0.268***
(Wetness index)	(0.106)	(0.105)	(0.095)	(0.095)
Share of pastoralism	0.536	0.546	0.550	0.488
	(0.449)	(0.446)	(0.471)	(0.436)
Standard deviation of		0.606		0.183
Disease environment		(0.181)		(0.161)

Notes: 1. See note 1 in Table (1).
2. In Panel A: the coefficient on *Disease Environment* is the coefficient on the wetness index from the regression of share of pastoralism on (average or minimum) parish-level wetness index, without and with the within-parish standard deviation of wetness index as a control variable. In Panel B: we examine whether or *not share of pastoralism* is a determinant of female age at first marriage and hence a potentially viable mechanism through which disease environment affects female age at first marriage. The coefficient on *Share of Pastoralism* is from the regression of age at first marriage on Share of Pastoralism. In Panel C: the coefficient on *Disease Environment* is the coefficient on the wetness index from the regression of age at first marriage on (average or minimum) parish-level wetness index, controlling for share of pastoralism, without and with the within-parish standard deviation of wetness index as a control variable. The sample consists of 630 pairs of parishes. Reported in parentheses are the bootstrapped standard errors taking into account the neighboring nature of the data based on 500 replications.

our results. Using records described below, we have constructed Crude Death Rates for 146 parishes in Kent for the last quarter of the 17th century and the last quarter of the 18th century. The results are presented in Table 4.

We first examine whether the disease environment is indeed related to mortality. Unsurprisingly, we find a significant correlation between the disease environment and the Crude Death Rate (Panel A). The effects are substantial. For example, in Column (2), the impact on crude death rate of average TWI, after controlling for its

Table 4. Investigating Channel B: *Mortality (Full Sample)*.

	Average TWI		Minimum TWI	
	(1)	(2)	(3)	(4)
Panel A: Outcome – Crude Death Rate				
Disease environment	8.704***	9.185***	8.601***	9.603***
(Wetness index)	(2.555)	(2.920)	(2.903)	(2.857)
Standard deviation of		−2.642		8.448**
Disease environment		(4.328)		(3.391)
Panel B: Outcome – Female Age at First Marriage				
Crude death rate	−0.017***			
	(0.004)			
Panel C: Outcome – Female Age at First Marriage				
Disease environment	−0.337***	−0.388***	−0.326***	−0.341***
(Wetness index)	(0.107)	(0.118)	(0.117)	(0.117)
Crude death rate	−0.014***	−0.013***	−0.014***	−0.014***
	(0.004)	(0.004)	(0.004)	(0.004)
Standard deviation of		0.231		−0.167
Disease environment		(0.245)		(0.224)
Panel D: Outcome – Female Age at First Marriage				
Disease environment	−0.429***	−0.486***	−0.429***	−0.446***
(Wetness index)	(0.103)	(0.112)	(0.112)	(0.112)
Standard deviation of		0.271		−0.235
Disease environment		(0.243)		(0.224)

Notes: 1. See note 1 in Table (1).
2. In Panel A: the coefficient on *Disease Environment* is the coefficient on the wetness index from the regression of crude death rate on (average or minimum) parish-level wetness index, without and with the within-parish standard deviation of wetness index as a control variable. The sample consists of 121 parishes. Robust standard errors are reported in parentheses.
3. In Panel B: we examine whether or not *mortality (Crude Death Rate)* is a determinant of female age at first marriage and hence a potentially viable mechanism through which disease environment affects female age at first marriage. The coefficient on *Crude Death Rate* is from the regression of age at first marriage on crude death rate. The sample consists of 2,772 individuals from 121 parishes. Robust standard errors are reported in parentheses.
4. In Panel C: the coefficient on *Disease Environment* is the coefficient on the wetness index from the regression of age at first marriage on (average or minimum) parish-level wetness index, controlling for crude death rate, without and with the within-parish standard deviation of wetness index as a control variable. The sample consists of 2,772 individuals from 121 parishes. Robust standard errors are reported in parentheses.
5. In Panel D: We replicate the results in Table (1) but with the same sample of 2,772 individuals from 121 parishes for which information on crude death rate is available.

standard deviation, is about 9.185. For an average parish in our data with 36.1949 per 1,000 at-risk population, such impact is equivalent to a more than 25% increase. Higher mortality rates are in turn associated with early marriage age (Panel B). When both the disease environment and the Crude Death Rates are included in the model, the disease environment continues to have a negative impact on FAFM, and so does the Crude Death Rate. In the meantime, the magnitude of the impact of the disease environment on FAFM decreases substantially, and the change of the impact signifies the important role of mortality as a channel in explaining the relationship between disease environment and FAFM. Remember that we have information on the Crude Death Rate only for a subset of the original sample, so to put the change in perspective, we re-estimate our baseline model using this subset of parishes (Panel D). By comparing the results in Panels C and D, we can see that the Crude Death Rate explains roughly 20% of the observed association between the disease environment and FAFM. The results are again robust to using the regression discontinuity approach (Table 5).

Table 5. Investigating Channel B: *Mortality (Neighboring Sample)*.

	Average TWI		Minimum TWI	
	(1)	(2)	(3)	(4)
Panel A: Outcome – Crude Death Rate				
Disease environment	5.902***	6.308***	5.950***	6.654***
(Wetness index)	(2.012)	(2.383)	(2.291)	(2.253)
Standard deviation of		−2.07		5.048*
Disease environment		(3.335)		(2.715)
Panel B: Outcome – Female Age at First Marriage				
Crude death rate	−0.029***			
	(0.008)			
Panel C: Outcome – Female Age at First Marriage				
Disease environment	−0.368**	−0.378**	−0.275	−0.329**
(Wetness index)	(0.151)	(0.172)	(0.176)	(0.164)
Crude death rate	−0.025***	−0.025***	−0.026***	−0.025***
	(0.008)	(0.008)	(0.008)	(0.008)
Standard deviation of		0.049		−0.345
Disease environment		(0.343)		(0.265)

Notes: 1. See note 1 in Table (1).
2. In Panel A: the coefficient on *Disease Environment* is the coefficient on the wetness index from the regression of crude death rate on (average or minimum) parish-level wetness index, without and with the within-parish standard deviation of wetness index as a control variable. In Panel B: the coefficient on *crude death rate* is the coefficient on the wetness index from the regression of age at first marriage on crude death rate. In Panel C: the coefficient on *Disease Environment* is the coefficient on the wetness index from the regression of age at first marriage on (average or minimum) parish-level wetness index, controlling for crude death rate, without and with the withinparish standard deviation of wetness index as a control variable. The sample consists of 203 pairs of parishes. Reported in parentheses are the bootstrapped standard errors taking into account the neighboring nature of the data based on 500 replications.

5.3 Further Correlational Analysis

Here, we briefly provide further preliminary evidence supporting our hypothesis, using alternative data sources at the county/regional level from England and Italy, respectively. Refined micro-level data like ours are generally not available, especially where they cover such stark variations in the disease environment. While these further results should be interpreted as correlational, rather than causal, these analyses are still indicative and strengthen our findings. We believe they could be of interest to many historical demographers and economic historians. We summarize the results here.

County-level Analysis, England. First, we make use of an existing county-level index of past malaria burden in England created by Kuhn et al. (2003). They tabulated deaths attributed to "ague" by county between 1840 and 1910 in the national records of the Registrar General and constructed an ague death rate per 100,000 population. Ague was a common term for an acute, intermittent fever, and it is a reasonable proxy for malaria burden. While the dataset covers a short period of time overlapping with the later 19th century, a period in which the prevalence of malaria had started to decline, the ague death rate by county captures historic regional variation; coastal, marshy areas and "fens" with traditional reputations as unhealthy exhibit higher index values. This regional-level variation appears to have been of long standing (Dobson, 2003; Gowland & Western, 2012; Kuhn et al., 2003).

We then deploy the county-level FAFM data previously used to support the pastoralism thesis in VV. The county-level data on FAFM come from the well-known study of Wrigley et al. (1997). Using family reconstitution methods, age at marriage was estimated for 26 parishes across England from 1580 to 1837. The aggregated FAFM estimates for each parish are then treated as representative samples for the 26 counties in which they lie and analyzed in conjunction with county-level data on, e.g., land-use. We again find a significant association between malaria burden and FAFM (Table 6). Using corrected figures for FAFM that account for the magnitude of the migration-censoring bias in each of

Table 6. Malaria Burden (Ague Rates) and Age at First Marriage (English Parish-Level).

	Outcome – Female Age at First Marriage					
	1600–1837			1600–1749		
	(1)	(2)	(3)	(4)	(5)	(6)
Ague rate	−0.020***	−0.020***	−0.009**	−0.026***	−0.026***	−0.017***
	(0.004)	(0.003)	(0.004)	(0.005)	(0.005)	(0.005)
Period fixed effects	No	Yes	Yes	No	Yes	Yes
Region fixed effects	No	No	Yes	No	No	Yes
N	112	112	112	66	66	66

Note: ***$p < 0.01$, **$p < 0.05$, *$p < 0.01$. Malaria burden is measured as ague rates discussed in the text. The sample consists of 4,843 valid observations.

Table 7. Pastoral Production, Ague Rates, and Age at First Marriage (English Parish-Level).

	Outcome – Female Age at First Marriage					
	1600–1837					
	OLS (1)	OLS (2)	OLS (3)	OLS (4)	IV (5)	IV (6)
Pastoral (1290)	4.036***	2.254*	5.973*	5.971*	8.085***	6.920***
	(0.876)	(0.930)	(2.935)	(2.892)	(1.345)	(1.692)
DMV	0.059***	0.026	0.075**	0.064*	0.093***	0.076**
	(0.017)	(0.018)	(0.025)	(0.026)	(0.020)	(0.024)
Ague rate		−0.015***		−0.007*		−0.006
		−0.004		−0.004		−0.005
N	112	112	112	112	112	112
	1600–1749					
	OLS (7)	OLS (8)	OLS (9)	OLS (10)	IV (11)	IV (12)
Pastoral (1290)	4.321***	1.964	6.817	6.533	7.759***	5.286*
	(1.237)	(1.263)	(4.384)	(4.092)	(1.786)	(2.074)
DMV	0.066**	0.022	0.067	0.048	0.091***	0.054
	(0.024)	(0.024)	(0.039)	(0.037)	(0.026)	(0.029)
Ague rate		−0.022***		−0.016**		−0.015*
		(0.005)		(0.005)		(0.006)
N	66	66	66	66	66	66

Note: ***$p < 0.01$, **$p < 0.05$, *$p < 0.01$. Malaria burden is measured as ague rates discussed in the text. The county-level data on FAFM come from Wrigley et al. (1997). Age at marriage was estimated for 26 parishes across England from 1580 to 1837. The data on pastoralism (Pastoral) are obtained from Voigtländer and Voth (2013).

the 26 counties Wrigley (1994), we also find that the relationship is generally robust to the inclusion of the pastoralism variable in VV (Table 7). Furthermore, introducing a county-level measure of the malaria burden as a control, we find that the effect of pastoralism is weakened or disappears (in terms of statistical significance), depending on model specifications.

Evidence from Italy. Italy is a significant test case because its historical documentation is reasonably rich and because malarial diseases were prevalent but with strong regional variation (see generally Bruce-Chwatt & de Zulueta, 1980; Snowden, 2008). In Italy, three main species of competent Anopheline vectors transmitted malarial diseases: A. sacharovi, A. labranchiae, and A. superpictus. The latter two were of greatest importance in central and southern Italy. A. labranchiae was probably the most important vector of malaria in Italy. It mostly breeds in fresh water and was common in coastal plains; it is not found north of 42-3°N; it is generally a good vector up to about 300 masl. It prefers regions with a minimum temperature of 14.3°C and an average diurnal temperature range of 12.7°C. It feeds on a range of species but prefers human blood. It will bite aggressively and eat indoors. Feeding behavior is most intense around sunset.

For Italy, we have constructed regional malaria-burden indices from late 19th-century national cause-of-death statistics. In Italy, national statistics become increasingly available after unification (in 1871). Large-scale malaria eradication efforts did not pick up pace until the very end of the 19th and beginning of the 20th century. There is thus a window of a few decades, before malaria was controlled, during which reasonably good official statistics exist. Before germ theory and modern diagnostics, nosological categories did not align perfectly with the actual infectious causes of various diseases. For the malaria-burden index, we have used a 6-year average of deaths from "malarial fevers and swamp wasting" during the years 1887–1892. Using the regional populations from the 1881 census, we take the average annual malaria deaths per 100,000 population to construct the index. The measurements span from Liguria, with a negligible 3.03 deaths per 100,000 from malaria, to Sardinia, at 308.60. As with the county-level data from England, the regions that had a historic reputation for being malarial also have the highest indices, suggesting that our measurement is not only valid but captures deep historic variations.

We have identified data for historical female age at first marriage in the existing historical demography literature, providing a reasonably representative sample of variation across Italy. We use syntheses by Rettaroli (Rettaroli, 1995) and by Dal Panta and Livi-Bacci (del Panta & Livi-Bacci, 1980) which report 42 regional measures from the 17th and 18th centuries. We also draw from an important dataset from southern Italy constructed by the historian Gerard Delille (Delille, 1977), who used a sample of parish records from the Kingdom of Naples between the 16th and 18th centuries to recover data about the social and demographic history of a number of villages.

Fig. 2 depicts the geographic distribution of malaria burden (annual deaths from malaria per 100,000 population) in Italy according to our index. Northern regions are generally associated with lower malaria burden than southern regions. Fig. 3 plots the density of age at first marriage by regions. In general, northern regions with low malaria incidence exhibit the EMP, while in southern regions with higher malaria burden, women married significantly earlier.

To quantify the actual impacts of malaria burden on marriage age, we perform regression analysis using our data. The results are presented in Table 8. The first column shows the bivariate association between malaria burden and age at first marriage. We confirm a strong negative relationship indicated in Fig. 3. When the malaria burden increases, age at first marriage indeed decreases. In other words, women marry early in unhealthy areas but delay their marriages in healthier environments. The effect is statistically significant. Every death per 100,000 could lead to a reduction of 0.051 in age at first marriage in the area. The average malaria burden is 102.07 and 14.27 per 100,000 in the Southern and Northern Italy, respectively. Using our estimated effect, such stark difference is translated into a difference of 4.47 years in age at first marriage between regions.

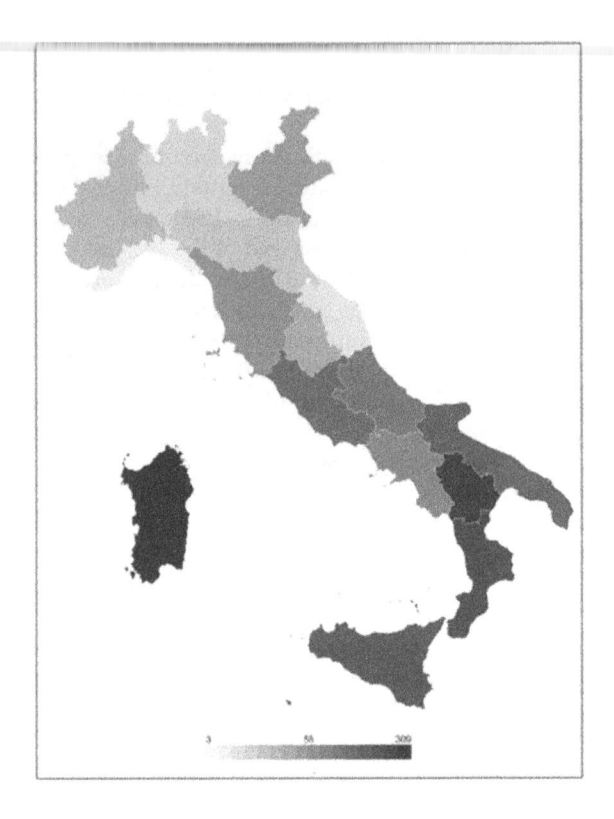

Fig. 2.   Annual Deaths From Malaria per 100,000 Population.

To further control for variation in possible underlying institutions and cultures, we also include region fixed effects (North vs South) in the Column (2). Our result continues to hold. The estimated effect is relatively stable, and the difference between the results in Columns (1) and (2) is statistically insignificant. One may be concerned about the systematic differences in measurements due to the sources of the data. We further control for such differences by adding the source fixed effects in Column (3), and the results remain unchanged. Finally, our results are also robust to inclusion of period fixed effects accounting for variation in age at first marriage over time (Column 4).

In Columns (5) and (6), we repeat our analysis with the full set of controls using only the Delille (1985) data. The data from Delille (1985) are primarily from Southern Italy and also have more refined year information from which age at first marriage is collected. This allows us to further control for any unobservable region-specific differences that cross-country analyses cannot. In Column (5), we continue to find a significant, negative relationship between malaria burden and age at first marriage. In Column (6), we also experiment with a linear time trend and find the same result. We report these findings only as correlations.

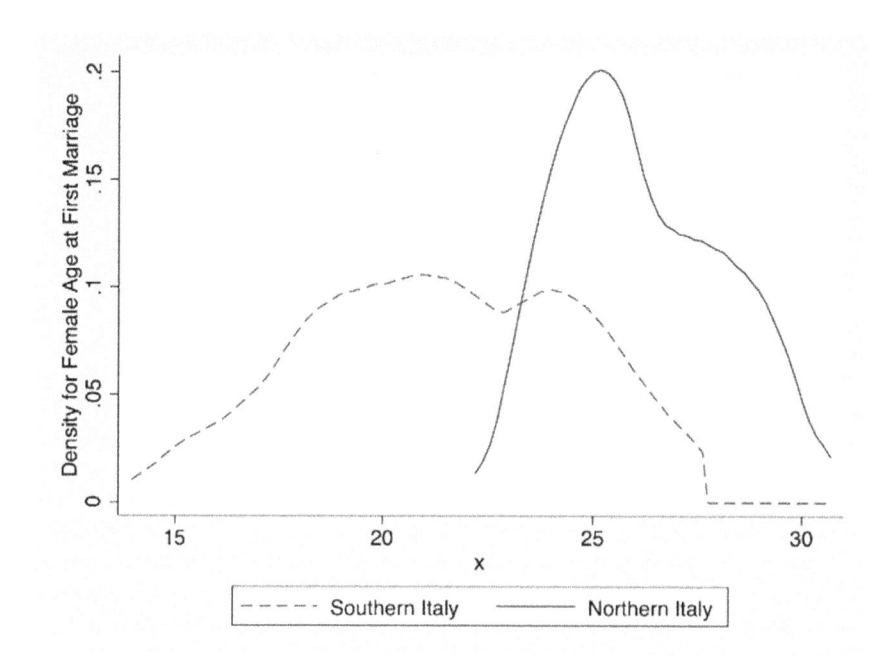

Fig. 3. Distribution of Age at First Marriage (Southern vs Northern Italy).

Table 8. Malaria Burden (Ague Rates) and Age at First Marriage (Italian Regional Level Data).

	Outcome – Female Age at First Marriage					
	All Sources			Delille (1985) Data Only		
	(1)	(2)	(3)	(4)	(5)	(6)
Malaria burden	−0.051***	−0.045***	−0.050***	−0.043***	−0.058***	−0.060***
	(0.005)	(0.009)	(0.008)	(0.009)	(0.015)	(0.014)
Region fixed effects	No	Yes	Yes	Yes	Yes	Yes
Source fixed effects	No	No	Yes	Yes	Yes	Yes
Period fixed effects	No	No	No	Yes	Yes	No
Linear time trend					No	Yes
N	73	73	73	73	31	31

Note: ***$p < 0.01$, **$p < 0.05$, *$p < 0.01$. Malaria burden is measured as ague rates discussed in the text. We use syntheses by Rettaroli (Rettaroli, 1995) and by Dal Panta and Livi-Bacci (del Panta & Livi-Bacci, 1980) which report 42 regional measures from the 17th and 18th centuries. We also draw from an important dataset from southern Italy constructed by the historian Gerard Delille (Delille, 1977), who used a sample of parish records from the Kingdom of Naples between the 16th and 18th centuries to recover data about the social and demographic history of a number of villages.

They are not only consistent with our findings from England but suggest that the exogenous disease environment can account for the marriage patterns in other parts of Europe and potentially beyond. In Italy, the correlations suggest that through some mechanism, geography exerted a powerful control on FAFM, and the disease environment is a plausible new hypothesis.

6. DISCUSSIONS

Our chapter contributes to the growing literature on the role of health in economic history in three different ways: empirically, methodologically, and substantively. Even though infectious diseases were the prime determinant of morbidity and mortality in premodern societies (Deaton, 2013; Fogel, 2004; Mercer, 2014), geographic variation in the disease burden has been neglected, mostly because data are hard to obtain. This general situation may represent more of a conundrum than has been fully admitted. Significant variation in the infectious disease burden existed before modern development; infectious diseases influence developmental pathways and in turn are influenced by development; yet, direct measures of the disease burden are all far downstream of economic development, obscuring the role of pre-existing variation in the infectious disease environment. To make matters worse, data on mortality and infectious disease are highly sensitive to bias resulting from systematic differences in national reporting systems, making cross-country analysis difficult (McCarthy et al., 2000). Our paper overcomes these empirical challenges by focusing on a disease that was important in past times and geographically structured in its prevalence. Malaria has been a major burden on human health, and historically, its spatial reach was far greater than it is today, including significant parts of Europe. The prevalence of malaria was persistent for millennia, determined in large part by physical geography. We are thus able to perform quantitative tests to study the impacts of a specific disease deeper into the past than is ordinarily possible.

Our effort to collect a large individual-level dataset also allows us to perform a more credible analysis of the effects of the disease environment. Unlike typical cross-country analysis, we apply the regression discontinuity method to exploit data from neighboring areas to isolate the main potential confounders that may impede us from drawing a causal conclusion regarding the impacts of the disease burden. This approach may be useful for many similar situations since historical data are oftentimes too limited to provide sufficient information to control for potentially confounding variables in empirical analyses, let alone test for plausible exogenous variations in the disease environment to identify the causal parameter.

Finally, our findings can contribute to the ongoing debates about the role of geography in economic history. Heavy disease burdens are strongly associated with poor economic performance, but it is debated whether infectious disease is the cause or consequence of poverty, with strong proponents on either side (16, 17). Much recent work demonstrates that the infectious disease burden has a direct effect on fertility, saving and investment, human capital formation, worker productivity, technology pathways, and state formation (Almond, 2006; Alsan, 2015; Baird et al., 2016; Bloom et al., 2014; Eppig et al., 2010; Lorentzen et al., 2008; Sachs & Malaney, 2002). These mechanisms, however, have mostly been demonstrated to work in shallow historical time, usually by comparing the relative success of national economies in achieving "catch-up growth" from the mid-20th century. It is uncontroversial that major population-level differences in the infectious disease burden and mortality preceded modern economic growth (Riley, 2005). Our study suggests a novel channel between the disease environment, and demographic and economic outcomes, via the EMP, that may have operated for centuries. In short, geographic variation in the infectious disease burden can be explored as a neglected but ultimate exogenous factor that might throw light on the deep origins of comparative development.

ACKNOWLEDGEMENT

We offer our sincere thanks to Katrin Kuhn, Becky Gowland, and Mary Dobson, each of whom generously shared data and ideas about the history of malaria. Corresponding author: Le Wang, Department of Ag and Applied Economics, Virginia Tech, VA, 24061. Email: le.wang.econ@gmail.com. The authors are listed alphabetically.

REFERENCES

Acemoglu, D., & Robinson, J. A. (2012). *Why nations fail: The origins of power, prosperity, and poverty*. Crown Books.

Almond, D. (2006). Is the 1918 influenza pandemic over? Long-term effects of in utero influenza exposure in the post-1940 US population. *Journal of Political Economy, 114*(4), 672–712.

Alsan, M. (2015). The effect of the tsetse fly on African development. *The American Economic Review, 105*(1), 382–410.

Appau, S., Churchill, S. A., Smyth, R., & Trinh, T. A. (2021). The long-term impact of the Vietnam War on agricultural productivity. *World Development, 146*, 105613.

Baird, J. K. (2013). Evidence and implications of mortality associated with acute Plasmodium vivax malaria. *Clinical Microbiology Reviews, 26*(1), 36–57.

Baird, S., Hicks, J. H., Kremer, M., & Miguel, E. (2016). Worms at work: Long-run impacts of a child health investment. *Quarterly Journal of Economics, 131*(4), 1637–1680.

Beven, K. J., & Kirkby, M. J. (1979). A physically based, variable contributing area model of basin hydrology [Un Modèle à Base Physique de Zone d'appel Variable de L'hydrologie Du Bassin Versant]. *Hydrological Sciences Journal, 24*(1), 43–69.

Bloom, D. E., Canning, D., & Fink, G. (2014). Disease and development revisited. *Journal of Political Economy, 122*(6), 1355–1366.

Bruce-Chwatt, L. J., & de Zulueta, J. (1980). *The rise and fall of malaria in Europe: A historico-epidemiological study*. Oxford.

Cohen, J. M., Ernst, K. C., Lindblade, K. A., Vulule, J. M., John, C. C., & Wilson, M. L. (2008). Topography-derived wetness indices are associated with household-level malaria risk in two communities in the western Kenyan highlands. *Malaria Journal, 7*(1), 40.

Cohen, J. M., Ernst, K. C., Lindblade, K. A., Vulule, J. M., John, C. C., & Wilson, M. L. (2010). Local topographic wetness indices predict household malaria risk better than land-use and land-cover in the western Kenya highlands. *Malaria Journal, 9*(1), 328.

De Moor, T., & Van Zanden, J. L. (2010). Girl power: The European marriage pattern and labour markets in the North Sea region in the late medieval and early modern period. *The Economic History Review*, *63*(1), 1–33.

Deaton, A. (2013). *The great escape: Health, wealth, and the origins of inequality*. Princeton University Press.

del Panta, L., & Livi Bacci, M. (1980). Le component naturali dell'evoluzione demografica nell'Italia del settecento. In *La popolazione italiana nel Settecento: relazioni e comunicazioni presentate al Convegno su La ripresa demografica del Settecento*, Bologna, 26–28 aprile 1979 (pp. 71–139).

Delille, G. (1977). *Agricoltura e demografia nel Regno di Napoli nei secoli XVIII e XIX*. https://cir.nii.ac.jp/crid/1130000795708066560

Delille, G. (1985). *Famille et propriété dans le royaume de Naples (XVe-XIXe siècle)* (Vol. 259, no. 1). Écoles françaises d'Athènes et de Rome.

Dennison, T., & Ogilvie, S. (2014). Does the European marriage pattern explain economic growth? *The Journal of Economic History*, *74*(3), 651–693.

Dobson, M. J. (2003). *Contours of death and disease in early modern England* (Vol. 29). Cambridge University Press.

Edwards, J., & Ogilvie, S. (2018). *Did the Black Death cause economic development by 'inventing' fertility restriction?* CESifo Working Paper Series. https://www.cesifo.org/en/publications/2018/working-paper/did-black-death-cause-economic-development-inventing-fertility

Eppig, C., Fincher, C. L., & Thornhill, R. (2010). Parasite prevalence and the worldwide distribution of cognitive ability. *Proceedings of the Royal Society B: Biological Sciences*, *277*(1701), 3801–3808.

Fogel, R. W. (2004). *The escape from hunger and premature death, 1700–2100: Europe, America, and the Third World* (Vol. 38). Cambridge University Press.

Foreman-Peck, J. (2011). The Western European marriage pattern and economic development. *Explorations in Economic History*, *48*(2), 292–309.

Gallup, J. L., & Sachs, J. D. (2001). The economic burden of malaria. *The American Journal of Tropical Medicine and Hygiene*, *64*(Suppl. l), 85–96.

Gowland, R. L., & Western, A. G. (2012). Morbidity in the marshes: Using spatial epidemiology to investigate skeletal evidence for malaria in Anglo-Saxon England (Ad 410–1050). *American Journal of Physical Anthropology*, *147*(2), 301–311.

Hajnal, J. (1965). European marriage patterns in perspective. In D. V. Glass & D. Eversley (Eds.), *Population in history* (pp. 101–146). Edward Arnold.

Hajnal, J. (1982). Two kinds of preindustrial household formation system. *Population and Development Review*, 449–494.

Hasted, E. (1798). *The history and topographical survey of the county of Kent* (Vol. 4). W. Bristow.

Kain, R. J. P., & Prince, H. C. (2006). *The tithe surveys of England and Wales* (Vol. 6). Cambridge University Press.

Kiszewski, A., Mellinger, A., Spielman, A., Malaney, P., Sachs, S. E., & Sachs, J. (2004). A global index representing the stability of malaria transmission. *The American Journal of Tropical Medicine and Hygiene*, *70*(5), 486–498.

Kuhn, K. G., Campbell-Lendrum, D. H., Armstrong, B., & Davies, C. R. (2003). Malaria in Britain: Past, present, and future. *Proceedings of the National Academy of Sciences*, *100*(17), 9997–10001.

Laslett, P. (1965). The history of population and social structure. *International Social Science Journal*, *17*(4), 582–593.

Lorentzen, P., McMillan, J., & Wacziarg, R. (2008). Death and development. *Journal of Economic Growth*, *13*(2), 81–124.

Lundh, C., & Kurosu, S. (2014). *Similarity in difference: Marriage in Europe and Asia, 1700–1900*. MIT Press.

McCarthy, D., Wolf, H., & Wu, Y. (2000). *The growth costs of malaria*. National Bureau of Economic Research.

McCord, G. C., Dalton, C., & Sachs, J. D. (2017). Malaria ecology, child mortality & fertility. *Economics and Human Biology*, *24*, 1–17.

Mercer, A. (2014). *Infections, chronic disease, and the epidemiological transition: A new perspective* (Vol. 31). Boydell & Brewer.

Mitton, T. (2016). The wealth of subnations: Geography, institutions, and within-country development. *Journal of Development Economics, 118*, 88–111.

Nordhaus, W. D. (2006). Geography and macroeconomics: New data and new findings. *Proceedings of the National Academy of Sciences, 103*(10), 3510–3517.

Outhwaite, R. B. (1973). Age at marriage in England from the late seventeenth to the nineteenth century. *Transactions of the Royal Historical Society, 23*, 55–70.

Rettaroli, R. (1995). L'età al matrimonio. In M. Barbagli & D. Kertzer (Eds.), *Storia della famiglia italiana, 1750–1950* (pp. 63–102).

Riley, J. C. (2005). Estimates of regional and global life expectancy, 1800–2001. *Population and Development Review, 31*(3), 537–543.

Ronsmans, C. (1996). Birth spacing and child survival in rural Senegal. *International Journal of Epidemiology, 25*(5), 989–997.

Ruggles, S. (1992). Migration, marriage, and mortality: Correcting sources of bias in English family reconstitutions. *Population Studies, 46*(3), 507–522.

Sachs, J. (2012). Reply to Acemoglu and Robinson's response to my book review. Review of Why Nations Fail, by Daron Acemoglu and James Robinson. Jeffrey Sachs. https://www.jeffsachs. org/journal-articles/z37yfg9bcx9k8atat8wez48aebtnzp

Sachs, J., & Malaney, P. (2002). The economic and social burden of malaria. *Nature, 415*(6872), 680–685.

Sachs, J. D. (2003). Institutions matter, but not for everything. *Finance and Development, 40*(2), 38–41.

Snowden, F. (2008). *The conquest of malaria: Italy, 1900–1962.* Yale University Press.

Voigtländer, N., & Voth, H.-J. (2013). How the west "invented" fertility restriction.. *The American Economic Review, 103*(6), 2227–2264.

Whiteman, A. (1986). *The Compton census of 1676: A critical edition.* Oxford University Press.

Wrigley, E. A. (1994). The effect of migration on the estimation of marriage age in family reconstitution studies. *Population Studies, 48*(1), 81–97.

Wrigley, E. A. (2018). No death without birth: The implications of English mortality in the early modern period. In *Problems and methods in the history of medicine* (pp. 133–150). Routledge.

Wrigley, E. A., Davies, R. S., Schofield, R. S., & Oeppen, J. E. (1997). *English population history from family reconstitution 1580–1837.* Cambridge University Press.

Wrigley, E. A., & Satchell, M. (2011). *The early English censuses.* British Academy.

Wupper, D. J., & Finger, R. (2022). Regression discontinuity designs in agricultural and environmental economics. *European Review of Agricultural Economics, 50*(1), 1–28. https://academic.oup.com/ erae/article/50/1/1/6749527

Yamana, T. K. (2015). *Mechanistic modelling of the links between environment, mosquitoes and malaria transmission in the current and future climates of West Africa.* PhD thesis. Massachusetts Institute of Technology.

Zanden, J. L. V., De Moor, T., & Carmichael, S. (2019). Capital women: The European marriage pattern. In *Female empowerment and economic development in Western Europe 1300–1800.* Oxford University Press.

ECONOMIC BONANZA AND WEALTH INEQUALITY: EVIDENCE FROM TAX RECORDS FOR LIMA, PERU

Luis Felipe Zegarra

Pontificia Universidad Católica del Perú, Lima, Peru;
CENTRUM Católica Graduate Business School, Lima, Peru

ABSTRACT

This chapter relies on tax records to estimate the distribution of wealth in 19th century Lima. In particular, by using real estate tax records of 1836 and 1857, I estimate the distribution of wealth of proprietors of Lima prior and during the Guano Era. I find that wealth inequality among proprietors remained practically the same in those two years. During this period of economic bonanza, social mobility was possible but did not change the distribution of wealth. Wealth inequality remained practically the same across real estate proprietors. On the other hand, a comparison of the wealth of proprietors and the labor income of laborers suggests that inequality between proprietors and low-skilled workers increased during the Guano Era.

Keywords: Wealth inequality; economic growth; Latin America; Peru; tax records

JEL Codes: N36; N96; N01; O15; R11

1. INTRODUCTION

For a long time, there has been debate about the relationship between economic growth and inequality. According to Kuznets (1963), as economies grow, inequality first increases then reaches a peak and then declines. The empirical support for the so-called Kuznets curve is mixed. Industrialization may increase

Research in Economic History, Volume 38, 53–75
Published under exclusive licence by Emerald Publishing Limited
ISSN: 0363-3268/doi:10.1108/S0363-326820250000038003

inequality by raising the earnings of those directly linked to fast-growing sectors. Over time, however, as production factors migrate from traditional to modern sectors, inequality may decline. There is some support for the positive relation between inequality and economic growth during industrialization processes (Lindert, 1986; Steckel & Moehling, 2001; Williamson & Lindert, 1980). There is also some support for a decline in inequality among advanced economies in the 20th century. This decline in inequality in that century, however, largely occurred due to government policies (Piketty et al., 2006). Moreover, in the last decades of the 20th century, inequality increased along economic growth (Aghion et al., 1999).

Census data, tax records, and probates allow the researcher to estimate wealth distribution.[1] Using census and tax records, Steckel and Moehling (2001) estimated wealth inequality in the United States in the 19th and early 20th centuries, considering all types of properties, not only real estate. Lindert (1986) used probate records to measure wealth inequality in England and Wales prior to 1900. Piketty et al. (2006) used estate tax records to estimate wealth inequality in France in the 19th and 20th centuries. Gelman and Santilli (2010) used economic censuses to estimate the distribution of land in rural Buenos Aires in 1839–1855. Djenderedjian and Martirén (2012) used census data as well as wills and inventories to estimate wealth inequality in Esperanza and Parana in Argentina in the 1860s.[2]

Peru is an interesting case of study for the relationship between economic growth and inequality. In the middle of the 19th century, the Peruvian economy experienced important changes. In the 1830s and 1840s, the Peruvian export sector remained stagnant. In the late 1840s, the exportation of guano changed the dynamics of the Peruvian economy.[3] Guano became the main export in the 1850s and 1860s: the participation of guano in total exports increased from 2.4% in 1845 to 63% in 1860. Total Peruvian exports increased from around 4.2 million dollars in 1835 to 9.2 million dollars in 1850 and 31 million in 1860. The Guano Era was one the periods of fastest export growth in Latin America. The economy of Lima benefited from the exportation of guano. Lima went through a period of economic bonanza due to the rapid increase in commercial activity.[4] What happened to distribution of wealth during this period?

In this chapter, I analyze the distribution of real estate wealth in Lima prior and during the Guano Era. In particular, I collected information from property tax records of 1836 and 1857 to estimate wealth distribution in Lima and determine whether wealth inequality changed during a period of rapid economic expansion. There was no economic census in 19th century Peru. Tax records constitute the most reliable source of information about wealth in Lima. The National Archives of Peru keep tax records of the 19th century. With those records, one can estimate the distribution of real estate wealth. Certainly, real estate was not the only type of wealth. However, since financial markets in Peru were very underdeveloped and the economy was not industrialized, real estate was probably an important type of wealth.[5]

The evidence suggests that wealth in Lima was very concentrated. When including all proprietors (natural and juridical persons), 1% richest proprietors owned 28% of the total real estate wealth of Lima in 1836 and 29% in 1857. The 10% richest proprietors owned 57% of the total real estate wealth of Lima in 1836 and 58% in 1857. When only including natural persons, the 1% richest proprietors owned 14% of total wealth in 1836 and 15% in 1857, whereas the 10% richest proprietors owned 48% of total wealth in 1836 and 49% in 1857.[6] Including all proprietors, the Gini coefficient was 0.67 in 1836 and 0.69 in 1857. Only including natural persons, the Gini coefficient was 0.61 in 1836 and 0.62 in 1857. Although real estate wealth in Lima was very concentrated, wealth inequality was not high for Latin American standards. For instance, the Gini coefficient in rural Buenos Aires was 0.66–0.67 in 1839–1855, whereas the Gini coefficient on land in several Brazilian counties was 0.63–0.82 in the late 19th and early 20th centuries.

During this Guano Era, a period of economic bonanza, real estate wealth inequality among proprietors remained practically the same in 1836–1857. The 1%, 10%, and 20% concentration ratios and the Gini coefficient barely changed during this period. On the other hand, there was some degree of social mobility during this period: some proprietors became richer and some became poorer. However, social mobility was usually limited to one quintile.

In addition, a comparison of the wealth of proprietors and the labor income of laborers suggests that inequality between proprietors and low-skilled workers increased during the Guano Era. Real estate increased in value during this period. Wages of low-skilled workers also increased but at a lower rate. Economic expansion did not change inequality within proprietors; but it seems economic growth increased inequality between real estate proprietors and the poorest residents of Lima.

The increase in inequality between real estate proprietors and low-income workers is consistent with other studies that show that inequality increases in early stages of economic development (Kuznets, 1963; Lindert, 1986; Steckel & Moehling, 2001; Williamson & Lindert, 1980). The guano boom increased inequality across different segments of the economy of Lima, between the owners of alternative production factors. Inequality among proprietors, however, remained the same during the Guano Era. Therefore, although an economic shock could increase inequality across different segments of the economy, it is possible it does not have any effect on inequality within economic segments, such as within the segment of estate owners.

Our findings show that the impact of economic growth on inequality depends on how growth affects the prices of production factors. By increasing the price of land, the guano boom made estate owners richer. Not only the richest proprietors became richer, the proprietors of small properties also became richer. Meanwhile, nominal salaries did not increase as rapidly as the value of land, so the differences between estate owners and low-income workers increased.[7]

This chapter contributes to our understanding of the linkages between economic growth and wealth inequality. First, this is the first study of wealth distribution for Peru during the Guano Era, a period of rapid growth of exports. Second, tax records have not been used for the study of wealth inequality in Peru. The use of tax records for the study of the history of Peru has been extremely limited in general.

2. HISTORICAL BACKGROUND

In the mid-19th century, Peru was a country of around 2 million inhabitants (Fuentes, 1858). Most Peruvians lived in the countryside. Only 20% of the population lived in urban areas and Lima and Arequipa were the only two cities with more than 10,000 inhabitants. Lima was the capital city and the largest city in Peru, with around 100,000 inhabitants. Lima was at the center of the political and economic life of colonial Peru. With the independence from Spain, Lima maintained a major role in the country.

Lima was divided into five districts. Around 20% of the population lived in each district. Each district was divided into neighborhoods (Table 1). With 11 neighborhoods, district 1 was located in downtown Lima. From colonial times, district 1 was at the center of the political and economic life of the capital city. The Presidential Palace and the Cathedral were located in this district. In addition, the main commercial streets of Lima, such as Portal de Escribanos and Mercaderes were part of this district. District 2 was located to the east of district 1, around San Francisco Church between districts 1 and 3. This district had 13 neighborhoods. It also had important commercial streets, such as Portal de Botoneros and Judios. District 3, also known as Barrios Altos, was located to the east of district 2. District 4 was located in the South of the city. District 5 was located in the north of the city, crossing the Rimac River.

Most residents of Lima worked in the secondary and tertiary sectors. In the late 1850s, merchants represented around 15% of the labor force of Lima, 25% were artisans and 40% were low-skilled workers (Fuentes, 1858). Low-skilled workers represented an important portion of the labor force. Laborers, servants, launderers, cooks and many other low-skilled workers offered their services for relatively low wages (Zegarra, 2020a). In addition, almost 12% of the labor force worked for the State, as public servants or members of the military. Farmers represented 1% of the labor force.

Peru has always been a main exporter of raw materials. During colonial times, Peru exported agricultural and mineral products. In the 1820s and 1830s, the export sector of Peru was stagnant. Independence wars and political instability that followed the change in regime in the 1820s hit the economy. The export sector experienced an important change in the late 1840s with the exportation of guano. Guano was extracted from islands in the southern coast of Peru. In the mid-19th century, guano became highly demanded as a natural fertilizer in Europe and the United States. Guano exports increased from 10,000 tons in 1845 to 188,000 tons in 1850 and more than 600,000 tons in 1857. In the following 13 years, annual exports of guano were 430,000 tons on average. The value of exports of guano increased from only 140,000 dollars in 1845 to more than 23 million dollars in 1857. The participation of guano in total exports increased from 2.4% in 1845 to 63% in 1860. Total exports increased rapidly in the 1850s. Total Peruvian exports increased from around 4.2 million dollars in 1835 to 9.2 million dollars in 1850 and 31 million in 1860 (Zegarra, 2018). In constant dollars of 1830, the value of exports of Peru increased from 4.5 million dollars in 1830 to 10.9 million dollars in 1850 and 33.9 million in 1860.[8]

Table 1. Real Estate Wealth and Number of Properties in Lima.

District	Neighborhoods	Real Estate Wealth (Million Pesos)		Number of Properties		Number of Doors		Value per Property (Pesos)		Value per Door (Pesos)		Adjusted Value per Door (Pesos)	
		1836	1857	1836	1857	1836	1857	1836	1857	1836	1857	1836	1857
All proprietors (natural and juridical persons)													
1	11	10.3	13.9	805	740	2,220	2,076	12,763	18,721	4,628	6,673	4,628	6,240
2	13	12.1	14.6	800	779	2,716	2,451	15,114	18,777	4,452	5,968	4,452	5,386
3	5	3.3	4.4	672	627	1,866	1,793	4,927	6,943	1,774	2,428	1,774	2,333
4	9	4.4	5.4	642	570	1,576	1,460	6,799	9,494	2,770	3,707	2,770	3,434
5	8	4.1	5.4	690	654	2,166	2,118	6,000	8,256	1,911	2,549	1,911	2,493
Total	46	34.2	43.6	3,609	3,370	10,544	9,898	9,471	12,951	3,242	4,409	3,242	4,139
Only natural persons													
1	11	8.0	9.6	603	535	1,657	1,430	13,207	17,975	4,806	6,723	4,806	5,804
2	13	9.6	9.9	596	510	1,989	1,527	16,109	19,460	4,828	6,499	4,828	4,991
3	5	2.2	2.8	480	442	1,241	1,130	4,573	6,284	1,769	2,458	1,769	2,239
4	9	3.5	4.0	504	427	1,216	1,062	6,849	9,388	2,838	3,776	2,838	3,296
5	8	3.3	4.1	554	490	1,770	1,588	5,946	8,423	1,862	2,599	1,862	2,333
Total	46	26.5	30.5	2,737	2,404	7,872	6,737	9,684	12,668	3,367	4,520	3,367	3,869

Notes: The table reports the real estate wealth, the number of properties, and the number of doors in Lima, according to the district.

The economy of Lima benefited from the expansion of economic activity. Commercial activity expanded in the city. There are no estimates of gross domestic product (GDP) for Lima. However, secondary sources suggest that commerce expanded in Lima during the Guano Era (Camprubí, 1957). In constant dollars of 1830, the value of credit expanded from around 400,000 dollars per year in 1835–1845 to 1.9 million dollars in 1855 (Zegarra, 2016). In response to the growth of the economy of Lima, the city witnessed the creation of the first banks in the early 1860s.

The evidence suggests that real wages of low skilled workers did not increase during the Guano Era (Arroyo-Abad, 2013b; Zegarra, 2020a, 2021). Since the economy expanded during the Guano Era, the fact that low skilled workers did not experience a significant improvement in living standards implies that other segments of the population received larger earnings. Other factors of production experienced an increase in real returns. In real terms, economic growth may have led to the growth of wages of skilled workers, the rental price of capital or the rental price of land. It is possible that *fincas* and houses in Lima became more valuable during this period and so that real estate proprietors became richer.

3. TAX RECORDS AND REAL ESTATE IN LIMA

Tax records constitute an important source of information about wealth. Real estate was taxed in 19th century Peru. According to the decree of January 2, 1827, urban tax properties were levied 3% of the annual "production" (Oviedo, 1870). The annual production referred to the actual rent or the appraisal of the rent. Rural proprietors were also charged 3% of the annual production. With tax records, one can determine the distribution of wealth in 19th century Lima.

The National Archives of Peru contain a wide variety of official records from colonial times. The Republic Section of the Archives keeps the original tax records of the 19th century. These records are manuscripts. I collected information from property tax records of Lima in 1836 and 1857. These are the only surviving real estate tax records corresponding to the proprietors in the city of Lima for 1830–1880.

Tax records include the name of the property owner and the address of the property. With respect to the address, the records specify the district, the neighborhood, the name of the street, and the door numbers.[9]

For each neighborhood, doors were enumerated consecutively. With the exception of a few neighborhoods, there was only one sequence of doors in each neighborhood. For a few neighborhoods, there were two or more sequences of doors. I calculated the number of doors in a neighborhood with one sequence of doors as $N_H - N_L + 1$, where N_H and N_L were the highest and lowest door numbers in the neighborhood reported in the tax records, respectively. The implicit assumption for this formula is that no door in the neighborhood had a lower number than N_L or higher than N_H. In neighborhoods with more than one sequence of doors, the total number of doors in the neighborhood was calculated as $\sum_{j=1}^{J} (N_{j,H} - N_{j,L} + 1)$, where $N_{j,H}$ and $N_{j,L}$ were the respective highest and lowest door numbers in the *j*-sequence of doors (as reported in the tax records), and *J* is the total number of sequences of doors in the neighborhood.

Over time, there were some changes in the enumeration of doors. Fewer doors were enumerated in 1857 than in 1836. For instance, in neighborhood 2 of district 1, doors were numbered from 1 to 188 in 1836 and from 1 to 177 in 1857. In neighborhood 5 of district 4, doors were numbered from 1 to 187 in 1836 and from 1 to 179 in 1857. I do not have an explanation on why fewer were enumerated in 1857. A possible explanation is that some doors were walled up after 1836.

On the other hand, some doors do not appear in the records. For instance, in the neighborhood 4 of district 1, the tax records do not list doors 154 and 173, whereas in the neighborhood 5 of the same district, the tax records do not list doors 6 and 8. However, missing doors account for a small percentage of the total number of doors: 3.4% in 1836 and 7% in 1857.

Tax records specify the amount of the annual "production" of the property and the tax amount.[10] Taxes and production are in pesos.[11] To estimate the value of real estate, I relied on annual production. In particular, I assume that the annual production was 3% the value of real estate.[12] Some properties were in ruins. Their taxable income was zero and so did not pay property taxes.

Some proprietors were exempted from paying property taxes. In particular, proprietors of estates of relatively low value did not have to pay property taxes. The decree of November 8, 1831, established that the urban proprietors with a total annual production of up to 30 pesos were exempted from the payment of urban property taxes. This exemption did not apply for people with other occupations. Two years later, on February 18, 1833, a new decree increased the exemption to the proprietors with a total annual production of 80 pesos or less.[13] In addition, a look at the tax records shows that some institutions (such as San Carlos school, as well as some convents and monasteries) were tax exempted, even though their production exceeded 80 pesos annually.

I argue that tax exemptions do not affect our estimates of real estate value in Lima. First, some proprietors with an annual production of less than 80 pesos appear in the tax records, even though they were exempted from tax payments. For instance, the tax records of 1836 report a production of less than 80 pesos and no taxes for Juan Tabara, Jose Sarabia, and Damacio Sánchez, among other proprietors. Second, tax records show the annual production of institutions with an annual production of more than 80 pesos, but that were tax exempted. For instance, the tax records of 1836 report several properties of San Carlos school with a production of more than 80 pesos, and for which the institution did not pay taxes.[14] A similar phenomenon occurred with several properties of monasteries and convents. Therefore, even if some proprietors were tax exempted, their annual production was still registered in tax records.[15] For these reasons, I argue that the total value of production registered in tax records provides an accurate estimate of the distribution of real estate value of Lima.

Property owners could be natural persons or juridical persons. Some proprietors were not identified because the records only indicate a first name or no name at all. Nonidentified proprietors represent around 2% of the total value of real estate in 1836 and less than 1% in 1857.

Table 2. OLS Estimates.

	Number of Lots in Natural Log	District 1 Dummy	District 2 Dummy	District 3 Dummy	District 4 Dummy	R2	N
Year 1836	0.751***	0.811***	0.816***	−0.151***	0.366***	0.46	3,490
Year 1857	0.599***	0.889***	0.831***	−0.132***	0.317***	0.39	3,356

Notes: The table reports the OLS estimates of a regression for the natural log of the value of the property was dependent variable. Observation unit = Taxable urban property in Lima. N = Number of observations. Significance levels: ***1%.
Dependent variable: Natural log of the value of the property.

It is possible that the number of doors was correlated with the size and thus the value of the property. In fact, a simple ordinary least squares (OLS) regression shows that the value of real estate was positively correlated to the number of doors (Table 2). In the regression, the dependent variable is the natural log of the value of a property. The explanatory variables are the natural log of the number of doors in the property and dummies for district. An increase in the number of doors by 10% causes an increase in the value of the property of 7.5% in 1836 and 6% in 1857. The effect is highly significant. Value also depended on the location. Properties in districts 1 and 2 were more valuable than in other districts, controlling for the number of doors. District 3 had the least valuable properties, controlling for the number of doors.

According to our calculations, the average value per door was 3,242 pesos in 1836 (Table 1). On average, properties were more valuable in districts 1 and 2. In 1836, the average value of real estate per door was 4,628 pesos in district 1 and 4,452 pesos in district 2. In contrast, the average value per door was 1,774 pesos in district 3, 2,770 pesos in district 4 and 1,911 pesos in district 5. Districts 3 and 5 were the districts with the lowest value per door in Lima. Since districts 1 and 2 also had more doors than other districts, the two districts accounted for most of the total real estate value of the city. In particular, district 1 accounted for 30% of the value of real estate of Lima; for district 2, the percentage was 35%. In 1857, the average value per door was 4,409 pesos. Districts 1 and 2 were still the districts with the highest value per door. In particular, the average value per door was 6,673 pesos in district 1 and 5,968 in district 2. In district 4, the average value per door was 3,707 pesos. In districts 3 and 5, the average value per door was less than 2,600 pesos. Of the total value of real estate in Lima, districts 1 and 2 accounted for 66%.

Real estate increased in value in 1836–1857. On average, the value per property increased from 9,471 pesos in 1836 to 12,951 pesos in 1857 at a rate of 37%. Meanwhile, on average, the value of real estate per door increased from 3,242 pesos in 1836 to 4,409 pesos in 1857 at a rate of 36%. The value of real estate per door increased in all districts in 1836–1857. In district 1, the value per door grew by 44%. In district 2, the value per door grew by 34%. In districts 3, 4, and 5, the value per door grew by 33%–36%.

As indicated previously, fewer doors were enumerated in 1857 than in 1836. It is possible that some doors were walled up in 1836–1857. The decline in the number of enumerated doors could bias the estimation of the value of real estate per door: a property of the same total value in 1836 and 1857 could have a higher value per door in 1857 if some of its doors were walled up. I then adjusted the value of real estate per door assuming that the number of doors did not decline in 1836–1857. On average, the adjusted value per door grew by 28% (instead of 35%) in 1836–1857. In districts 1, 3 and 5, the adjusted value per door grew by 30%–35%; whereas in districts 2 and 4, the adjusted value per door increased by 21%–24%.

The increase in the value of real estate is consistent with other sources. Some sources suggest that rent increased during this period. For instance, according to Armas (2007), the monthly rent of a room in the *callejones* of the Monastery of Mercedarias increased from 1.5–2 pesos in the early 1830s to 2–3 pesos in the early 1850s.[16]

There was no high inflation in this period: the consumer price index increased by 7.1% between 1836 and 1857 (Gootenberg, 1990) and the nominal cost of subsistence increased by 3% between 1835–1840 and 1855–1860 (Zegarra, 2021).[17] Therefore, the increase in the value of real estate per door cannot be attributed to a general trend of prices: there was inflation in Lima during this period, but the value of real estate increases much faster than prices.

Table 3 reports the real estate wealth by category of proprietor. The Catholic Church was an important proprietor in Lima. Monasteries, convents and churches had 3.4 million pesos worth of real estate in 1836 and 3.8 million pesos in 1857. Those amounts represented 10% of total value of real estate in Lima in 1836 and 8.6% in 1857. Other organizations of the Catholic Church also owned

Table 3. Distribution of Real Estate Properties and Real Estate Wealth by Categories.

	1836				1857			
	Number of Properties		Real Estate Wealth (Pesos)		Number of Properties		Real Estate Wealth (Pesos)	
		%		%		%		%
Monasteries, convents, and churches	402	11.1	3,434,667	10.0	372	11.0	3,751,133	8.6
Cofradias and other Catholic organizations	127	3.5	936,200	2.7	146	4.3	1,542,300	3.5
Hospitals	51	1.4	702,600	2.1	23	0.7	447,367	1.0
Education institutions	2	0.1	14,000	0.0	2	0.1	14,167	0.0
Government	43	1.2	368,533	1.1	13	0.4	618,467	1.4
Companies	1	0.0	2,000	0.0	4	0.1	221,667	0.5
Testamentary trusts	40	1.1	652,900	1.9	235	7.0	3,950,600	9.1
Men	1,654	45.8	16,300,000	47.7	1,570	46.6	20,800,000	47.7
Women	1,083	30.0	10,200,000	29.8	834	24.7	9,622,367	22.1
Others	68	1.9	961,933	2.8	144	4.3	2,365,200	5.4
Nonidentified	138	3.8	603,567	1.8	27	0.8	279,400	0.6
Total	3,609	100.0	34,176,400	100.0	3,370	100.0	43,612,667	100.0

Notes: The table reports the number of properties and the value of real estate for a number of categories. I only take into account properties that have a positive value.

valuable real estate. In total, *cofradías*, brotherhoods, and other Catholic organizations had real estate worth nearly 1 million pesos in 1836 and 1.5 million pesos
in 1857. Meanwhile, hospitals, schools, and the State accounted for 3.1% of the
total value of real estate in Lima in 1836 and for 2.4% of the total value in 1857.

Natural persons owned a large fraction of real estate of Lima. In 1836, men
owned around 48% of total real estate wealth; women owned 30%. In 1857, the
percentages were 48% for men and 22% for women. The role of women as proprietors was very important. Widows, single women, and married women could
legally own properties.[18] Some of the proprietors may have belonged to the same
household. It is possible that the distribution of wealth among households was not
the same as the distribution among natural persons. Unfortunately, I do not have
information on the relationship between the different proprietors or even about their
marital status to calculate the distribution of wealth among households.

4. DISTRIBUTION OF REAL ESTATE WEALTH

Tax records allow us to infer about wealth distribution in Lima. Was wealth
highly concentrated? Did Lima experience changes in the distribution of wealth
during the Guano Era?

In 1836, there were 1,777 identified proprietors of real estate in Lima with a
total value of 32 million pesos (Table 4). On average, the value of real estate per
proprietor was 18,244 pesos in 1836. With a standard deviation of 109,000 pesos,
the coefficient of variation was 6.0.[19] There was then a large variability in wealth
among proprietors. In addition, since the median wealth was lower than the
mean, it is clear that very large values had an impact on the mean. In particular,
the value of real estate of the Catholic Church was very large: the value of the
Church's real estate (the maximum value in the distribution) was 4.4 million
pesos, 240 times the average. Not surprisingly, the distribution of wealth was
highly skewed. In 1836, the skewness coefficient was above 35, a very large value.
On the other hand, around 40% of proprietors in 1836 had real estate wealth of
5,000 pesos or less (Fig. 1), 23% of proprietors had real estate worth 5,001–10,000
pesos, 26% of proprietors had real estate worth 10,001–30,000 pesos, and 11%
owned real estate with a value of more than 30,000 pesos.

The value of real estate per proprietor increased over time: the average value of
real estate per proprietor in 1857 was greater than in 1836. However, there were
important similarities between 1836 and 1857. In particular, the coefficient of
variation in 1857 was 5.7, still very large. Like in 1836, in 1857 the median was also
far lower than the mean due to the presence of very large values. The distribution was
also highly skewed: the coefficient of skewness was 30. On the other hand, around
32% of proprietors had real estate worth up to 5,000 pesos, 21% owned real estate
worth 5,001–10,000 pesos, 29% had wealth of 10,001–30,000 pesos and 17% owned
real estate worth more than 30,000 pesos.

Much of the variability and skewness of real estate wealth can be explained by the
presence of the Catholic Church. Consider the distribution of real estate among
natural persons. In this case, the coefficient of variation was 1.9 in 1836 and 1.9 in

Table 4. Descriptive Statistics of Real Estate Wealth per Proprietor.

	Unit	All Proprietors (Natural and Juridical Persons)		Only Natural Persons (Excluding the Church and Other Organizations)	
		1836	1857	1836	1857
Statistics					
Average	Pesos	18,244	26,317	14,721	20,208
Median	Pesos	7,200	10,000	6,800	10,000
Standard deviation	Pesos	109,916	149,315	27,412	38,475
Coefficient of variation		6.0	5.7	1.9	1.9
Skewness		35.5	30.2	8.2	7.6
Kurtosis		1,390	1,026	107	92
Maximum	Pesos	4,370,867	5,293,434	465,533	615,000
Minimum	Pesos	0	400	0	400
Percentiles					
Percentile 95	Pesos	56,667	75,000	53,733	67,300
Percentile 90	Pesos	32,560	48,333	31,800	46,400
Percentile 80	Pesos	20,000	26,667	19,693	26,667
Percentile 70	Pesos	13,333	18,627	13,333	16,667
Percentile 60	Pesos	10,000	13,333	10,000	13,333
Percentile 50	Pesos	7,200	10,000	6,800	10,000
Percentile 40	Pesos	5,120	6,667	5,000	6,667
Percentile 30	Pesos	4,000	5,000	4,000	5,000
Percentile 20	Pesos	2,400	3,333	2,400	3,333
Percentile 10	Pesos	1,600	2,400	1,600	2,400
Percentile 5	Pesos	1,200	1,667	1,200	1,667
Concentration ratios					
Top 20%		0.70	0.70	0.64	0.66
Top 10%		0.57	0.58	0.48	0.49
Top 1%		0.28	0.29	0.14	0.15
Gini coefficient		0.67	0.69	0.61	0.62
Number of proprietors		1,777	1,541	1,722	1,437

Notes: The table reports the descriptive statistics of wealth per proprietor.

1857. In contrast, as indicated previously, such coefficient was 6.0 in 1836 and 5.7 in 1857 when including all proprietors (natural and juridical persons). The coefficient of skewness is also lower when only including natural persons. In this case, the coefficient of skewness was 8.2 in 1836 and 7.6 in 1857. In contrast, when including all proprietors, the coefficient of skewness was above 30. Since the Church was a very rich proprietor, the average value of real estate per proprietor also declines when excluding the Church from the calculations.

A common indicator of wealth inequality is the proportion of wealth owned by the richest proprietors. The k-concentration ratio measures the wealth of the k % richest proprietors as a proportion of the total real estate wealth of Lima.

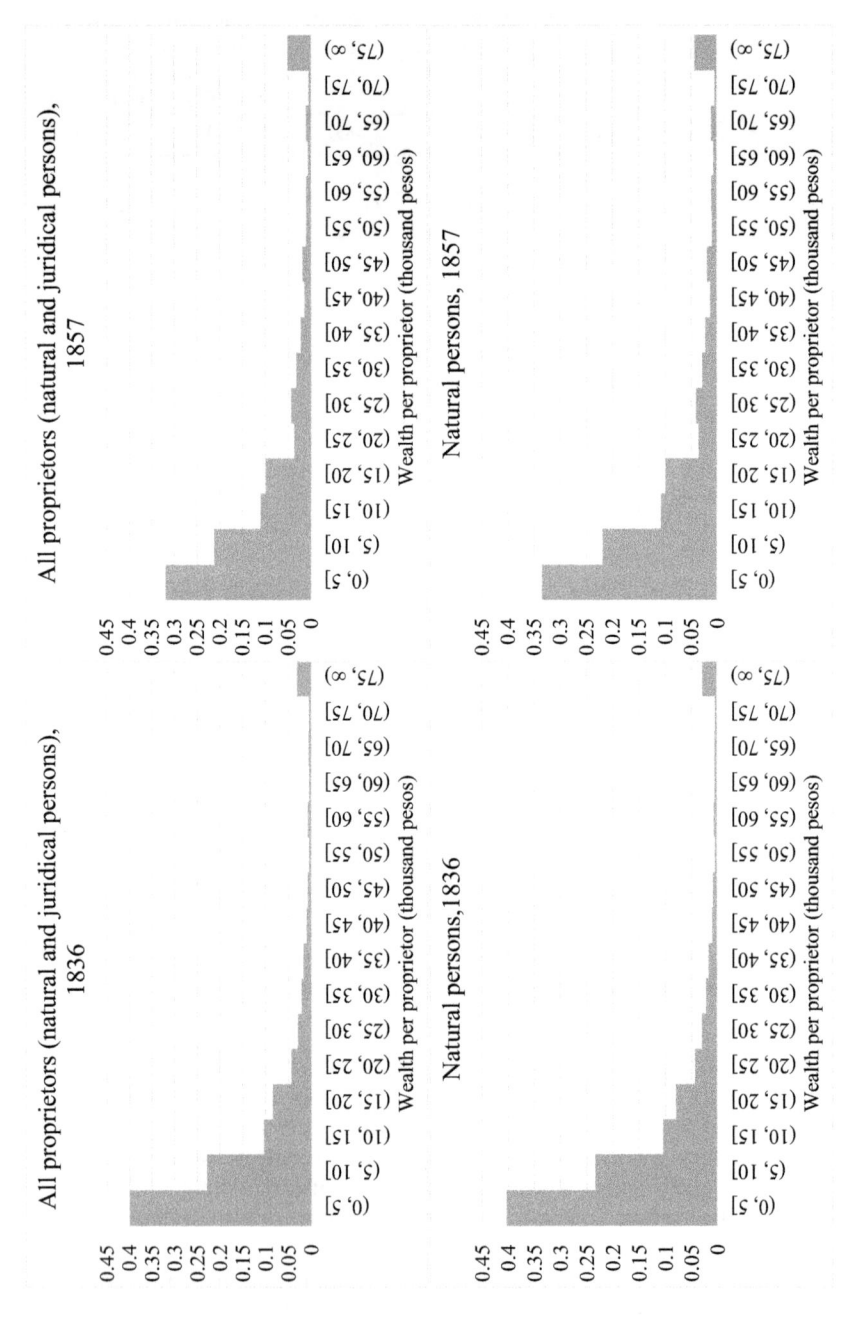

Fig. 1. Distribution of Real Estate Wealth by Proprietor.

Notice that I do not include people who did not own real estate; so if real estate were the only source of wealth, then our estimates would underestimate the actual wealth inequality among residents of Lima.

In 1836, the 1% richest proprietors had nearly 9 million pesos worth of real estate. The 1%-concentration ratio of taxable income was 0.28, so the 1% richest proprietors owned 28% of the total real estate wealth of Lima. The 10%-concentration ratio was 0.57, so the 10% richest proprietors owned 57% of the total real estate wealth of Lima. Meanwhile, the 20%-concentration ratio was 0.7. In 1857, the 1%-, 10%-, and 20%-concentration ratios were 0.29, 0.58, and 0.7. Wealth was very concentrated in 1836 and 1857. Importantly, the concentration ratios practically remained the same in 1836 and 1857. The guano boom did not cause important changes in the concentration of real estate wealth.

The Church was an important real estate proprietor. Since the Church owned more than 10% of total wealth, it may explain much of the wealth concentration in Lima. Let us calculate the concentration ratio excluding the Church. I also exclude other juridical persons from the calculations. As expected, when only including natural persons, the concentration ratio among real estate owners was lower. In 1836, the 1%-concentration ratio was 0.14 instead of 0.28; the 10%-concentration ratio was 0.48, instead of 0.57; and the 20%-concentration ratio was 0.64, instead of 0.7. For 1857, the concentration ratios among real estate owners were also lower when only including natural persons.

One limitation of the concentration ratios is that they only measure the differences in wealth between the richest proprietors and the rest of proprietors. Those ratios do not take into account the differences within the richest proprietors nor the differences within those who are not at the top. In contrast, the Gini coefficient is a measure of inequality at all levels. The Gini coefficient takes values between 0 and 1, where a higher value implies higher inequality. A value of 1 implies absolute concentration, i.e., one proprietor owns all wealth, whereas a value of 0 implies that all proprietors have exactly the same wealth.

I calculated the Gini coefficient using the following formula: $\text{Gini} = 2\frac{\sum_{i=1}^{N}\rho_i y_i}{N\sum_{i=1}^{N}y_i} - \frac{N+1}{N}$, where N is the number of proprietors, y_i is the real estate wealth of proprietor i, and ρ_i is the position of proprietor i in the ranking of proprietors, from the bottom to the top. For the proprietor with the lowest level of wealth, ρ_i is equal to 1. For the proprietor with the highest level of wealth, ρ_i is equal to N.[20]

Including all proprietors (natural and juridical persons), the Gini coefficient was 0.67 in 1836 and 0.62 in 1857. Only considering natural persons, the Gini coefficient was 0.61 in 1836 and 0.62. Therefore, there was no much change in wealth inequality among proprietors between 1836 and 1857. Wealth inequality among real estate proprietors did not change during this period of economic bonanza.

How does Lima compare to other Latin American cities and regions? Wealth in Lima was very concentrated. However, wealth inequality among proprietors in Lima was not high for Latin American standards (Table 5). In 1839–1855, the Gini coefficient in rural Buenos Aires was 0.66–0.67. In addition, the 20% richest proprietors owned 70% of total real estate.[21] In comparison, the Gini coefficient

Table 5. Wealth Inequality in Latin America.

City/Region	Country	Period	Type of wealth	Concentration Ratios		Gini Coefficient
				10%	20%	
Cuiabá	Brazil	1889–1937	All types of wealth	0.72	0.84	0.76 to 0.78
Cuiabá	Brazil	1911–c.1930	Land			0.68 to 0.73
Bela Vista	Brazil	c.1920	Land			0.63
Aquidauana	Brazil	c.1920	Land			0.67
Corumbá	Brazil	1911–c.1930	Land			0.78 to 0.79
Corumbá	Brazil	c1920	Cattle			0.53
Cáceres	Brazil	1911–c.1930	Land			0.77 to 0.82
Cáceres	Brazil	c.1920	Cattle			0.74
Tres Lagoas	Brazil	c.1920	Land			0.81
Tres Lagoas	Brazil	c.1920	Cattle			0.70
Campo Grande	Brazil	c.1920	Land			0.76
Campo Grande	Brazil	c.1920	Cattle			0.59
Paraná	Argentina	1862–1863	All types of wealth			0.78
Esperanza	Argentina	1864	All types of wealth			0.38
Rural Buenos Aires	Argentina	1839	Land		0.70	0.67
Rural Buenos Aires	Argentina	1855	Land		0.70	0.66

Notes: The table reports indicators of wealth inequality among proprietors in Latin America. The sources are Gelman and Santilli (2010), Frank (2004), Djenderedjian, and Martirén (2012).

in Lima was 0.61–0.67 in 1836 and 0.62–0.69 in 1857 (depending on whether the Church was included), and the richest 20% proprietors owned 64%–70% of total wealth. Lima was as unequal as rural Buenos Aires.[22] Inequality in some regions in the North of Brazil was even higher than in Lima. In the late 19th and early 20th centuries, the Gini coefficient on land in several Brazilian counties was 0.63–0.82.[23] In Cuiabá, for example, the Gini coefficient ranged between 0.68 and 0.73 in 1911–1930. In Bela Vista, the Gini coefficient circa 1920 was 0.63. In Corumbá, the Gini coefficient in 1911–1930 was 0.78–0.79.

Importantly, the expansion of the economic activity in Lima did not change the distribution of real estate wealth in Lima. Before the Guano Era and after several years of export boom, wealth inequality among proprietors remained practically the same. The guano boom did not increase inequality among proprietors, but it did not reduce it either.

5. SOCIAL MOBILITY

Even though wealth inequality among proprietors did not change, there could have been social mobility. For instance, it is possible that the poorest proprietors in 1836 became the richest proprietors in 1857. If the new rich concentrated the same proportion of total wealth in 1857 as the old rich did in 1836, then wealth inequality would have remained the same.

I look at the sample of proprietors of 1836 that remained proprietors in 1857. Consider the proprietors that belonged to the first quintile in 1836 (the richest proprietors). Taking into account those who remained proprietors in 1857, nearly 60% belonged to the first quintile of 1857 and around 20% belonged to the second quintile (Table 6). Consider now the proprietors who belonged to the second quintile in 1836 (the second richest quintile). Among those who remained as proprietors in 1857, 37% remained in the second quintile in 1857, 25% move up to the first quintile, and 22% moved down to the third quintile. Consider now the proprietors who belonged to the fifth quintile of 1836 (the poorest proprietors).

Table 6. Distribution of Natural Persons Who Owned Real Estate in 1836 and 1857.

	Quintile in 1857					
	1	2	3	4	5	Total
Quintile in 1836						
1	58.4	19.8	8.9	7.9	5.0	100.0
2	25.0	36.5	21.9	12.5	4.2	100.0
3	13.6	15.9	33.0	22.7	14.8	100.0
4	1.3	10.7	22.7	44.0	21.3	100.0
5	1.6	6.5	11.3	12.9	67.7	100.0

Notes: The table reports the distribution of natural persons that owned real estate in 1836 and 1857.

Among those who remained proprietors in 1857, nearly 68% remained in the fifth quintile in 1857. Most of the poorest proprietors of 1836 who still owned a property in 1857 did not move up in the distribution of wealth.

These results show that there was some degree of social mobility in 1836–1857. Some proprietors became richer and some became poorer. Social mobility, however, was usually limited to one quintile. Consider the case of the proprietors who belonged to the second, third, and fourth quintiles, i.e., those who could move up or down in the distribution of wealth. Among them, around 80% stayed in the same quintile, moved up one quintile, or moved down one quintile.

In spite of the social mobility among real estate proprietors of Lima, the poorest proprietors of 1836 did not necessarily move up in the distribution of wealth. For instance, some proprietors in the fourth quintile moved up in the distribution of wealth; others, however, moved down to the fifth quintile. In addition, although it was possible for some proprietors to move out of their quintiles, it was very unlikely for proprietors to move up or down two or more quintiles. For the proprietors in the fifth quintile, it was very unlikely to move up two or more quintiles. Similarly, it was very unlikely for the proprietors in the first quintile to move down two or more quintiles.

These results do not imply that the poorest proprietors became poorer over time, but that their accumulation of wealth did not occur at higher rates than that of the richest proprietors. Considering only the proprietors of 1836 that remained proprietors in 1857, the growth of real estate value did not depend on the quintile (Table 7). For instance, the proprietors who belonged to the first quintile experienced an increase of 40% in their real estate wealth in 1836–1857. For those who belonged to the second, third, fourth, and fifth quintiles, the growth rates were 32%, 31%, 27%, and 46%, respectively. The expansion of commerce and

Table 7. Real Estate Wealth of Natural Persons Who Owned Real Estate in Both Years, 1836 and 1857.

	Average Value of Real Estate per Proprietor			Average Number of Doors per Proprietor			Average Value of Real Estate per Door per Proprietor		
	1836	1857	g (%)	1836	1857 1/	g (%)	1836	1857 1/	g (%)
By quintile in 1836									
1	47,316	66,410	40.4	10.4	11.9	14.0	6,568	8,417	28.1
2	13,540	17,874	32.0	4.3	4.3	1.2	4,605	6,869	49.2
3	7,253	9,500	31.0	3.3	3.0	−8.3	3,053	4,755	55.8
4	3,966	5,041	27.1	2.4	2.1	−9.3	2,269	3,118	37.5
5	1,591	2,314	45.5	1.5	1.7	12.7	1,408	1,842	30.8

Notes: The table reports the value of real estate per proprietor, the adjusted number of doors per proprietor, and the value of real estate per door per proprietor in 1836 and 1857. The value of real estate per door is calculated as the value of real estate divided by the number of doors (the number of doors adjusted for 1857). g = Growth rate between 1836 and 1857. 1/ For 1857, the number of doors was adjusted, following the procedure explained in the text.

economic growth provided opportunities to accumulate wealth to the richest proprietors and the poorest proprietors.

The increase in real estate wealth can be explained by the increase in the total area of the properties or the increase in the unit value of land. Were there differences in the size of the properties or the value of real estate per unit of land across quintiles?

I do not have information on the size of properties. However, one could use the number of doors as a proxy (although imperfect) for the size of the properties and so the value of real estate per door as a proxy of the value per unit of land. However, as indicated previously, fewer doors were enumerated in 1857 than in 1836, probably because some doors were walled up. Then, in order to estimate the change in the value of real estate per unit of land in 1837–1856, I adjusted the number of doors for each property for 1857. To do so, I calculated the growth rate of the number of doors in 1836–1857 in each neighborhood. This rate was usually negative. Denote this rate as g. Then, for each property in 1857, I calculated the adjusted number of doors as the actual number of doors in 1857 divided by $1 + g$. For 1857, the adjusted value of real estate per door for each proprietor was calculated as the total value of real estate divided by the adjusted number of doors. For 1836, I did not adjust the number of doors.

Table 7 reports the adjusted number of doors per proprietor and the adjusted value of real estate per door per proprietor in 1836 and 1857. These figures correspond to natural persons who owned real estate in both years. The results show that the growth of real estate value for all quintiles largely depended on the increase in the adjusted value of real estate per door. In general, the growth of real estate value per door exceeded the growth of the number of doors.

These results are consistent with the information per district. As mentioned previously, the value of land grew all over Lima, not only the top districts of the city. The value of real estate per door increased in all districts. In 1836–1857, the adjusted value of real estate per door increased by 30%–35% in districts 1, 3, and 5 and by 21%–24% in districts 2 and 4 (Table 1). Properties became more valuable all over the city, not only in the most high-value streets of Lima. The richest proprietors accumulated wealth due to the increase in the value of land. The proprietors of the poorest districts of Lima, however, also became richer as their properties became more valuable.

6. COMPARING PROPRIETORS AND WORKERS

Real estate was not the only type of wealth. Unfortunately, I do not count with information on other types of wealth. Since some residents of Lima could have owned capital in different forms, not only as real estate, I cannot compute the distribution of wealth for all inhabitants of Lima. Nevertheless, real estate was probably an important type of wealth. Owning real estate was presumably an important mode of accumulating capital.

To have a sense of the differences in living standards in Lima, one can analyze how hard it was for low-income residents to reach the same level of income or the same level of wealth as real estate proprietors. How long did low-skilled workers need to work to accumulate the same level of income or real estate wealth as proprietors?

Laborers, servants, and other low-skilled workers were among those with the lowest salaries in Lima and had severe difficulties to cover their basic expenses. The average wage of laborers was around 0.9 pesos per day in 1835–1840 and 1 peso per day in 1855–1860 (Zegarra, 2021). Assuming that laborers worked 250 days per year, their salary would have been around 250 pesos per year.[24]

Let us calculate some indicators of inequality between proprietors and laborers. One of them is the ratio annual rent of a proprietor/annual income of a laborer (Table 8). The ratio measures the income inequality between proprietors and laborers, assuming that the only source of income of proprietors was the rent of real estate. The average annual rent of a proprietor was 1.1 times the annual income of a laborer in 1836 and 1.2 times in 1857. Real estate proprietors may have had alternative sources of income in addition to rent, so the ratio annual rent of a proprietor/annual income of a laborer may underestimate the differences in income between proprietors and laborers.

Table 8. Differences Between Real Estate Wealth and Laborers? Income.

	Annual Income of a Proprietor Divided by the Annual Income of a Laborer		Wealth of a Proprietor Divided by the Annual Income of a Laborer		Wealth of a Proprietor Divided by s Times the Annual Income of a Laborer	
	1836	1857	1836	1857	1836	1857
Statistics						
Average	1.1	1.2	63.8	78.9	212.5	197.2
Standard deviation	1.3	1.3	118.7	150.2	395.8	375.5
Maximum	13.0	12.5	2016.4	2,400.5	6,721.2	6,001.4
Minimum	0.0	0.0	0.0	1.6	0.0	3.9
Percentiles						
Percentile 90	2.3	2.7	137.7	181.1	459.1	452.8
Percentile 80	1.6	1.8	85.3	104.1	284.3	260.2
Percentile 70	1.1	1.2	57.8	65.1	192.5	162.6
Percentile 60	0.9	1.0	43.3	52.0	144.4	130.1
Percentile 50	0.6	0.8	29.5	39.0	98.2	97.6
Percentile 40	0.5	0.6	21.7	26.0	72.2	65.1
Percentile 30	0.4	0.5	17.3	19.5	57.8	48.8
Percentile 20	0.3	0.4	10.4	13.0	34.7	32.5
Percentile 10	0.2	0.2	6.9	9.4	23.1	23.4

Notes: The table reports the results for three indicators, the ratio of annual income of a proprietor/annual income of a laborer, the ratio of wealth/annual income of a laborer, and the ratio of wealth divided by s times the annual income of a laborer, where s is the portion of the annual income that a laborer saved. s is assumed to be 0.3 in 1836 and 0.4 in 1857.

Another indicator of inequality between proprietors and workers is the ratio wealth of a proprietor/annual income of a laborer. This ratio measures the number of years an average laborer would have to work to reach the same level of wealth as a proprietor, if the laborer saved his entire annual income.[25] The assumption that a laborer saved his entire income is certainly not realistic. The calculation of this ratio, however, still allows us to determine the differences between wealth of proprietors and the labor income of low-skilled workers. One must take into account that laborers spent a portion of their income to calculate the actual number of years a laborer would need to work.

The average wealth of a proprietor was equivalent to 64 times the annual income of a laborer in 1836 and 79 times in 1857 (Table 6). To reach the same level of wealth of the richest proprietor in 1836, a laborer would have to work 2,016 years if he saved his entire income. To reach the wealth of the richest proprietor in 1857, a laborer would have to work more than 2,400 years, also assuming he did not spend any portion of his income. To reach the same level of wealth as the proprietor with the median wealth in 1836 (percentile 50), a laborer would have to work almost 30 years, saving his entire income. To reach the wealth of the median proprietor in 1857, the laborer would have to work almost 40 years. To exceed the wealth of the 20% poorest proprietors in 1836, a laborer would have to work at least 10.4 years; to do the same in 1857, a laborer would have to work at least 13 years.

These figures show that there were large differences between the wealth of proprietors and the labor income of low-skilled workers. Proprietors owned valuable *fincas* and houses. Laborers could have spent their entire life saving their entire income and yet would have not been able to reach the same level of wealth as a large number of proprietors.

Importantly, the differences between the wealth of proprietors and the labor income of laborers increased between 1836 and 1857. On average, the ratio wealth/annual income of laborers increased by 24% in 1836–1857. The guano boom expanded the differences in wealth and income between the rich and the poor. Proprietors experienced an increase in wealth and laborers experienced an increase in wages. However, the value of real estate increased more rapidly than wages. In the previous section, I showed that wealth inequality did not change within proprietors. Across residents of Lima (proprietors and nonproprietors), however, it seems inequality increased during the Guano Era.

The finding that the differences between wealth of proprietors and labor income of low-skilled workers expanded during the Guano Era should not be surprising. In fact, the evidence suggests that economic growth was associated with larger inequalities in the 19th and early 20th centuries. For other countries, Arroyo-Abad (2013a) and Williamson (1999) found that inequality between renters and low-skilled workers increased due an increase in terms of trade and immigration. As stated by the Heckscher-Ohlin model, increasing terms of trade in a land-abundant region (such as Latin America) and massive immigration would lead to a reduction in the wage/rental ratio.

The ratio wealth of a proprietor/annual labor income of a laborer underestimates the number of years a laborer would need to work to reach the same level of wealth as the proprietor. Laborers had to use a portion of their income to cover basic expenses, so they could not save their entire salary. Recent estimates suggest that if workers spent only at subsistence levels, they would have saved around 30% of their income in 1835–1840 and 40% in 1855–1860 (Zegarra, 2021).[26] Denote s as the proportion of their incomes that workers could save. Then the number of years that a low-skilled worker would need to work to reach the same wealth of a proprietor, when saving a portion s of their income, is equal to the ratio wealth divided by s times the annual salary. Following Zegarra's estimates, assume $s = 0.3$ in 1836 and $s = 0.4$ in 1857.[27]

The results show that to reach the same level of wealth as the average proprietor in 1836, a laborer would have to work 213 years. In 1857, the estimate was 197 years. Laborers would have to work around two centuries to reach the same level of wealth as the average proprietor in 1836 and 1857. In order to reach the wealth of the richest proprietor in 1836 and 1857, a laborer would have to work more than 6,000 years. To reach the same level of wealth as the proprietor with the median wealth, a laborer would have to work almost a century. To exceed the wealth of the 20% poorest proprietors, a laborer would have to work more than 30 years. There were then very large differences between the wealth of real estate proprietors and the annual income of low-skilled workers in Lima.

7. CONCLUSIONS

Real estate was very concentrated in Lima. In particular, including all proprietors (natural and juridical persons), the 10% richest proprietors owned 57% of the total real estate wealth of Lima in 1836 and 58% in 1857. When only including natural persons, the 10% richest proprietors owned 48% of total wealth in 1836 and 49% in 1857. However, even though real estate in Lima was highly concentrated, wealth inequality among proprietors was not high for Latin American standards.

Importantly, inequality among proprietors remained practically the same in Lima during this period of economic bonanza. Economic growth could have provided opportunities to a large number of people to expand their incomes and accumulate wealth. However, economic growth could have provided better opportunities not only to the poorest proprietors but also to the richest proprietors. There was some social mobility, but that was usually limited to one quintile.

I do not count with information on other types of wealth to compare the distribution of wealth for the entire population of Lima. However, the results show that the differences between the wealth of real estate proprietors and the labor income of low-skilled workers increased during the Guano Era. Real estate became more valuable at a time when wages did not increase much. Wealth inequality among real estate proprietors did not change during the Guano Era. However, inequality in living standards between real estate owners and low-skilled workers expanded during this period.

NOTES

1. Income tax records and surveys have made it possible to estimate income inequality for the 20th century. Prior to 1900, however, information on household income has been hard to obtain. Therefore, most historical studies have focused on estimations of wealth inequality.

2. Other studies on wealth inequality are Williamson and Lindert (1980), De Meere (1983), James (1988), and Shammas (1993).

3. Guano was the accumulated excrement of sea birds.

4. The State, as owners of guano, experienced a substantial expansion of revenues. Those resources were largely spent on public works, payments of public debt, and government salaries (Tantaleán, 1983; Yepes, 1981).

5. Industrialization implies that wealth could be composed of machinery. Investment in machinery increased in the 1860s and 1870s, with the creation of mortgage banks and the expansion of long-term credit to plantations. In countries with developed financial markets, financial investments may be an important fraction of total wealth. In Lima, however, the financial market was very underdeveloped. In other countries, real estate has been an important type of wealth. Real estate was the main type of wealth in the United States and United Kingdom prior to 1900 (Lindert, 1986; Steckel & Moehling, 2001). In the 19th century, real estate in Paris represented more than 60% of total wealth in the early 19th century, but then declined in importance over the rest of the century (Piketty et al., 2006).

6. In this case, I exclude juridical persons, i.e., companies, organizations, and institutions. Among juridical persons, the State and the Catholic Church were important proprietors of real estate.

7. The Heckscher-Ohlin theory may explain the increase in the price of land with respect to the price of labor during the Guano Era. According to this theory, an increase in terms of trade leads to a decline in the wage-rental ratio in land-abundant economies and to an increase in the ratio in labor-abundant economies. In Latin America, a land-abundant region, terms of trade increased in the 19th century. The increase in terms of trade contributed to the growth of the economy but also increased inequality between landowners and workers (Arroyo-Abad, 2013a; Williamson, 1999). In labor-abundant regions, an increase in terms of trade led to an increase in the wage-rental ratio (O'Rourke et al., 1996).

8. To deflate the export figures, I use the US CPI index from Williamson (2021).

9. I use the term district to refer to "cuartel".

10. One possible problem of the data is that fiscal valuation is not necessarily the same as market valuation. One might then question the validity of tax records as source of information about wealth. Scattered evidence, however, shows that market valuation was not far from fiscal valuation. For instance, in 1836, Agustín Cruzate rented a small house in Imprenta street for 7 pesos per month during 6 months (Notary of José de Selaya, Protocolo 699). According to the fiscal valuation, the annual production was 75 pesos, equivalent to 6.25 pesos per month. Mariano Soriano rented a house in Mercaderes street for 48 per month (Notary of Eduardo Huerta, Protocolo 268). According to the fiscal valuation, the annual production of the property was 700 pesos or 58 pesos per month. There were some differences between the market and fiscal valuations. However, it seems the properties with a higher market value also had a higher fiscal valuation.

11. The silver peso was the monetary unit from colonial times. In 1863, it was replaced by the silver sol, of similar mineral content.

12. An analysis of real estate sales prices and rental prices in the valleys of Lima suggests that rental was around 3% of the value of the property (Zegarra, 2020b). I assume the rate was the same in the city of Lima.

13. A look at the data shows that some proprietors had a taxable income of less than 80 pesos and paid property taxes. It is possible that those proprietors had other sources of income, and so their total income (including all sources of revenue) exceeded 80 pesos per year.

14. The school only paid taxes for one property.
15. In addition, only a small number of doors do not appear in the tax records. as shown previously, less than 8% of doors do not appear in the tax records.
16. *Callejones* were properties composed of an alley and several rooms, rented to low-income families. Pardo et al. (1870) also indicate that rent increased in Lima in the 1850s and 1860s.
17. Prices increased at a faster rate later in the 1860s and 1870s.
18. They could also conduct different types of financial transactions. In fact, a large number of women participated in the credit market as lenders and borrowers.
19. The minimum value in 1836 is zero because some proprietors had real estate worth zero. Those properties were usually in ruins.
20. Our estimates of the Gini coefficient measure inequality within the real estate owner class, not among all residents of Lima.
21. Information on real estate inequality in Buenos Aires comes from Gelman and Santilli (2010).
22. Meanwhile, Djenderedjian and Martirén (2012) show that in the early 1860s wealth inequality (using not only real estate) in Paraná and Esperanza in Argentina was 0.78 and 0.38, respectively.
23. Information on wealth inequality for the North of Brazil comes from Frank (2001).
24. This is a standard assumption to determine the standards of living of laborers.
25. I do not take into account the interest rate. A positive interest rate would reduce the number of years a laborer would need to work to accumulate the same level of wealth as the proprietor. However, inflation would increase the price of real estate, increasing the number of years a laborer would need to work.
26. In the 1860s and early 1870s, inflation led to the decline in real wages of low-skilled workers. During the Guano Era, low-skilled workers experienced a decline in their living standards in spite of the commercial boom (Zegarra, 2020a, 2021).
27. Notice that the ratio of wealth divided by the portion s of the laborer's income declined between 1836 and 1857. The decline of this ratio can be explained by the increase in s from 0.3 to 0.4. Since s increased during this period, the ratio of wealth divided by the portion s of the laborer's income declined even though wealth increased more rapidly than labor income.

REFERENCES

Aghion, P., Caroli, E., & García-Peñalosa, C. (1999). Inequality and economic growth: The perspective of the new growth theories. *The Journal of Economic Perspectives, 37*(4), 1615–1660.
Armas, F. (2007). *Iglesia: Bienes y rentas. Secularización liberal y reorganización patrimonial en Lima 1820-1950*. Instituto Riva Agüero/Pontificia Universidad Católica del Perú/Instituto de Estudios Peruanos.
Arroyo-Abad, L. (2013a). Persistent inequality? Trade factor endowments, and inequality in Republican Latin America. *The Journal of Economic History, 73*(1), 38–78.
Arroyo-Abad, L. (2013b). Failure to launch: Cost of living and living standards in Peru during the 19th century. *Journal of Iberian and Latin American Economic History, 32*, 47–76.
Camprubí, C. (1957). *Historia de los bancos en el Perú*. Editorial Lumen.
De Meere, J. (1983). Long-term trends in income and wealth inequality in the Netherlands 1808–1940. *Historical Social Research, 27*, 8–37.
Djenderedjian, J., & Martirén, J. (2012). La Distribución de la Riqueza Rural entre tradición y modernidad. Los casos de la colonia Esperanza y el distrito de Paraná durante la década de 1860. *Población & Sociedad, 19*(2), 125–154.
Frank, Z. (2001). Exports and inequality: Evidence from the Brazilian frontier, 1870-1937. *The Journal of Economic History, 61*(1), 37–58.
Fuentes, M. (1858). *Estadística General de Lima*. Tipografía Nacional de M. N. Corpancho.

Gelman, J., & Santilli, D. (2010). Una creciente desigualdad. La propiedad de la tierra en Buenos Aires entre 1839 y 1855. *Investigaciones de Historia Económica, 6*, 11–33.

Gootenberg, P. (1990). Carneros y Chuño: Price levels in nineteenth-century Peru. *Hispanic American Historical Review, 70*(1), 1–56.

James, J. (1988). Personal wealth distribution in late eighteenth-century Britain. *The Economic History Review, 41*(4), 543–565.

Kuznets, S. (1963). Quantitative aspects of the economic growth of nations. *Economic Development and Cultural Change, 11*(2), 1–80.

Lindert, P. (1986). Unequal English wealth since 1670. *Journal of Political Economy, 94*(6), 1127–1162.

O'Rourke, K., Taylor, A., & Williamson, J. (1996). Factor price convergence in the late nineteenth century. *International Economic Review, 37*(3), 499–530.

Oviedo, J. (1870). *Colección de Leyes, Decretos y Ordenes publicadas en el Perú desde el año de 1821 hasta 31 de diciembre de 1859* (Vol. XV). Manuel A. Fuentes.

Pardo, M., Salinas, A., Laos, D., Rosas, F., & Arosemena, M. (1870). *Datos e Informes sobre las Causas que han Producido el Alza de Precios de los Artículos de Primera Necesidad que se Consumen en la Capital.* Imprenta del Estado.

Piketty, T., Postel-Vinay, G., & Rosenthal, J. (2006). Wealth concentration in a developing economy: Paris and France, 1807-1994. *The American Economic Review, 96*(1), 236–256.

Shammas, C. (1993). A new look at long-term trends in wealth inequality in the United States. *The American Historical Review, 98*(2), 412–431.

Steckel, R., & Moehling, C. (2001). Rising inequality: Trends in the distribution of wealth in industrializing New England. *The Journal of Economic History, 61*(1), 160–183.

Tantaleán, J. (1983). *Políticas Económico-Financiera y la Formación del Estado: Siglo XIX.* Centro de Estudios para el Desarrollo y la Participación.

Williamson, J. (1999). Real wages, inequality and globalization in Latin America before 1940. *Journal of Iberian and Latin American Economic History, 17*(S1), 101–142.

Williamson, S. (2021). The annual consumer price index for the United States, 1774-Present. *MeasuringWorth.* https://www.measuringworth.com/datasets/uscpi/. Accessed on November 5, 2021.

Williamson, J., & Lindert, P. (1980). *American inequality: A macroeconomic history.* Institute for research on poverty monograph series. Academic Press.

Yepes, E. (1981). *Perú 1820-1920. ¿Un siglo de desarrollo capitalista?* Signo Universitario.

Zegarra, L. F. (2016). Political instability and non-price loan terms in Lima, Peru: Evidence from notarized contracts. *European Review of Economic History, 20*, 478–525.

Zegarra, L. F. (2018). Reconstruction of export series for Peru before the great depression. *Journal of Iberian and Latin American Economic History, 36*(3), 393–421.

Zegarra, L. F. (2020a). Living costs and real wages in nineteenth century Lima: Levels and international comparisons. *Australian Economic History Review, 60*(2), 186–219.

Zegarra, L. F. (2020b). *Trade flows, relative factor prices and the Heckscher-Ohlin theory: The case of a land-intensive economy.* CENTRUM Católica Working Paper.

Zegarra, L. F. (2021). Economic growth, nutrition and living standards in 19th century Lima: New estimates of welfare ratios using a linear programming model. *América Latina en la Historia Económica, 28*(3), 1–32.

CAN LAND INEQUALITY NEGATIVELY AFFECT HUMAN CAPITAL? THE AMERICAN CASE, 1950–1970

Bárbara Tundidor

University Carlos III of Madrid, Spain

ABSTRACT

The present chapter analyzes land inequality's role in expanding mass literacy between North and South America. According to the central claims, countries with low land inequality, organized in family farms linked to commercial elites, such as the United States, have consistently shown higher literacy levels than latifundia countries with high land inequality and landed elites, such as Latin American countries, where literacy has tended to be blocked. To analyze this hypothesis, a new and original database of landginis, large holding ratio, and illiteracy rates has been calculated from the original censuses of each country, offering the most extensive collection of data on land inequality and literacy for America in this period. By employing panel ordinary least squares, fixed and random effects approach, it is found that, historically, countries with higher land inequality and latifundia systems had worse literacy levels. Nevertheless, not all Latin American countries had latifundia systems, high land inequality, and high illiteracy.

Furthermore, in the United States, some states had higher levels of land inequality and illiteracy than some Latin American regions. Moreover, the results suggest that land inequality accentuated illiteracy more among adults than younger ones. Land inequality acted as a barrier to literacy.

Keywords: Land inequality; human capital; Latin America; subnational states; comparative economics

JEL Codes: I24; N50; N56; O13

Research in Economic History, Volume 38, 77–126
Copyright © 2025 Bárbara Tundidor
Published under exclusive licence by Emerald Publishing Limited
ISSN: 0363-3268/doi:10.1108/S0363-326820250000038004

1. INTRODUCTION

Some authors argue that the success of the United States over Latin America is due to the unequal distribution of land in Latin American countries. This land inequality had adverse effects on human capital and was one of the reasons for the reversal of fortune in Latin America; this hypothesis is presented and defended mainly by the authors Galor et al. (2009).[1]

Historically, countries with high land inequality and latifundia systems have been united with powerful landed elites who have blocked democracy and the expansion of mass education (Acemoglu & Robinson, 2006; Wegenast, 2009). These landed elites, linked to land inequality and latifundia, have tended to understand mass education as a threat to their economic and political interests. At the time of Latin American independence from Europe, many Latin American countries fit these characteristics exhibiting high land inequality, a latifundia system, and landed elites. These circumstances in Latin American countries during their independence led to the creation of new institutions and constitutions designed according to landed oligarchies' preferences, which blocked literacy expansion and established voting requirements based on literacy or landowner-ship to avoid mass participation of the population in the decision-making processes. This reality seems to have survived for more than a century after independence, generating a legacy of asset inequality and high illiteracy in Latin America. While in the United States, a low land inequality model, small-medium family farms, and business-commercial style elites rather than landlords always prevailed. Commercial elites have always tended to tolerate mass education and private property more than landed elites since these commercial elites have not seen education as an economic or social threat to their interests. This framework promoted that the institutions designed in the United States were, from the beginning, more inclusive and facilitated human capital formation. However, one of the main findings of this paper is to show that not all Latin American countries, nor all states of the United States, fit this description. At the time of the creation of some Latin American countries, there was a predominance of family farms, low land inequality, and commercial elites. In these countries, more inclusive institutions were designed; there was no tendency to block the expansion of literacy or the mass participation of their population, leaving a more egalitarian legacy and higher levels of human capital. While in some states of the United States, there were high levels of land inequality and powerful, politically influential landed elites, which were able to block the expansion of mass literacy and fostered the transmission and survival of inequality and low human capital formation.

According to the literature, this past would have influenced the land distribution and human capital well into the 20th century. To empirically corroborate these findings, the main contribution of this paper is to provide an extensive collection of original data at national and sub-national level on land distribution and literacy for 11 Latin American countries and the United States for benchmark years 1950, 1960, and 1970.[2] Exploiting the original data from agricultural and population censuses from each country, I can offer new and original landgini estimations, a new large holding ratio, and illiteracy rates for each country and each sub-national level. Thanks to this extensive collection of data, this paper shows America's largest database on land inequality and illiteracy in the mid-20th century. Besides, these data affirm empirically that, as previously defended, even though Latin America generally had high levels of land inequality and illiteracy, not all Latin American countries had the same characteristics. The second contribution of this paper is to show the mechanisms through which land inequality could affect literacy, showing the effect that different agrarian systems and elites can have on human capital formation.

To my knowledge, no one has thoroughly investigated how land inequality and illiteracy in America at the national and sub-national levels relate. Nor has anyone made a relevant empirical contribution to the discussion of this topic or has contributed with new estimates of landgini, large holding ratio, and illiteracy rates at sub-national levels in these years.

The remainder of the paper is organized as follows: in Section 2, I provide a literature review on how land inequality affects human capital. Section 3 briefly explains land inequality and illiteracy in Latin America, focusing on historical cases most relevant to the hypothesis. Section 4 discusses the methodological approach to measuring land inequality and illiteracy and introduces the new landgini estimates, large holdings ratio, and illiteracy rates. Section 5 shows the results of the OLS, FE, and RE models using the recent estimates. Section 6 concludes.

2. RELATED LITERATURE

Different authors have investigated how land inequality and landed oligarchies have persistently affected human capital formation. Bowles (1978) was one of the first scholars to study how a powerful landed elite can affect human capital. In the struggle between landed elites and capitalists, landlords prefer illiterate workers to maintain a high level of cheap labor in the countryside, thus having incentives to block mass education. Lindert (2004a, 2004b), with cross-sectional regressions in the late 19th and early 20th centuries, shows how landed elites tend to oppose and block public financing of mass education, highlighting that the backwardness in primary education is essentially a consequence of landed oligarchies. Banerjee and Iyer (2005), using district data for India, explore how those districts that were historically under the domination of landed elites had lower levels of schooling and agricultural productivity than those districts in which agriculture was organized in small and medium-sized farms. Galor et al. (2004, 2009) examine how landlords and industrial elites differ in the optimal level of education for the workforce. They argue that, historically, the countries with high land inequality and landed elites offered fewer literacy opportunities, affecting the population's human capital, technological progress, and per capita income levels across countries. According to Galor, Moav, and Vollrath, low land inequality could influence the reversal of fortune. In countries with low land inequality, organized in small-medium family farms and with commercial elites, the population was better qualified to take advantage of the advances of the Industrial Revolution, fostering the industrialization process and the transition to modern growth.[3]

Comparing Latin America with Asia, Wegenast (2009) uses the composition of the countries' exports to study agrarian structures and land inequality. He explores how countries characterized by a latifundia system and high land inequality were linked to politically influential landed elites, which used their influence to perpetuate inequality and restrict access to education. In a later work, Wegenast (2010) examines federal units in Brazil to show that in states with high land inequality and politically influential landed elites, institutions encouraged less education, and landowners were strongly opposed to the expansion of mass education. Meanwhile, in states where historically small and medium-sized farms predominated, there was greater access to education and higher literacy levels.

Studying education across the United States from 1890 to 1930, Ramcharan (2010) and Vollrath (2013) find that land inequality negatively impacted investment and school spending. More recently, Beltrán Tapia and Martínez-Galarraga (2018) exhaustively analyze the relationship between access to land ownership, political power, and education in preindustrial Spain. They show how land concentration acted as a barrier to human capital development in areas with high land inequality and powerful landed elites. They also point out how these elites resisted and limited the implementation of educational policies.

Relatedly, Goñi (2016, 2022) examines the relationship between land inequality and education in England and Wales at the end of the 19th century. While Goñi highlights how most landowners opposed the provision of public education, only those with political power could oppose and block the expansion of education.

In a case study of Prussian regions in the 19th century, Cinnirella and Hornung (2016) show that areas with high land inequality and strong landed oligarchies were negatively associated with registration rates. Only the erosion of the feudal oligarchy and the emancipation of the peasantry fostered higher levels of registration in areas where there was initially high land concentration and powerful landed elites.

Despite the extensive literature that negatively relates land inequality and human capital, it is worth highlighting a recent line of research that emphasizes that land inequality and landed elites did not always negatively affect human capital. For example, Reis (2005) considers that it is not the agrarian structure or the political power of landed oligarchies that hold back mass literacy. Rather, high education costs, in his case in primary education, held back enrollment and access to training. Clark and Gray (2014), using microlevel data, examine the agrarian social structure and school achievement in 19th-century England; they show that rural inequality poorly explains the differences in literacy levels, being other cultural factors that could have influenced the expansion of literacy.[4] Pennock (2014) studies an international sample at the end of the 20th century and points out that landed oligarchies opposed education development only in industrialized countries where landlords had to compete with commercial elites for cheap labor. While in rural countries, landed oligarchies, thanks to the absence of rival elites, promoted education to improve productivity in the countryside.

In line with this latest paper is the exciting study by Andersson and Berger (2016, 2019), which analyzes Swedish municipalities in the 19th century and shows that local agrarian elites were not always a barrier to expanding mass education. Their findings show how some rural elites realized the benefits of promoting education to maintain social order, consolidate national identity, or benefitted from a more educated workforce.

Against this background, it is difficult to predict whether, in the Latin American countries organized in small-medium farms linked to commercial elites, education was encouraged more than in those characterized by latifundia systems and powerful landed elites, where it is assumed that there was an educational delay. Whether or not a state promotes the expansion of mass education will depend on whether elites see the training of the population as a threat to their interests or an economic opportunity (Andersson & Berger, 2016, 2019). In what follows, I describe the first attempts to expand mass literacy in Latin America, the evolution of land inequality, and the evolution of elites until the middle of the 20th century. I then quantitatively explore whether the countries and sub-national levels with historically high land inequality and landed elites experienced worse literacy levels.

3. LAND INEQUALITY AND HUMAN CAPITAL IN LATIN AMERICA: EXPLAINING THE LINK BETWEEN LAND DISTRIBUTION, LANDED OLIGARCHIES, AND ILLITERACY

The first attempts at mass literacy in Latin America came from religious orders (Jesuits, Franciscans, and Piarists). In colonial times, these orders established parochial schools that mainly taught to pray and evangelized the population.[5] Some schools also taught reading, writing, and other higher notions. However, these advances did not reach the entire population due to the low number of schools, the high costs, and because the primary targets tended to be children of the rural aristocracy.

In the 19th century, with the independence of Latin America, the new free states assumed the function of increasing literacy (Teaching State).[6] At this crucial moment, thanks to the new distribution of political and economic power, the Latin American elites had the opportunity to influence mass education. Whether elites try to block mass education will depend on whether education implies a risk to their interests. At the time of Latin American independence, there were two types of elites. First, powerful landed elites were linked to latifundia systems with high land inequality and cheap labor. Second, commercial elites were linked to family farm systems with small-medium holdings and low land inequality.

The landed elites refused to promote mass education; they saw literacy as an economic and political risk. Economically, landowners were aware that spreading literacy required funds. For this reason, they did not support literacy because they would have to bear higher taxes on their assets. It is necessary to remember that land is the primary and most accessible tax asset in rural economies (Acemoglu & Robinson, 2006). Furthermore, better-trained workers may migrate to cities to find other higher-paying and more challenging jobs, causing labor shortages and raising rural wages. Besides, attending school would keep children and young people from working in fields (Galor et al., 2009).

Politically, landowners had incentives to keep the population illiterate. An illiterate population allowed the new ruling elites to maintain power because the franchise had a literacy requirement (Andersson & Berger, 2016) (see Appendix A, Table A1, for a complete chronology of voting rights in Latin America).

Additionally, blocking the expansion of education was a tool to prevent the mobilization of labor and political organizations against landlord interests.[7] In many cases, the central governments of the new Latin American countries neglected education, decentralizing it to local governments (Wegenast, 2010) (See Appendix A, Table A2, for a summary of the centralization or decentralization of primary educational policies in Latin America during this period).

With these objectives and interests, landed oligarchies directly influenced the drafts of the constitutions of the new Latin American countries, establishing voting requirements based on literacy or landownership, which caused land inequality to affect the new distribution of political power and the expansion of education.

The commercial elites did not tend to block mass education. The commercial elites were made up of merchants and were characteristic of countries with low land inequality and organized in small-medium farms. When these countries were founded, land inequality did not influence the new distribution of political power or educational policies. These countries even passed laws promoting settlement and private landownership, similar to the laws of the United States of America (Nugent & Robinson, 2010). The commercial elites in Latin American focused on the trade of agricultural products, so their wealth did not depend on large holdings or cheap labor; for these elites, the expansion of literacy was not a threat to their economic or political interests. During the constitutional development of these states, commercial elites did not block voting rights or literacy to maintain power (see Appendix B, Fig. B1, for the general mechanism of land distribution affecting mass literacy).

In what follows, I present historical evidence comparing various Latin American countries. These comparisons are complicated due to different institutions, immigrant populations, and colonial masters.[8] However, despite these factors, the comparison of these countries is coherent to the extent that all of them share similar characteristics: all were colonies, all became independent, and after their independence, all can be classified according to two types of structures agrarian and two types of elites, which allows us to make a comparison and see if the difference in land distribution and elites can leave a mark on human capital.

3.1 Countries With High Land Inequality, Landed Elites, and Illiteracy

A representative example within this group of countries is Brazil. At the time of its independence, most of the states in Brazil had a plantation-style system, cheap coerced labor, and a powerful landed elite. Most political representatives were linked to the landed elite and defended their interests. The elite influenced the democratic norms establishing literacy as a requirement to vote, elaborating constitutions where free and compulsory education was abolished, and where the decentralization of the educational system was promoted to avoid the central state educational responsibilities. However, this decentralization helped mass education progress in those minority states where small-medium holdings predominated since the commercial elites that dominated these states could influence state education.

Throughout Brazilian history, many attempts were made to make the population literate, and most failed due to the constant political blockade of landowners. This situation lasted until the middle of the 20th century when a new democratic system was established, and there was a significant decrease in illiteracy levels (Hagopian, 1996; Wegenast, 2010). Nevertheless, despite this improvement, illiteracy levels in Brazil remained among the highest in Latin America (see Appendix A, Table A4).

Chile is another illustrative historical case. At the time of its independence, it was characterized by a latifundia system and a powerful landed elite. From the beginning, literacy and landownership requirements were established as a condition for voting, and land expropriation without compensation payment at the market price was considered unconstitutional (Thiesenhusen, 1995, p. 96). Despite everything, the Chilean landowner elite did not have as much political influence as the Brazilian one, but Chilean landowners opposed mass education, especially rural education, with the same intensity. Examples are the Obligatory Primary Education law of 1902 and the experimental plan for rural education San Carlos in the 1940s. With these projects, an attempt was made to improve teaching quality and offer the population free education. Both projects were boycotted, and the last one was paralyzed by the Conservative Party, which was strongly linked to the landed elite. The constant blockade of any initiative that promoted mass education continued until the mid-1960s when educational reforms were approved to improve educational access and quality. However, the military regime suspended or postponed these reforms (1973–1990), decentralizing education and promoting private education.

3.2 Countries With Low Land Inequality, Commercial Elites, and Illiteracy

Countries like Costa Rica, Panama, and Colombia are prototypes of countries with low land inequality and commercial elites. At their independence, Costa Rica and Panama were characterized by small-medium holdings and commercial elites as ruling elites. In Panama, there was never a powerful landed elite (Wegenast, 2009, p. 95).

In the case of Costa Rica, there were influential commercial elites in different cities, which caused these elites to compete among themselves to attract political support; with this aim, subsidies and land ownership rights were offered to small farmers. These elites barely established literacy requirements for voting or prevented mass education. In fact, in the mid-19th century, Costa Rica enjoyed a substantial expansion of human capital without impediments from dominant elites (Nugent & Robinson, 2010).

Colombia was characterized by regional diversity. In some departments, commercial elites focused on trading goods and products from small-medium farmers. In contrast, in other departments, a latifundia style prevailed together with a powerful landed elite. Elites in regions where the latifundia style predominated showed more reluctance to promote education.[9]

Venezuela is a case characterized by its tragic change of direction. Upon gaining independence, the nation initially bore similarities to Costa Rica. Commercial and banking activities characterized the Venezuelan elites, and competition between elites favored small-medium farms, and not mass literacy was blocked. However, from 1899 until the 20th century, several dictatorships destroyed small properties, increased land concentration, and created a strong landed elite (Nugent & Robinson, 2010; Yarrington, 1997).

Mexico is the opposite case of Venezuela. In its beginnings, as an independent country, it was characterized by a latifundia structure and landed elites. However, the 1910 Revolution made the landed oligarchy lose relevance, the latifundia system was largely dismantled, and free and compulsory public education was established. Despite these changes, regional differences remained. In northern states, where a more egalitarian land distribution already prevailed, literacy increased more rapidly than in southern states, where more landlord tradition and coerced labor had been employed (Galor et al., 2009).

Finally, the Argentine case is atypical. Argentina was characterized by a latifundia system and wealthy landed elites in the first years as an independent country. Nevertheless, land inequality was not as pronounced as in other latifundia countries, landed elites did not oppose mass education, and voting requirements were soon eliminated (see Appendix A, Table A1). A possible explanation for the Argentine situation may be that the main economic activity of landowners was raising and selling cattle. Cattle activity requires little labor. These landowners did not need as much cheap work as those who ran large estates.[10] Perhaps, for this reason, Argentine landowners did not see labor mobility or the political participation that literacy fosters as a threat. In addition, certain economic activities derived from the livestock industry, such as leather processing and trade, required specific skills and training in part of the workforce. Argentine landowners came to promote mass literacy by encouraging the expansion of primary schools (Elis, 2011).

4. THE NEW DATA

How to measure latifundia or smallholding tradition? How do we analyze levels of land inequality in a country? And what about human capital? Data on land distribution and illiteracy are scarce, both published and unpublished, especially at the sub-national level. For this reason, one of the main contributions of this paper is to offer the most extensive compilation of data on land inequality and illiteracy for the American continent in the mid-20th century. I exploit the data from the original population and agriculture censuses for each country in the sample. The use of these official sources allows me to create a new and original database both at the national and sub-national levels (see Appendices, Table A4, for access to the disaggregated database and an explanation about it, and Fig. B2).[11]

Concerning how to measure land inequality and the latifundia tradition in a country, most studies to date use land distribution as an indicator to find out if the land was unevenly distributed and if it was concentrated in the hands of a small percentage of the population since high land inequality was linked to strong landed elites (Rajan & Ramcharan, 2009).

To obtain this original data on land distribution at the national and sub-national levels, extensive archiving and compilation work has been necessary and the agricultural censuses of each country have been used. These censuses are published every 10 years and provide information on the number and size of all holdings, including holdings exploited, nonexploited, privately owned, rented, and state-owned. All these holdings are distributed in the following hectare category or size bins: Latin American censuses range from less than 1 to 5 hectares up to 100,000 hectares and more. The US censuses range from 1–10 acres (0.4–3.6 ha) up to 2,000 acres and more (809,371 ha and more) (see Appendix A, Tables A3 and A4, and its comments for a further explanation of the data, its collection, and its sources). Using these agricultural censuses allows me to contribute to the literature with new landgini and large holding ratio estimates and a unique and original land distribution dataset for Latin America and the United States for the period studied (see Appendix A, Table A4, for access to the disaggregated database and an explanation about it).

On the other hand, to measure land distribution, there are several options.[12] In this case, the Gini coefficient applied to land distribution (landgini) is used to analyze the levels of unequal land distribution. The landgini is a coefficient that measures land distribution between values 0 (equality) and 1 (inequality). The formula is as follows:

$$G = \frac{\sum\limits_{i=1}^{n} \sum\limits_{j=1}^{n} |x_i - x_j|}{2n^2 \mu}$$

where x_i and x_j are the percentage shares of the land of n deciles ($n=10$) and μ is $1/n$ (Frankema, 2008; Nunn, 2008).[13] The reasons why this index has been chosen over the other options are simple: first, it is the most used index in the literature to analyze land inequality.[14] Second, it has a straightforward interpretation (Summerhill, 2010). Third, this index captures land owned by governments, collectively, or distributed in cooperatives, and it measures all registered land and includes the size and number of all holdings. Finally, it is an index without units of measurement, which allows and facilitates comparisons within and across states, regions, and countries around the world; for that reason, it is the most appropriate measure to meet the comparative purpose of this study.

Nevertheless, it is necessary to emphasize that this index measures inequality between landowners. It does not distinguish between tenants and owners, nor does it capture individuals who do not own land (Frankema, 2008; Funari, 2017). However, these typical landgini features need not be detrimental to this analysis. On the contrary, a high landgini shows that in a society, a minority of owners own most of the land, while the rest of the great majority owns a small portion of land. On the other hand, a lower landgini would show a more egalitarian society, where the vast majority of owners own approximately the same amount of land without giving rise to minorities that can impose themselves on the rest of the community.

However, due to the possible limitations that the landgini may have as the only measure to analyze land inequality and the latifundia tradition, another complementary variable is calculated to help analyze land distribution. This measure is the Large Holding ratio, which indicates the percentage of large holdings in a given national or sub-national level for the period studied. Similarly, to landgini, this ratio is bounded between 0 and 1. The formula is as follows:

$$\text{Large Holding}_{i,t} = \frac{\text{Number of holdings with a surface} > 100 \text{ hectares}}{\text{Total number of holdings}}$$

The objective of this measure is to show the percentage of holdings that can be considered large holdings, that is, latifundia. This same index with similar purposes has been used previously by Cinnirella and Hornung (2016), analyzing, in their case, the link between land inequality and the expansion of mass education in 19th-century Prussia.[15] With this index, the authors defend that it is intuitive that the largest holdings depend on nonfamily workers, that is, forced or paid labor, so they argue that a higher percentage of large holdings will indicate that a higher percentage of the population is subject to coercive institutions in regions where land inequality is very high.[16]

Although there are no clear minimum or maximum dimensions for large holdings, according to the agrarian structure of Latin America in these years, it is possible to begin to consider as large holdings those with an area greater than 100 hectares (see Appendix A, Table A3).

To measure human capital, I use the illiteracy rate, as defined by the population censuses of each country. The officially accepted definition defines illiterate as anyone *unable to read and write a simple paragraph in any language*. Since 1950, there has been consensus on the comparability of illiteracy data for American countries, thanks to the initiative of international organizations to homogenize statistics.[17]

Censuses provide information to analyze two age groups, most countries offer illiteracy data for ages 14+, and others provide data for ages 5–10+. Two illiteracy rates will be calculated: an illiteracy rate for ages 14+ and another for ages 5–10+. Therefore, the first illiteracy rate is calculated as the number of illiterate people aged 14+ in the population corresponding to that age group. And the second rate is calculated as the number of illiterate people aged 5–10+ in the population corresponding to that age group:[18]

$$(\text{I}) \text{ Illiteracy Rate (for ages } 14+) = \frac{\text{Illiteracy Population for ages } 14+}{\text{Population for ages } 14+}$$

$$(\text{II}) \text{ Illiteracy Rate (for ages } 5-10+) = \frac{\text{Illiteracy Population for ages } 5-10+}{\text{Population for ages } 5-10+}$$

The illiteracy rate for ages 14+ is the definition of adult illiteracy most widely employed, while the rate for ages 5–10+ is most used in the analysis of child–adult illiteracy.[19] These two illiteracy rates will allow us to see if land inequality was negatively related to adult illiteracy, child illiteracy, or both or neither.

For this purpose, landgini indices, large holding ratios, and illiteracy rates for each country and each sub-national level are calculated for the whole sample for the years 1950, 1960, and 1970. In total, my data include 618 landginis and large holding ratios and 547 illiteracy rates (see Appendix A, Table A4, to access the disaggregated database and to see landgini estimates, large holding ratio, and illiteracy rates by countries and by sub-national level for each country, and for a further discussion about results). This extraordinary data collection offers the most complete and remarkable portrait of land inequality and human capital in Latin America and the United States from 1950 to 1970.

Furthermore, these data provide a unique opportunity to investigate whether sub-national levels organized into latifundia systems with high land inequality exhibited worse literacy levels.

The levels of land inequality and illiteracy by regional blocks are graphed in Fig. 1. The left panel contains the levels of landgini for the United States, Mexico, and Central and South America.[20] The right panel shows the illiteracy rate of 14+ for the same regions, all from 1950 to 1970. Generally, the regional blocks with

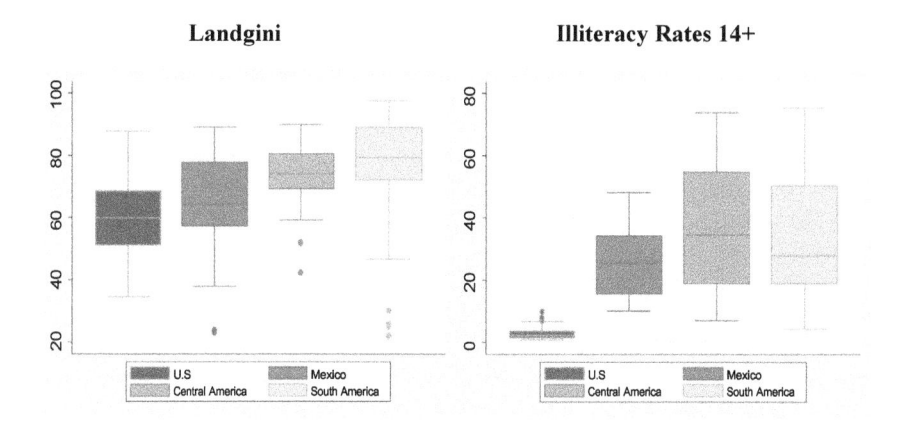

Fig. 1. Landgini and Illiteracy Rates by Regional Blocks, 1950–1970.
Source: Author's elaboration; Agricultural and Population Censuses, 1950–1970.
Note: The shares rectangle represents the interquartile range, which contains the
median – the solid line. Dots beyond this range are possible outliers.

high landgini also tended to show higher illiteracy rates. Specifically, the area of South America reaches levels of land inequality close to 98%, as is indicated by the landgini index, and an illiteracy rate close to 80%. Exceptions within the South American area are represented by the minimum values, which represent some sub-national levels from Argentina, Colombia, or Brazil where, according to historical evidence, the smallholder tradition and commercial elites predominated.

These results highlight the regional difference within the countries. For example, since the independence, the Brazilian states characterized by a strong landed oligarchy, which were reluctant to mass literacy, still show high levels of landgini and illiteracy in this period.[21] While other states, such as Santa Catarina or Espirito Santo, characterized by being organized around family farms and commercial elites, registered relatively low levels of land inequality and illiteracy within the general trend of Brazil.[22] Similar regional differences can be observed within Colombia, where departments characterized by growing coffee on small farms and by commercial elites show lower levels of both land inequality and illiteracy than those that, in the past, were organized around large holdings and landed elites (see Appendix A, Table A4, for access to the disaggregated database and an explanation about it).[23]

Despite reducing land inequality and illiteracy since the Revolution, Mexico is also distinguished by its regional disparity. Some states suffered significant land redistributions and investments in human capital leading to lower levels of inequality and illiteracy. For example, in Baja California, the landgini decreased from 88.5% in 1950 to 71.9% in 1970, and its illiteracy rate dropped from 15.1% to 12.6%.[24] However, the southern states, historically dominated by landowners and distinguished by latifundia systems and coerced labor, resisted the changes brought by the new regime and did not experience a significant decrease in land inequality or illiteracy. For instance, in the 1970s, the southern state of Oaxaca still showed an illiteracy rate of 45.7% and a landgini of 89.1%.

Furthermore, these data preliminarily support the hypothesis proposed by Galor et al. (2009), which argues that the United States had lower levels of land inequality and, consequently, less illiteracy than Latin America. In fact, within the United States, we can find the same variation; Fig. 2 graphs the landgini and illiteracy rate by regional blocks in the United States from 1950 to 1960.[25]

The states in New England, Middle Atlantic, East North Central, and West North Central regions show lower levels of land inequality and illiteracy because they were mainly organized around family farms. In contrast, higher land inequality was characteristic of the southern states, historically organized in latifundia with coerced labor and slavery, which, according to historical evidence, led to higher levels of illiteracy.[26] However, the states from the mountain and Pacific regions show high levels of land inequality and low levels of illiteracy. This inverse relationship between land inequality and illiteracy may be because rural elites in these states did not have as much influence as in the southern states or other Latin American countries (Wright, 1986), perhaps due to the presence of other powerful industries and competing elites, such as commercial and industrial. It is also worth noting that in the mountainous region, there are states such as Montana, Wyoming, or Colorado, which are characterized by having a cattle-raising tradition, and some studies argue that landed elites focused on cattle-raising do not negatively affect literacy (see Droller & Fiszbein, 2021; Elis, 2011).

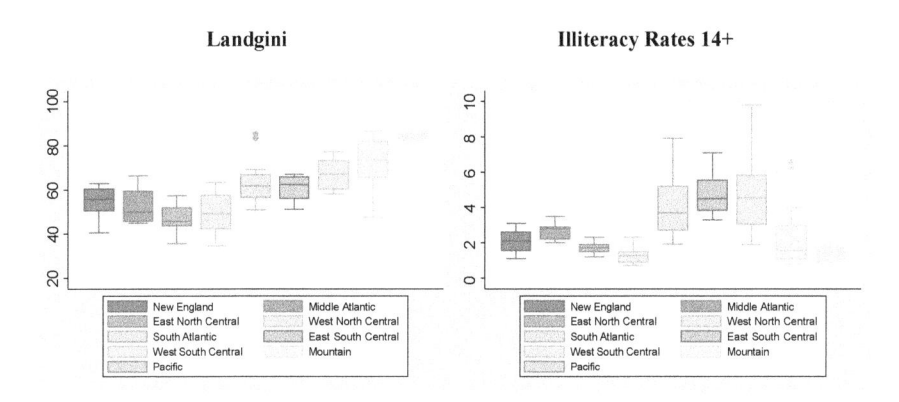

Fig. 2.   Landgini and Illiteracy Rates 14+ in the United States by Regional Blocks, 1950–1960. *Source:* Author's elaboration; Agricultural and Population Censuses, 1950–1960. *Note:* The shares rectangle represents the interquartile range, which contains the median – the solid line. Dots beyond this range are possible outliers.

In any case, these states would challenge the hypothesis Galor et al. (2009) suggested. They would be more in line with studies that argue that some rural oligarchies may have more interests in promoting education for self-interest than smallholder societies, by productive interests, for example, or with those studies that find no relationship between land inequality and human capital (in the Appendix B, see Fig. B2).[27]

Despite everything, there is a decreasing evolution of land inequality across countries and subnational levels (both Latin America and the United States) for this period. Illiteracy rates also have a similar downward trend for both age groups. It is due to increased industrialization, urbanization, economic globalization, and the advancement of democracy in some countries, which fostered agrarian and educational reforms and the weakening of the landed oligarchy.[28]

These generally decreasing trends in land inequality and illiteracy can be best seen in Figs. 3 and 4. Fig. 3 contains the evolution of the landgini for the period from 1950 to 1970 by countries. Fig. 4 shows the development of illiteracy for ages 14+ in the same countries in the same period.

In general, the countries experienced a decrease in land concentration, especially in the 1960s and 1970s. We can see a decreasing trend in countries such as Chile, Costa Rica, Ecuador, Mexico, and Venezuela. On the other hand, we can see a consistent trend in countries such as Brazil and Colombia, where landgini levels do not change much over the period. We can also appreciate a slight increase in landgini for Argentina, Honduras, Panama, and the United States, except for Argentina, not reaching highly high values. About Nicaragua, lamentably, for this period, there is only information at the country level for the year 1960 (see Appendix A, Table A4).

A similar trend shows the illiteracy rate for ages 14+ graphed in Fig. 4. There was a decrease in illiteracy in the 60s, but it was in the 70s that we can see a more

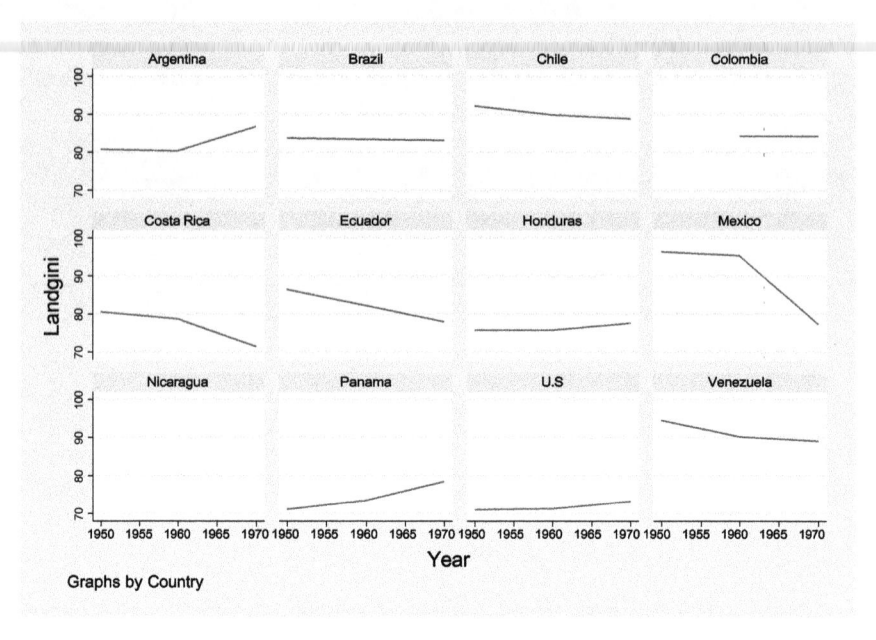

Fig. 3.   Landgini Evolution, 1950–1970. *Source:* Author's elaboration;
Agricultural and Population Censuses, 1950–1970.

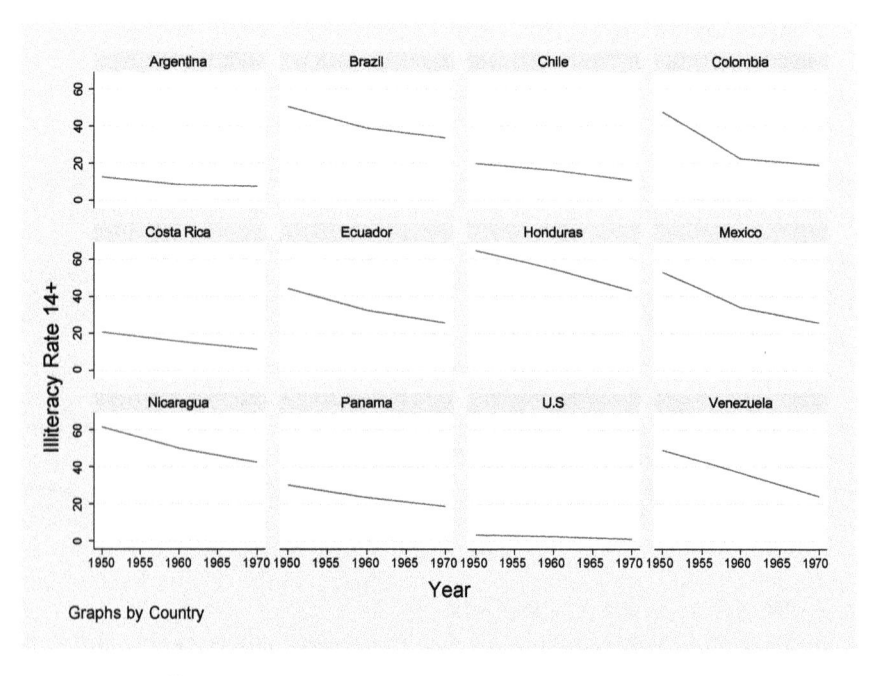

Fig. 4.   Illiteracy Rate Ages 14+ Evolution, 1950–1970. *Source:* Author's
elaboration; Population Censuses, 1950–1970.

significant drop in illiteracy. Interestingly, the countries with the most significant decrease in illiteracy are those with the greatest reduction in land inequality: Chile, Costa Rica, Ecuador, and Mexico (see Appendix A, Table A4 to see data from Figs. 3 and 4 by country and the comparison with estimates of other authors). Another illiteracy measure for ages 5–10+ experienced the same decrease for this period (see Appendix B, Fig. B3).

Other attractive illiteracy measures to analyze would be rural and urban illiteracy rates.

Unfortunately, in this period, most censuses fail to provide much data on rural and urban illiteracy. However, it has been possible to extract some illiteracy rates for some countries in some years (see Appendix B, Fig. B4). Rural illiteracy rates are generally higher than urban ones. And both rural and urban rates tend to decrease throughout the period studied.

5. METHODOLOGY AND ECONOMETRIC RESULTS

The central hypothesis is that the subnational levels historically organized into latifundia systems linked to landed elites and with high land inequality may have left long-lasting footprints on literacy. Specifically, exhibiting worse levels of literacy than other subnational levels organized in smallholdings, with low land inequality, and linked to commercial elites. A preliminary exploration of these new data confirms that there may be a positive association between land inequality and illiteracy, as indicated by Fig. 5.

Fig. 5 plots the landgini against illiteracy rates; it documents a positive association between the two variables. Generally, subnational levels with high land inequality tended to have higher illiteracy rates.

However, other factors can drive these associations. To test if land inequality was positively associated with illiteracy, I estimate an econometric model as specified below:

For ages 14+:

$$(1) \ \text{IlliteracyRate}_{i,t} = \ \beta_0 + \beta_1 \text{landgini}_{i,t} \Big/ \text{Ratiolargeholding}_{i,t} + \beta_2 \text{lurbanpop}_{i,t}$$
$$+ \beta_3 \text{lchilddependency}_{i,t} + \beta_4 \text{Catholics}_{i,t} + \beta_5 \text{ldensity}_{i,t}$$
$$+ \beta_6 \text{ldistance}_{i,t} + \beta_7 \text{landlocked}_i + \beta_8 \text{geocontrols}_i + u_{i,t}$$

For ages 5–10+:

$$(2) \ \text{IlliteracyRate}_{i,t} = \ \beta_0 + \beta_1 \text{landgini}_{i,t} \Big/ \text{Ratiolargeholding}_{i,t} + \beta_2 \text{lurbanpop}_{i,t}$$
$$+ \beta_3 \text{lchilddependency}_{i,t} + \beta_4 \text{ldensity}_{i,t} + \beta_5 \text{ldistance}_{i,t}$$
$$+ \beta_6 \text{landlocked}_i + \beta_7 \text{geocontrols}_i + u_{i,t}$$

(Table A5 in the Appendix A presents all details about variables and their summary statistics).

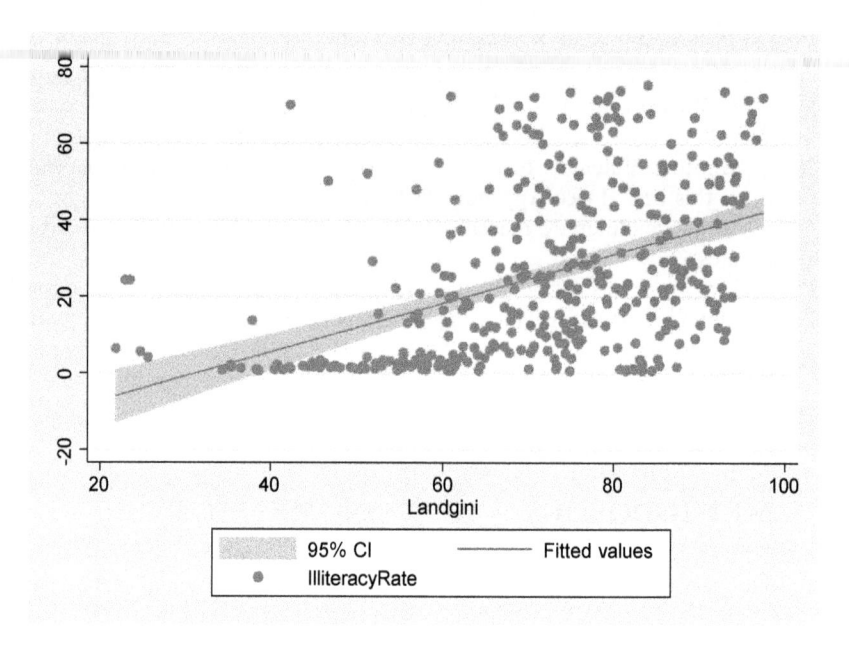

Fig. 5.   Landgini and Illiteracy Rates, 1950–1970. *Source:* Author's
elaboration; Agricultural and Population Censuses, 1950–1970.

I use an unbalanced panel dataset for 11 Latin American countries and the United
States, a total of 372 observations from 1950 to 1970.[29] I use the illiteracy rates by
subnational levels for ages 14+ and 5–10 + as the dependent variables. I use these
illiteracy rates because they capture the share of the population that is unable to read
and write a simple paragraph in any language. They also allow me to differentiate
between adult illiteracy and child illiteracy. These rates are used in the literature by
other authors to analyze human capital in a country (Arroyo-Abad, 2016; Núñez,
2005b). Higher values show a higher share of illiteracy.

As a key independent variable, I use the landgini variable at the subnational level
to measure land inequality. In addition, I use the ratio of large holdings, as previously defined. The remaining independent variables and controls, widely used in
studying human capital and land inequality, have also been obtained from each
country's population census. Following the literature (Albertus, 2017; Galor et al.,
2009), the percentage of urban population at each subnational level has been estimated to control the possible effect of urbanization, industrialization, and the
demand for human capital in the urban sector can have on illiteracy. According to
preliminary studies, there is a greater demand for education in urban-intensive
regions; more education is demanded to perform more skilled jobs. Furthermore,
the level of urban population captures the economic importance of agriculture and
serves as a proxy for industrialization (Albertus, 2017, p. 252). Finally, the urban
population also aims to capture the demand factor (Beltrán Tapia &
Martínez-Galarraga, 2018, p. 87).

The logarithm of child dependency, for each subnational level, is also included to measure the potential need for social and economic support for the child and youth population by the working-age population. Theoretically, a higher share of children and the young population is likely to put more pressure on the education system. Besides, if a family's resources are limited, a larger offspring can limit each child's options for enrolling at school (Beltrán Tapia & Martinez- Galarraga, 2018, p. 88).

I also include a measure of whether a region is predominately Catholic. Some studies argue that Catholicism may not be beneficial for mass education. It is mentioned above that although the first attempts to teach the population to read and write came from religious orders, they focused more on evangelizing the people than instructing them. Furthermore, due to the high costs of establishing schools and the fact that the main beneficiaries were the children of the rural aristocracy, these literacy efforts did not reach the entire population. However, in the Protestant religion, greater educational autonomy was encouraged; Alter and Clark (2010) mention that literacy was higher in Protestant countries since each individual was expected to read the Bible on their own.[30]

Logarithms of population density and distance to the capital city of each country are used to control access to urban areas and markets and capture demand factors.[31] In addition, the literature maintains that the distance to the capital is a tool for analyzing the central government's influence on regional elites. The further away the province is, the less likely the central government will be able to exercise control (Arroyo-Abad, 2016).

I also include an indicator variable that measures whether the location is land-locked. The logic behind this variable is the capture of openness to trade and cultural flows due to better access to the sea, which could affect literacy (Mariella, 2022).

Finally, I include several geographic controls, such as area, latitude, and longitude for each subnational level, are added to account for regional and climatic diversity (Angeles & Elizalde, 2017; Mariella, 2022).

To claim the robustness of the results and to follow the recent literature, models with ordinary least squares (OLS), fixed and random effects (FE and RE) are estimated (Pennock, 2014; Wegenast, 2009) for both illiteracy rates. Fixed and random effects estimations help consider unobserved heterogeneity and time-invariant factors. Furthermore, year dummies are also included in all models to control the temporal heterogeneity along years. The Hausman test will be applied to determine the most appropriate estimation. In addition, due to the heterogeneity of all subnational levels, the estimate includes standard error clustering at subnational levels and bootstrap methods, given the common institutions and serial correlation within subnational levels (Arroyo-Abad, 2016).

5.1 Econometric Results

Table 1 reports the results from the estimations of Eqs. (1) and (2) via OLS, FE, and RE. Column (1) presents the specification with OLS, and columns (2) and (3) show the specification with fixed and random effects, respectively. Columns (4), (5), and (6) represent the same specifications but with standard errors clustered at the country-state level. Columns (7) and (8) show the FE and RE estimations

Table 1. Effect of Land Inequality (Landgini) on Illiteracy Rate.

	Dependent Variable: Illiteracy Rate (14+)								Dependent Variable: Illiteracy Rate (5–10+)							
	Model 1 (OLS)	Model 2 (FE)	Model 3 (RE)	Model 4 (OLS)	Model 5 (FE)	Model 6 (RE)	Model 7 (FE)	Model 8 (RE)	Model 9 (OLS)	Model 10 (FE)	Model 11 (RE)	Model 12 (OLS)	Model 13 (FE)	Model 14 (RE)	Model 15 (FE)	Model 16 (RE)
$Landgini_{i,t}$	0.28*** (0.05)	0.14** (0.05)	0.16*** (0.04)	0.28*** (0.05)	0.14 (0.10)	0.16** (0.07)	0.14 (0.11)	0.16** (0.07)	−0.21** (0.09)	0.06* (0.03)	0.02 (0.04)	−0.21 (0.13)	0.06 (0.05)	0.02 (0.04)	0.06 (0.05)	0.02 (0.05)
$UrbanPop_{i,t}$	−0.45*** (0.04)	0.038 (0.05)	−0.19*** (0.04)	−0.45*** (0.05)	0.038 (0.04)	−0.19*** (0.04)	0.038 (0.05)	−0.19*** (0.04)	−0.35*** (0.05)	0.0029 (0.02)	−0.04* (0.02)	−0.35** (0.10)	0.0029 (0.01)	−0.04 (0.03)	0.0029 (0.05)	−0.043 (0.06)
$lChildDependency_{i,t}$	−12.2** (4.07)	11.8*** (1.61)	8.32*** (1.78)	−12.2*** (3.48)	11.8*** (1.33)	8.32*** (1.67)	11.8*** (1.26)	8.32*** (1.64)	10.7 (9.39)	12.01** (4.68)	18.7*** (4.40)	10.7 (11.7)	12.01** (3.84)	18.7*** (3.91)	12.01* (6.17)	18.7*** (5.48)
$Catholics_{i,t}$	39.3*** (4.29)		40.9*** (4.79)	39.3*** (6.48)		40.9** (5.64)		40.9*** (5.37)								
$lDensity_{i,t}$	2.38*** (0.71)	0.85 (1.80)	1.08 (0.84)	2.38** (0.86)	0.85 (1.77)	1.08 (0.86)	0.85 (1.73)	1.08 (0.86)	−0.53 (0.83)	0.98 (2.34)	−1.82* (1.07)	−0.53 (1.01)	0.98 (2.52)	−1.82 (1.13)	0.98 (3.19)	−1.82 (1.23)
$lDistance_{i,t}$	4.97*** (0.86)		4.51*** (1.15)	4.97*** (1.13)		4.51*** (1.30)		4.51*** (1.33)	−4.2** (1.34)		−6.34*** (1.76)	−4.2** (1.64)		−6.34** (2.09)		−6.34*** (1.98)
$Landlocked_i$	−1.04 (1.43)		−1.33 (1.88)	−1.04 (1.66)		−1.33 (1.95)		−1.33 (2.02)	−2.85 (2.00)		−5.08* (2.78)	−2.85 (2.67)		−5.08 (3.26)		−5.08 (3.85)
$lArea_i$	0.58 (0.82)		−1.08 (1.01)	0.58 (1.01)		−1.08 (1.28)		−1.08 (1.21)	−1.42 (0.87)		−2.77** (1.10)	−1.42 (1.35)		−2.77 (1.91)		−2.77 (1.80)
$Latitude_i$	0.39*** (0.04)		0.46*** (0.05)	0.39*** (0.09)		0.46*** (0.07)		0.46*** (0.06)	0.49*** (0.05)		0.54*** (0.06)	0.49*** (0.06)		0.54*** (0.06)		0.54*** (0.07)
$Longitude_i$	0.37*** (0.06)		0.35*** (0.07)	0.37*** (0.07)		0.35*** (0.07)		0.35*** (0.07)	0.83*** (0.06)		0.93*** (0.07)	0.83*** (0.07)		0.93*** (0.07)		0.93*** (0.07)
Year dummies	YES	YES	YES	YES	YES	YES	YES	YES	YES	YES	YES	YES	YES	YES	YES	YES
Standard errors clustered	NO	NO	NO	YES	YES	YES	NO	NO	NO	NO	NO	YES	YES	YES	NO	NO
Bootstrap methods	NO	NO	NO	NO	NO	NO	YES	YES	NO	NO	NO	NO	NO	NO	YES	YES
Observations	273	273	273	273	273	273	273	273	150	150	150	150	150	150	150	150
R^2 (within/between)	0.75	0.69/0.31	0.61/0.72	0.75	0.69/0.31	0.61/0.72	0.69/0.31	0.61/0.72	0.71	0.90/0.008	0.89/0.62	0.71	0.90/0.008	0.89/0.62	0.90/0.008	0.89/0.62
Prob > F	0.0000	0.0000		0.0000	0.0000				0.0000	0.0000		0.0000	0.0000			
Prob > chi²			0.0000			0.0000	0.0000	0.0000			0.0000			0.0000	0.0000	0.0000

Source: Author's elaboration.

applying bootstrap methods. The rest of the columns follow the same order previously mentioned but use the illiteracy rate for ages (5–10+) as the dependent variable. In all these estimates, the key independent variable is the landgini.

Starting with the estimates with the illiteracy rate 14+ as the dependent variable, it is worth emphasizing that the sign and statistical significance of the independent key variable, landgini, hardly changes between specifications from 1 to 3. In all these models, the landgini has a positive effect on the illiteracy rate, and in all of them, it has statistical significance. According to column 1, the OLS model, an increase in landgini implies a rise of 0.20 percentage points in the illiteracy rate (14+). In columns 2 and 3, FE and RE models, an increase in the landgini suggests a rise of 0.10 and 0.11 percentage points in the illiteracy rate (14+), respectively.

The coefficients of the other variables included in the models also provide interesting insights. In model 1, estimated with OLS, we can see that the percentage of urban population and the logarithm of child dependency have a negative effect on illiteracy levels. However, these effects change in the estimate with fixed effects (model 2). In this model 2, we can also see that the landgini and child dependency variables have a positive and statistically significant impact on illiteracy, which is expected. On the one hand, the hypothesis presented here, and defended mainly by the literature, is that higher land inequality could increase illiteracy; on the other hand, an economically dependent young population always increases the pressure on educational systems, being able to promote illiteracy due to lack of resources. About the remaining variables, the coefficients of the percentage of Catholic population and density also show, according to the literature, a positive effect on illiteracy levels in models 1 and 3. For their part, the distance and landlocked variables also show interesting results. Distance has a positive and significant effect on illiteracy, which could indicate that, according to some authors, the further a subnational level is from the central government, the more influential the local elites will be, and if these local elites are against the mass education, we will find worse results in literacy.[32] While the landlocked variable negatively affects illiteracy since greater cultural and trade openness seems to promote literacy; however, it is not statistically significant in any model.

After analyzing these results, our attention should focus on the changes in signs of the urban population and child dependency variables when they are estimated with fixed effects. This is because all the omitted variables that do not fluctuate over time are eliminated with the fixed-effects estimation.[33] The change in sign and significance of these variables indicates that the estimation with OLS could present a particular bias due to omitted variables that are eliminated when estimating with fixed effects. The Hausman test is applied to determine which estimate is the most appropriate, and according to the results, the estimation with fixed effects is the most accurate.[34] In the estimation with fixed effects, we can observe the positive and statistically significant impact of landgini on illiteracy levels. The same impact and significance have the logarithm of child dependency. However, the density and percentage of the urban population lose statistical significance.

Nevertheless, despite these results, due to the heterogeneity of all subnational levels and to the common institutions and serial correlation within subnational levels, estimates with standard cluster errors and bootstrap methods are also aggregated and presented in columns 4–8. In these estimates, we can see that, in all of them, the effects of the variables do not change, and in most of them, their statistical significance does not change either. Only in the case of the landgini, we can appreciate that it loses statistical significance in the estimates with fixed effects (models 5 and 7), although it maintains the same effect as in the previous estimates. This loss of significance may be due to the possible diversity and lack of data in some countries. An example is the lack of data for the 1970s in countries like Chile or Nicaragua.[35] This distortion caused by the characteristics of this international analysis is included in these new estimates. However, it is necessary to mention that the positive effect of landgini on illiteracy does not change.

On the other hand, if we analyze the effect of land inequality on the 5–10+ illiteracy rate in models 9 to 16, we can again see exciting results. The most noticeable change is the sign and statistical significance of the landgini in these specifications. The landgini shows a negative sign in the models estimated with OLS (models 9 and 12). In contrast, in the rest of the models, the landgini has a positive sign with statistical significance in the estimated model with fixed effects (model 10). According to model 9, an increase in landgini implies a reduction of 0.11 percentage points in the illiteracy rate (5–10+). While in the models estimated with FE and RE (models 10 and 11), an increase in the landgini suggests an increase of 0.03 and 0.01 percentage points, respectively, in the illiteracy rate (5–10+).

These results show that, again, OLS could present a certain bias. Following the previous methodology, FE and RE are estimated to account for unobserved heterogeneity and time-invariant factors. The Hausman test is also applied, and again, it indicates that the estimation with fixed effects is the most appropriate (model 10). In this model, we can observe that the sign of the landgini and child dependency is positive, with statistical significance. At the same time, the urban population and the density lose statistical significance.

After these results, once again, to go a little further, the same models are estimated with standard errors clustered at subnational levels and bootstrap methods (models from 12 to 16). We can see that the landgini loses statistical significance, although it maintains the same positive effect on illiteracy. Only the child dependency variable keeps a positive and statistically significant impact in all estimates, except in the estimates with OLS (models 9 and 12), where it does not show significance.

Table 2 reports the results from the estimations of Eqs. (1) and (2) via OLS, FE, and RE, but with the large holding ratio as the key independent variable. The order is the same as previously mentioned: Column (1) presents the specification with ordinary least squares, and columns (2) and (3) show the specification with fixed and random effects, respectively.

Columns 4, 5, and 6 represent the same specifications but with standard errors clustered at the country-state level. Columns 7 and 8 show the FE and RE

	Model 1 (OLS)	Model 2 (FE)	Model 3 (RE)	Model 4 (OLS)	Model 5 (FE)	Model 6 (RE)	Model 7 (FE)	Model 8 (RE)	Model 9 (OLS)	Model 10 (FE)	Model 11 (RE)	Model 12 (OLS)	Model 13 (FE)	Model 14 (RE)	Model 15 (FE)	Model 16 (RE)
	Dependent Variable: Illiteracy Rate (14+)								Dependent Variable: Illiteracy Rate (5–10+)							
$Ratiolargeholding_{l,t}$	-0.041 (0.05)	0.075 (0.08)	-0.001 (0.05)	-0.041 (0.05)	0.075 (0.07)	-0.001 (0.04)	0.075 (0.08)	-0.001 (0.04)	0.0001 (0.078)	-0.03 (0.02)	-0.032 (0.02)	0.0001 (0.071)	-0.03 (0.03)	-0.032 (0.03)	-0.03 (0.04)	-0.032 (0.04)
$UrbanPop_{l,t}$	-0.40*** (0.04)	0.023 (0.05)	-0.18*** (0.04)	-0.40*** (0.05)	0.023 (0.04)	-0.18*** (0.04)	0.023 (0.04)	-0.18*** (0.05)	-0.36*** (0.05)	0.002 (0.02)	-0.045* (0.02)	-0.36** (0.11)	0.002 (0.01)	-0.045 (0.03)	0.002 (0.05)	-0.045 (0.06)
$ChildDependency_{l,t}$	-8.85** (4.22)	11.9*** (1.75)	9.35*** (1.81)	-8.85** (3.85)	11.9*** (1.39)	9.35*** (1.65)	11.9*** (1.43)	9.35*** (1.65)	7.91 (9.55)	11.8*** (4.76)	18.83*** (4.44)	7.91 (12.3)	11.8** (4.08)	18.83*** (4.03)	11.8* (6.42)	18.83*** (5.54)
$Catholics_{l,t}$	46.7*** (4.36)		44.9*** (5.20)	46.7*** (6.58)		44.9*** (5.58)		44.9*** (4.94)								
$Density_{l,t}$	2.56** (0.83)	1.00 (2.04)	1.15 (0.94)	2.56** (1.08)	1.00 (1.96)	1.15 (0.99)	1.00 (1.85)	1.15 (1.00)	-0.84 (0.94)	0.46 (2.40)	-2.00* (1.07)	-0.84 (1.18)	0.46 (2.73)	-2.00* (1.14)	0.46 (3.58)	-2.00 (1.24)
$Distance_{l,t}$	5.34*** (0.90)		4.56*** (1.18)	5.34*** (1.15)		4.56*** (1.33)		4.56*** (1.42)	-3.96** (1.38)		-6.26*** (1.74)	-3.96** (1.71)		-6.26** (2.07)		-6.26** (2.00)
$Landlocked_l$	-0.23 (1.51)		-0.85 (1.93)	-0.23 (1.72)		-0.85 (2.00)		-0.85 (2.12)	-3.33 (2.02)		-5.05* (2.74)	-3.33 (2.70)		-5.05 (3.23)		-5.05 (3.80)
$Area_i$	1.06 (0.85)		-0.83 (1.04)	1.06 (1.09)		-0.83 (1.34)		-0.83 (1.21)	-2.10** (0.84)		-2.73** (1.08)	-2.10 (1.44)		-2.73 (1.95)		-2.73 (1.87)
$Latitude_i$	0.40*** (0.04)		0.46*** (0.05)	0.40*** (0.10)		0.46*** (0.07)		0.46*** (0.06)	0.503*** (0.06)		0.53*** (0.064)	0.503*** (0.05)		0.53*** (0.06)		0.53*** (0.07)
$Longitude_i$	0.28*** (0.06)		0.31*** (0.08)	0.28*** (0.08)		0.31*** (0.07)		0.31*** (0.07)	0.86*** (0.070)		0.92*** (0.077)	0.86*** (0.073)		0.92*** (0.071)		0.92*** (0.079)
Year dummies	YES	YES	YES	YES	YES	YES	YES	YES	YES	YES	YES	YES	YES	YES	YES	YES
Standard errors clustered	NO	NO	NO	YES	YES	YES	NO	NO	NO	NO	NO	YES	YES	YES	NO	NO
Bootstrap methods	NO	NO	NO	NO	NO	NO	YES	YES	NO	NO	NO	NO	NO	NO	YES	YES
Observations	273	273	273	273	273	273	273	273	150	150	150	150	150	150	150	150
R^2 (within/between)	0.73	0.66/0.08	0.60/0.71	0.73	0.66/0.08	0.60/0.71	0.66/0.08	0.60/0.71	0.70	0.90/0.0003	0.89/0.62	0.70	0.90/0.0003	0.89/0.62	0.90/0.0003	0.89/0.62
Prob > F	0.0000	0.0000		0.0000	0.0000		0.0000		0.0000	0.0000		0.0000	0.0000		0.0000	
Prob > chi²			0.0000			0.0000		0.0000			0.0000			0.0000		0.0000

Source: Author's elaboration.

Note: All regressions include a constant. Robust standard errors in parentheses, $***p < 0.001$, $**p < 0.05$, $*p < 0.1$. Sample in Model (5–10+) only includes LACs.

estimations applying bootstrap methods. The rest of the columns follow the same order previously mentioned but use the illiteracy rate for ages (5–10+) as the dependent variable.

Starting again with the illiteracy variable for those over 14 years of age, the first thing that stands out when using the large holding ratio as a variable to measure land inequality and latifundia tradition is the sign changes in this variable in the estimates with fixed effects (models 2, 5, and 7). We can see a positive impact on these estimates with fixed effects; a higher percentage of large estates would imply a higher illiteracy rate, although without statistical relevance.

On the other hand, the effect and statistical relevance of the rest of the variables are similar to the previous results using the landgini index. The urban population changes sign again, from negative to positive in the estimation with fixed effects, and loses significance. Child dependency shows a similar behavior, changes its sign to positive, and maintains statistical relevance. The catholic and distance variables repeat their significance and positive effect on illiteracy. Density shows a positive and statistically relevant effect on the OLS estimates (models 1 and 4), a relevance that it loses in the rest of the estimates. And landlocked, again, is negative and without statistical significance in all models. Once again, the Hausman test is applied to find out which estimate is the most accurate among the models 2–3; again, the most appropriate estimate is fixed effects (model 2). About the remaining models (4–8), we see the same coefficients and statistical significance for all variables in the estimates with standard errors and bootstrap.

On the other hand, analyzing the models with the dependent variable illiteracy 5–10+ (models 9 to 16), we see that the large holding ratio is not statistically significant. And in the estimates with fixed effects, it even changes its sign, negatively impacting illiteracy. Child dependency is the only variable that continues to show a positive and statistically significant effect on illiteracy.

However, it is necessary to remember that in the sample, Latin American subnational levels are being compared with those of the United States; the latter, although they have low land inequality, show a larger size for the average holding.[36] For this reason, the United States has been dropped out from the sample, and the same models have been estimated again, showing the results in Table 3. In addition, in this way, an effort is made to try to avoid the possible distortion that the comparison with the United States may cause. The aim is to homogenize the sample by comparing only the Latin American countries.

In Table 3, we can see the results of the estimations of Eq. (1) via OLS, FE, and RE, with both independent variables: the landgini index and the large holding ratio. Eq. (2) is not estimated again since, as indicated at the bottom of Tables 1 and 2, the sample only includes some Latin American countries (LACs), which are the only ones that offer illiteracy data for the age group 5–10+. The order is the previously mentioned: Column (1) presents the specification with ordinary least squares, and columns (2) and (3) show the specification with fixed and random effects, respectively. Columns 4, 5, and 6 represent the same specifications but with standard errors clustered at the country-state level. Columns 7 and 8 show the fixed and random effects estimations applying bootstrap methods.

Table 3. Effect of Land Inequality on Illiteracy Rate, Only Latin American Countries.

	Dependent Variable: Illiteracy Rate (14+)															
	Model 1 (OLS)	Model 2 (FE)	Model 3 (RE)	Model 4 (OLS)	Model 5 (FE)	Model 6 (RE)	Model 7 (FE)	Model 8 (RE)	Model 9 (OLS)	Model 10 (FE)	Model 11 (RE)	Model 12 (OLS)	Model 13 (FE)	Model 14 (RE)	Model 15 (FE)	Model 16 (RE)
Landgini$_{i,t}$	0.21**	0.17*	0.16**	0.21**	0.17	0.16*	0.17	0.16								
	(0.08)	(0.08)	(0.07)	(0.08)	(0.11)	(0.08)	(0.12)	(0.11)								
Ratiolargeholding$_{i,t}$									0.005	0.33*	−0.003	0.005	0.33**	−0.003	0.33**	−0.003
									(0.070)	(0.18)	(0.08)	(0.073)	(0.13)	(0.06)	(0.16)	(0.06)
UrbanPop$_{i,t}$	−0.56***	0.09	−0.32***	−0.56***	0.09	−0.32***	0.09	−0.32***	−0.53***	0.11	−0.31***	−0.53***	0.11*	−0.31***	0.11	−0.31***
	(0.06)	(0.08)	(0.05)	(0.06)	(0.07)	(0.06)	(0.08)	(0.06)	(0.06)	(0.08)	(0.05)	(0.06)	(0.06)	(0.06)	(0.09)	(0.06)
lChildDependency$_{i,t}$	−20.0***	17.8**	−0.90	−20.0***	17.8**	−0.90	17.8*	−0.90	−19.1***	24.6***	1.21	−19.1***	24.6***	1.21	24.6**	1.21
	(5.62)	(5.98)	(5.05)	(5.39)	(5.76)	(6.61)	(9.57)	(5.61)	(5.84)	(5.90)	(5.10)	(5.90)	(7.12)	(7.00)	(10.6)	(5.33)
Catholics$_{i,t}$																
lDensity$_{i,t}$	1.01	2.29	0.23	1.01	2.29	0.23	2.29	0.23	1.31	1.40	0.14	1.31	1.40	0.14	1.40	0.14
	(0.97)	(3.72)	(1.12)	(1.17)	(3.05)	(1.14)	(4.00)	(1.36)	(1.05)	(3.59)	(1.22)	(1.38)	(3.55)	(1.29)	(5.07)	(1.51)
lDistance$_{i,t}$	5.37***		4.42**	5.37***		4.42**		4.42**	5.25***		4.06**	5.25***		4.06**		4.06**
	(1.24)		(1.56)	(1.53)		(1.74)		(1.76)	(1.26)		(1.59)	(1.57)		(1.79)		(1.73)
Landlocked$_i$	−3.03		−2.77	−3.03		−2.77		−2.77	−3.66*		−2.95	−3.66		−2.95		−2.95
	(2.03)		(2.40)	(2.28)		(2.26)		(2.46)	(2.06)		(2.45)	(2.26)		(2.32)		(2.60)
lArea$_i$	−1.40		−2.72**	−1.40		−2.72		−2.72	−1.31		−2.76*	−1.31		−2.76		−2.76
	(1.22)		(1.39)	(1.65)		(1.79)		(1.74)	(1.25)		(1.42)	(1.72)		(1.86)		(1.76)
Latitude$_i$	0.51***		0.52***	0.51***		0.52***		0.52***	0.53***		0.52***	0.53***		0.52***		0.52***
	(0.05)		(0.06)	(0.04)		(0.05)		(0.05)	(0.05)		(0.06)	(0.05)		(0.05)		(0.05)
Longitude$_i$	0.70***		0.61***	0.70***		0.61***		0.61***	0.74***		0.65***	0.74***		0.65***		0.65***
	(0.12)		(0.14)	(0.13)		(0.13)		(0.14)	(0.13)		(0.14)	(0.13)		(0.13)		(0.14)
Year dummies	YES	YES	YES	YES	YES	YES	YES	YES	YES	YES	YES	YES	YES	YES	YES	YES
Standard errors clustered	NO	NO	NO	YES	YES	YES	NO	NO	NO	NO	NO	YES	YES	YES	NO	NO

(Continued)

Table 3. *(Continued)*

	Model 1 (OLS)	Model 2 (FE)	Model 3 (RE)	Model 4 (OLS)	Model 5 (FE)	Model 6 (RE)	Model 7 (FE)	Model 8 (RE)	Model 9 (OLS)	Model 10 (FE)	Model 11 (RE)	Model 12 (OLS)	Model 13 (FE)	Model 14 (RE)	Model 15 (FE)	Model 16 (RE)
						Dependent Variable: Illiteracy Rate (14+)										
Bootstrap methods	NO	NO	NO	NO	NO	NO	YES	YES	NO	NO	NO	NO	NO	NO	YES	YES
Observations	177	177	177	177	177	177	177	177	177	177	177	177	177	177	177	177
R^2 (within/between)	0.66	0.72/ 0.02	0.51/0.63	0.66	0.72/ 0.02	0.51/0.63	0.72/ 0.02	0.51/0.63	0.65	0.71/ 0.008	0.51/0.62	0.65	0.71/ 0.008	0.51/0.62	0.71/ 0.008	0.51/0.62
Prob $> F$	0.0000	0.0000		0.0000	0.0000				0.0000	0.0000		0.0000	0.0000			
Prob $>$ chi^2			0.0000			0.0000	0.0000	0.0000			0.0000			0.0000	0.0000	0.0000

Source: Author's elaboration.
Note: All regressions include a constant. Robust standard errors in parentheses, ***$p < 0.001$, **$p < 0.05$, *$p < 0.1$.

In Table 3, in the first models (models from 1 to 3), we can see that the results do not change much when the United States has been dropped from the sample. The landgini is shown to be statistically significant and with a positive effect. According to the Hausman test, the most appropriate estimate is the estimate with fixed effects (model 2). Apart from the landgini, in the estimates with fixed effects, the child dependency variable is the only statistically relevant and positively impacts illiteracy. In the rest of the estimates (models 4 to 8), the variables repeat in effect and significance. Finally, when the standard errors clustered at the country-state level and bootstrap methods are applied, the landgini loses significance in the estimates with fixed effects (models 5 and 7). Nevertheless, it maintains the same positive impact throughout all the estimates.

Regarding the variable large holding ratio results, we can see more disparate results once the United States is dropped from the sample.

The large holding ratio loses its negative effect on illiteracy in most estimates. It shows statistical significance in all the estimates with fixed effects, again indicated as the most appropriate by the Hausman test. The child dependency variable again shows a constant positive impact with statistical significance in all estimates with fixed effects. The Catholic variable does not show results, either with the landgini or the large holding ratio, since in all Latin American subnational levels, more than 50% of the population is Catholic. Density and distance show a positive effect, the latter being the only one with statistical significance.

Finally, the landlocked variable negatively affects illiteracy with hardly any statistical significance.

To sum up, when comparing all estimated models with the illiteracy rate (14+) and the illiteracy rate (5–10+) for these three decades, it can be seen that land inequality, measured by both the landgini and the large holding ratio, appears to negatively affect literacy, above all more in the adult population than among the young one. Perhaps these results are due to illiteracy affecting the adult population more negatively than young people (Núñez, 2005b).

6. CONCLUSIONS

Taking into account the limitations that an international analysis may have, this comparative study of the Latin American countries and the United States of America offers light on the inequalities that still existed in the middle of the 20th century. A century after independence, Latin America still had high levels of land inequality. This inequality was not all due to the colonial legacy but was also influenced by the new Latin American ruling elites. Furthermore, the levels of land inequality in Latin America were generally higher than in the United States. On the other hand, it seems that the hypothesis of Galor et al. (2009) still held in the middle of the 20th century. The subnational levels with the highest land inequality had higher illiteracy, especially those with latifundia past and powerful landed elites with political influence to perpetuate this inequality. Moreover, it is an exciting finding that some states in the southern United States share specific characteristics with Latin America, such as high levels of land inequality, a landlord's past, and high levels of illiteracy. In general, however, land inequality and illiteracy levels declined in the mid-20th century, leading to an expansion in mass literacy and a decline in land inequality.

Future investigations should focus on investigating and understanding more deeply the channels through which elites can affect mass education, as well as the relationship between industrial, commercial, and landlord elites and their effect on education, not only in countries underdeveloped but also in developed countries, helping to have a complete vision of how inequality and elites can affect the formation of human capital.

STATISTICAL SOURCES

Agricultural Censuses

Argentina

Dirección Nacional de Estadística y Censos, 1953. Censo Agropecuario, 1952. República Argentina. Ministerio de Hacienda. Buenos Aires.

Dirección Nacional de Estadísticas y Censos, 1964. Censo Nacional Agropecuario, 1960. República Argentina. Poder Ejecutivo Nacional. Secretaría de Estado de Hacienda. Buenos Aires.

Instituto Nacional de Estadística y Censos, 1969. Censo Nacional Agropecuario, 1969. Datos del Relevamiento Agrícola. República Argentina. Ministerio de Economía. Secretaría de Estado de Programación y Coordinación Económica, Buenos Aires.

Brazil

Conselho Nacional de Estatística Serviço Nacional de Recenseamento, 1956. VI Recenseamento Geral Do Brasil, Censo Agrícola,1950. I.B.G.E, Rio de Janeiro.

Conselho Nacional de Estatística Serviço Nacional de Recenseamento, 1966–1967. VII Recenseamento Geral Do Brasil, Censo Agrícola, 1960. I.B.G.E, Rio de Janeiro.

Fundação Instituto Brasileiro de Geografia e Estatística, 1975. VIII Recenseamento Geral Do Brasil, Censo Agrícola, 1970. Secretaría de Planejamento Da Presidência Da República, Rio de Janeiro.

Chile

Dirección de Estadística y Censos, 1955. III Censo Nacional Agrícola Ganadero, 1955, República de Chile. Ministerio de Economía Santiago de Chile.

Dirección de Estadística y Censos. Santiago,1966–1970. IV Censo Nacional Agrícola Ganadero, 1964–1965. República de Chile.

Instituto Nacional de Estadísticas. Santiago, 1981. V Censo Nacional Agrícola Ganadero, 1975–1976. República de Chile. Ministerio de Economía, Fomento y Reconstrucción.

Colombia
Directorio Nacional de Explotaciones Agropecuarias, 1964. Censo Agropecuario, 1960. República de Colombia. Departamento Administrativo Nacional de Estadística. Bogotá.
Departamento Administrativo Nacional de Estadística, 1974. Censo Nacional Agropecuario, 1970–1971. República de Colombia. Bogotá.

Costa Rica
Dirección General de Estadística y Censos, 1953. Censo Agropecuario, 1950. Ministerio de Economía y Hacienda., San José.
Dirección General de Estadística y Censos, 1965. Censo Agropecuario, 1963. Ministerio de Economía y Hacienda, San José.
Dirección General de Estadística y Censos, 1974. Censo Agropecuario, 1973. Ministerio de Economía, Industria y Comercio, San José.

Ecuador
Ministerio de Economía. Banco Nacional de Fomento, 1956. Primer Censo Agropecuario Nacional, 1954. República del Ecuador, Banco Central del Ecuador, Quito.
Food and Agriculture Organization of the United Nations (FAO):
Food Agriculture Organization, 1955; Report 1950 World Census of Agriculture, Rome.
Food Agriculture Organization, 1971; Report 1960 World Census of Agriculture, Rome.
Food Agriculture Organization, 1981; Report 1970 World Census of Agriculture, Rome.

Honduras
Dirección General de Censos y Estadísticas, 1954. I Censo Agropecuario, 1952. República de Honduras, Ministerio de Gobernación, El Salvador.
Dirección General de Estadísticas y Censos, 1967–1968. II Censo Agropecuario, 1965–1966. República de Honduras, Secretaría de Economía y Hacienda, El Salvador.

México
Dirección General de Estadística, 1956. III Censo Agrícola Ganadero y Ejidal, 1950. Estados Unidos Mexicanos, Secretaría de Economía, México D.F.
Dirección General de Estadística, 1965. IV Censos Agrícola Ganadero y Ejidal, 1960. Estados Unidos Mexicanos, Secretaría de Industria y Comercio, México D.F.
Dirección General de Estadística, 1975. V Censos Agrícola Ganadero y Ejidal, 1970. Estados Unidos Mexicanos, Secretaría de Industria y Comercio, México D.F.

Nicaragua
Dirección General de Estadística y Censos, 1966. Censo Nacional Agropecuario, 1963. Ministerio de Economía, Managua.

Panamá

Dirección de Estadística y Censo, 1954. I Censo Agropecuario, 1950. República de Panamá, Contraloría General de la República, Panamá.
Dirección de Estadística y Censo, 1961. II Censo Agropecuario, 1960. República de Panamá, Contraloría General de la República, Panamá.
Dirección de Estadística y Censo, 1971. Censo Agropecuario, 1970. República de Panamá, Contraloría General de la República, Panamá.

United States

US Bureau of the Census, 1960. US Census of Agriculture, 1959. US Government Printing Office, Washington, D.C.
US Bureau of the Census, 1967. Census of Agriculture, 1964. US Government Printing Office, Washington, D.C.
US Bureau of the Census, 1973. Census of Agriculture, 1969. US Government Printing Office, Washington, D.C.
US Bureau of the Census, 1978. Census of Agriculture, 1974. US Government Printing Office, Washington, D.C.

Venezuela

Dirección General de Estadística y Censos Nacionales, 1959. II Censo Nacional Agropecuario, 1950. República de Venezuela, Ministerio de Fomento, Caracas.
Dirección General de Estadística y Censos Nacionales, 1967. III Censo Agropecuario, 1961. República de Venezuela, Ministerio de Fomento, Caracas.
Dirección General de Estadística y Censos Nacionales, 1976. IV Censo Agropecuario, 1971. República de Venezuela, Ministerio de Fomento, Caracas.

Population Censuses

Argentina

Dirección Nacional de Servicios Técnicos del Estado y Dirección General de Servicio Estadístico Nacional, 1951. IV Censo General de la Nación, 1947. Resultados Generales del Censo de Población, Buenos Aires.
Consejo Nacional de Educación, 1946. Censo Escolar de la Nación, 2o edición, Buenos Aires.
Dirección Nacional de Estadística y Censos, 1961.Censo Nacional de Población, 1960, Total País y Tomos Provinciales II- IX, Buenos Aires.

Brazil

Conselho Nacional de Estatística. Serviço Nacional de Recenseamento, 1956. Censo Demográfico Série Nacional, Volume I. Rio de Janeiro.
Departamento de Estatística de População, 1967. VII Recenseamento Geral Do Brasil, 1960. Série Nacional, Volume I Censo Demográfico, Fundação Instituto Brasileiro de Geografia e Estatística. Rio de Janeiro.
Ministério do Planejamento e Coordenação Geral, 1971. VIII Recenseamento Geral Do Brasil, 1970. Série Nacional, Volume I Censo Demográfico. Rio de Janeiro.

Conselho Nacional de Estatística, 1951. Anuário Estatístico do Brasil, 1950. Instituto Brasileiro de Geografia e Estatística (IBGE). Rio de Janeiro.
Conselho Nacional de Estatística, 1960. Anuário Estatístico do Brasil, 1960. Instituto Brasileiro de Geografia e Estatística (IBGE). Rio de Janeiro.
Ministério Do Planejamento e Coordenação Geral, 1971. Anuário Estatístico do Brasil, 1971. Instituto Brasileiro de Geografia e Estatística (IBGE). Rio de Janeiro.

Chile
Servicio Nacional de Estadística y Censos, 1952. XII Censo General De Población y I de Vivienda, Tomo I Resumen País. Santiago.
Dirección de Estadística y Censos, 1960. XIII Censo de Población y II de Vivienda, Resumen País. Santiago.
Instituto Nacional de Estadísticas, 1970. XIV Censo de Población y III de Vivienda, Resumen País. Santiago.

Colombia
Departamento Administrativo Nacional de Estadística, 1951. Censo de Población de Colombia, 1951, Resumen. Bogotá D. E.
Departamento Administrativo Nacional de Estadística, 1967. XIII Censo Nacional de Población, Resumen General. Bogotá, D.E.
Departamento Administrativo Nacional de Estadística, 1973. La Población en Colombia 1973, XIV Censo Nacional de Población y III de Vivienda, Muestra de Avance. Bogotá D.E.

Costa Rica
Ministerio de Economía y Hacienda y Dirección General de Estadística y Censos, 1953. Censo de Población de Costa Rica, 1950, San José.
Dirección General de Estadística y Censos, 1966. Censo de Población de Costa Rica, 1963. San José.
Dirección General de Estadística y Censos, 1974. Censo de Población de Costa Rica, 1973. Tomo I, San José.

Ecuador
Dirección Nacional de Estadística y Censos, 1952. Información Censal: Resumen de los resultados definitivos del Censo Nacional de Población, 1950. Quito.
División de Estadística y Censos, 1964. II Censo de Población y Primer Censo de Vivienda, 1962. Tomo I, Junta Nacional de Planificación y Coordinación Económica, Quito.

Honduras
Dirección General de Censos y Estadísticas, 1952. Resumen General del Censo de Población, 1950. Tegucigalpa.
Dirección General de Estadística y Censos, 1964. Censo de Población de Honduras, 1961. Secretaria de Economía y Hacienda, Tegucigalpa, D.C.

México
Secretaría de Economía Y Sección General de Estadística, 1952. VII Censo General de Población, 1950. Resumen General, México, D.F.

Secretaría de Economía, Sección General de Estadística, 1962. VIII Censo General de Población, 1960. Resumen General, México, D. F.

Secretaría de Industria y Comercio, Dirección General de Estadística, 1972. IX Censo General de Población, 1970. Resumen General, México, D. F.

Nicaragua
Ministerio de Economía Y Dirección General de Estadística y Censos, 1964–1965. Censos Nacionales 1963, Volumen I y II: Población Managua.

Panamá
Dirección de Estadística y Censo 1954. V Censo de Población de Panamá, 1950. Volumen II: Características Educativas, Panamá.

Dirección de Estadística y Censo, 1954. V Censo de Población de Panamá, 1950. Volumen I: Características Generales, Panamá.

Dirección de Estadística y Censo, 1964. VI Censo de Población de Panamá y II de Vivienda, 1960. Volumen VI: Características Educativas, Panamá.

Dirección de Estadística y Censo, 1971–1972. VII Censo de Población de Panamá, 1970. Volumen III: Compendio General de Población. Panamá.

United States
US Bureau of the Census, 1954. Statistical Abstract of the United States, 1954. 75th edition Washington D.C.

US Bureau of the Census, 1967. Statistical Abstract of the United States, 1967. 88th Edition Washington, D.C.

Venezuela
Dirección General de Estadística y Censos Nacionales, 1966. XI Censo General de Población, 1961. Resumen General de la República, parte A. Ministerio de Fomento, Caracas.

Dirección General de Estadística y Censos Nacionales, 1967. XI Censo General de Población, 1961. Resumen General de la República, parte B y C. Ministerio de Fomento, Caracas.

Dirección General de Estadística y Censos Nacionales, 1974. X Censo de Población y Vivienda, 1974. Resumen General. Ministerio de Fomento, Caracas.

ACKNOWLEDGMENTS

This paper was presented at seminars and conferences in Madrid, Santiago de Compostela, and the Young Scholar Initiative. I would like to thank the feedback obtained here. I also gratefully acknowledge the comments received from the editors, Carl T. Kitchens and Shawn Kantor, and the referees.

NOTES

1. Some authors defend the hypothesis that human capital formation is the actual reason behind the different growth patterns between the United States and Latin America. In turn, land inequality would influence human capital formation (Galor et al., 2009, pp. 161–162).

2. This paper uses the largest administrative divisions of each American country below the national level as a unit of analysis. Each country uses a different term for its largest administration divisions: states in Mexico and the United States, departments in Colombia, provinces in Argentina, and so on. I use the term "sub-national levels" to refer to all these administrations (Angeles & Elizalde, 2017).

3. Núñez (2005a) exposes how farmers with small-medium holdings and properties appreciate education more than landless workers, who do not see benefits in investing in education due to a lack of prospects and self-profit.

4. Specifically, areas in the north of England close to Scottish areas with solid educational systems demanded higher levels of education, regardless of local inequality.

5. Schools of the First Letters (Escuelas de las Primeras Letras), networks of educational centers in charge of religious orders where children (indigenous included) were evangelized and learned the Catholic doctrine. Establishing schools was a slow process; first, the Viceroy and then the King had to approve the foundation of new schools. Sometimes, this system entailed a high bureaucratic and economic cost.

6. It is called Teaching State (Estado Docente) to the role that new governments exercise in controlling the education system, planning, and implementing educational policies determined by the government and its institutions. The new role of the states was developed in Latin America throughout the 19th and early 20th centuries (Arroyo-Abad, 2016).

7. Some studies affirm a positive relationship between education, labor mobilization, voting participation, and political activity. See Brady et al. (1995), Krishna (2002), Kuenzi (2006), or Wegenast (2009).

8. Nugent and Robinson (2010), analyzing whether factor endowments influence the subsequent growth of Latin American coffee economies, make an international comparison of different Latin American countries, including Brazil, that had other colonial institutions and a different homeland.

9. An example is the federal government's initiative in 1870 to implement a centralized education system with compulsory attendance for children; local landowners showed strong resistance and political opposition through the Conservative party (Wegenast, 2009).

10. Frankema (2008) indicates that countries like Argentina and Uruguay had large land extensions and little labor. For this reason, these countries specialized in livestock products and grain.

11. Disaggregated data are available upon request.

12. Family Farm Index (Vanhanen, 1997), Agricultural Population per Holding (Erickson & Vollrath, 2004), Fraction of Farm Labourers over the total Agricultural Population (Beltrán Tapia & Martínez-Galarraga, 2018), Labor-Dependent Agriculture (Albertus, 2017), Percentage of agricultural laborers as a proportion of the active agricultural population (Beltrán Tapia et al., 2021).

13. The calculation of these formula can be made using Stata programs ineqdec and ineqdec0.

14. This index has been widely used by many authors throughout the literature such as Erickson and Vollrath (2004), Acemoglu et al. (2007), Nunn (2008), Ziblatt (2008), Frankema (2008), Ramcharan (2010), Vollrath (2013), Funari (2017), and Albertus et al. (2018). The few studies that do not include this index are due to lack of data. For example, in some cases, there is not information about the size of holdings to calculate landgini index (Beltrán Tapia & Martínez-Galarraga, 2018, p. 85); in other cases, data about area of holdings are missing (Cinnirella & Hornung, 2016, p. 140).

15. Recently, Ricci and Zanibelli (2021) have also used a similar measure to analyze land distribution in Italy in 1930s, considering large holdings larger than 100 ha.

16. These authors even interpret that the percentage of the largest holdings could also capture a dimension of political inequality since political power was mainly proportional to the size of the possessed land (Cinnirella and Hornung, 2016, p. 140).

17. Organizations such as the United Nations, the International Commission for the Improvement of International Statistics (COINS), the Inter-American Institute of Statistics (IASI), or the recommendations of the Alliance for Progress program for Latin American countries encouraged and helped most of the countries of the region to coordinate efforts and follow a standard methodology at the moment of elaborating their censuses (Núñez, 2005b).

18. Note that some countries offer illiteracy rates already calculated and explaining their preparation for some years, for example, countries as the United States or Ecuador. The vast majority provides information on illiterate population, literate population and total population, and separately rates have to be calculated.

19. See Núñez (2005b), Wegenast (2010), Arroyo-Abad (2016), and databases of the World Bank and the UNESCO as well.

20. For clarity, American Central includes Costa Rica, Panama, Honduras and Nicaragua; South America contains Argentina, Chile, Colombia, Venezuela and Brazil.

21. It is the case of Brazilian states as Pernambuco or Alagoas (see Appendix A, Table A4, for access to the disaggregated database and an explanation about it).

22. Wegenast (2010, pp. 116–121) points out that the Brazilian states with an equal land distribution exhibited higher primary school matriculations at the end of the 19th century.

23. Colombian departments as Caldas or Quindio (Nugent & Robinson, 2010).

24. Similar decreases in landgini and illiteracy rates occurred in Baja California Sur, Coahuila, Chihuahua, and Durango from 1950 to 1970 (see Appendix A, Table A4, for access to the disaggregated database and an explanation about it).

25. Galor et al. (2009) argue that there is a causal adverse effect between land concentration and education spending across American states during the high-school movement (1880–1940).

26. Wright (1986) mentions that the governments of the southern states were strongly influenced by landowners, who lobbied to avoid mass education for fear that better-educated workers would move north in search of better job opportunities. And Goldin (1998) notes that from 1920 to 1930, the South lagged behind the rest of the nation in educational attainment and enrollment rates.

27. See Reis (2005), Clark and Gray (2014), and Andersson and Berger (2016).

28. See Thiesenhusen (1995), Frankema (2008), and Albertus (2015).

29. The total sample when only illiteracy rates and land inequality are analyzed is 372 observations. However, the sample size changes when the other variables (urban population, child dependency, etc.) are included in the models since for these variables, in some cases, data are missing for some subnational levels.

30. Becker and Woessmann (2010), analyzing the effect of Protestantism on human capital in nineteenth-century Prussia, argue that Protestant areas had better human capital formation than Catholic ones. Because Luther's drive to read the Bible without intermediaries created human capital that then facilitated industrial development. On the other hand, Beltrán Tapia and Martínez-Galarraga (2018) show that in some countries like Spain, the Catholic Church did not actively encourage education, although in places with shortage of teachers, local priests offered certain educational services. Nevertheless, they also highlight that in Catholic educational systems, women suffered discrimination in access to education, which fostered higher levels of illiteracy in general.

31. Beltrán Tapia and Martínez-Galarraga (2018) argue that higher population density would allow economies of scale to be exploited in the supply of schooling.

32. See Arroyo-Abad (2016).

33. An example of these omitted variables would be the number of teachers at the sub-national level, which can affect school supply and demand (Beltrán Tapia & Martinez-Galarraga, 2018, pp. 81–82). The training of these teachers, the parent's education level, the average family income, and the school infrastructure all affect the supply and demand

of education and literacy. Unfortunately, they cannot be included in this analysis due to a lack of data.

34. Pennock (2014), carrying out an empirical analysis similar to this paper, decides to consider the estimation of random effects the most appropriate due to with fixed effects the variables that do not change over time are not shown, which the author considers a significant loss of relevant information for his research. In this paper, it has been decided to show the result of both estimations and to use the Hausman test to find out which estimate is the most appropriate.

35. In Chile, after the coup d'état, there was an interruption in the preparation of some statistics that, in some cases, lasted until the early 1990s. In Nicaragua, the second agricultural census was carried out in 1971, but the databases, formularies, and all the census information were lost because of an earthquake. In Colombia, the first agricultural census was carried out in the 1960s, missing data for the 1950s.

36. An example is the state of Minnesota, which for the 1960s shows a very low landgini of 41.5%, an illiteracy rate of only 1%, and a high large holding ratio of 45.3%, indicating a higher percentage of medium-large sized farms with an equal land distribution (Appendix B, see Fig. B2).

37. Disaggregated data are available upon request. To request the database directly, write to tundidorbarbara@gmail.com, or go to the link indicated in the text.

38. The Mexican agrarian reform is one of the world's longest and most ambitious reforms and the first to be developed on the American continent. It started with the 1910 Revolution and continued until 1992, at least 103 million hectares were reallocated (De Janvry et al., 2014).

39. Partly because an agrarian reform was also beginning to be applied in Colombia in the 1960s and 1970s, see Balcázar et al. (2001).

40. During the mandate of President Alessandri (1958–1964), the Chilean agrarian reform was known as the "plot reform" due to its little development and scope (see Thiesenhusen, 1995).

41. Goldin (1998) shows that between 1920 and 1935, the advancement of secondary education was remarkably rapid in the nonsouthern states.

REFERENCES

Acemoglu, D., Bautista, M. A., Querubin, P., & Robinson, J. A. (2007). *Economic and political inequality in development: The case of Cundinamarca, Colombia.* National Bureau of Economic Research Working Paper No.13208. https://www.nber.org/papers/w13208. Accessed on March 20, 2021.

Acemoglu, D., & Robinson, J. A. (2006). *Economic origins of dictatorship and democracy.* Cambridge University Press.

Albertus, M. (2015). *Autocracy and redistribution: The politics of land reform.* Cambridge University Press.

Albertus, M. (2017). Landowners and democracy. The social origins of democracy reconsidered. *World Politics Review, 69*(2), 233–276.

Albertus, M., Brambor, T., & Ceneviva, R. (2018). Landholding inequality and rural unrest: Theory and evidence from Brazil. *Journal of Conflict Resolution, 62*(3), 557–596.

Albertus, M., Diaz-Calleros, A., Magaloni, B., & Weingast, B. R. (2016). Authoritarian survival and poverty traps: Land reform in Mexico. *World Development, 77*, 154–170.

Alter, G., & Clark, G. (2010). The demographic transition and human capital. In S. Broadberry & K. H. O'Rourke (Eds.), *The cambridge economic history of modern Europe, Vol. 1: 1700–1870* (pp. 43–69). Cambridge University Press.

Andersson, J., & Berger, T. (2016). *Elites and the expansion of education in 19th-century Sweden. Lund papers in economic history: Education and the labour market.* Department of Economic History, Lund University Working Paper No. 149. https://lup.lub.lu.se/search/ws/files/13625993/LUP149.pdf. Accessed on June 5, 2021.

Andersson, J., & Berger, T. (2019). Elites and the Expansion of Education in 19th-century Sweden. *The Economic History Review, 72*(3), 897–924.

Angeles, L., & Elizalde, A. (2017). Pre-colonial institutions and socioeconomic development: The case of Latin America. *Journal of Development Economics, 124*, 22–40.

Arroyo-Abad, L. (2016). The limits of the Estado Docente: Education and political participation in Peru 1876–1940. *Revista de Historia Económica [Journal of Iberian and Latin American Economic History], 34*(1), 81–109.

Balcázar, A., López, N., Orozco, M., L., & Vega, M. (2001). *Colombia: Alcances y Lecciones de su Experiencia en Reforma Agraria.* Red de Desarrollo Agropecuario, CEPAL, Working Paper No.109. Santiago de Chile. https://repositorio.cepal.org. Accessed on May 24, 2021.

Banerjee, A., & Iyer, L. (2005). History, institutions, and economic performance: The legacy of colonial land tenure systems in India. *The American Economic Review, 95*(4), 1190–1213.

Becker, S. O., & Woessmann, L. (2010). The effect of Protestantism on education before industrialization: Evidence from 1816 Prussia. *Economics Letters, 107*(2), 224–228.

Beltrán Tapia, F. J., Diez Minguela, A., Martínez-Galarraga, J., & Tirado-Fabregat, D. A. (2021). *The roots of land inequality in Spain.* Instituto Figuerola de Historia y Ciencias Sociales, Universidad Carlos III de Madrid Working Paper No 2021-01. https://e-archivo.uc3m.es/bitstream/handle/. Accessed on July 10, 2021.

Beltrán Tapia, F. J., & Martínez-Galarraga, J. (2018). Inequality and education in pre-industrial economies: Evidence from Spain. *Explorations in Economic History, 69,* 81–101.

Bowles, S. (1978). Capitalist development and educational structure. *World Development, 6*(6), 783–796.

Brady, H. E., Verba, S., & Schlozman, K. L. (1995). Beyond SES: A resource model of political participation. *American Political Science Review, 89*(2), 271–294.

Cinnirella, F., & Hornung, E. (2016). Landownership concentration and the expansion of education. *Journal of Development Economics, 121,* 135–152.

Clark, G., & Gray, R. (2014). Geography is not destiny: Geography, institutions and literacy in England, 1837–63. *Oxford Economic Papers, 66*(4), 1042–1069.

Colomer, J. M. (2004). Taming the tiger: Voting rights and political instability in Latin America. *Latin American Politics and Society, 46*(2), 29–58.

De Janvry, A., Gonzalez-Navarro, M., & Sadoulet, E. (2014). Are land reforms granting complete property rights politically risky? Electoral outcomes of Mexico's certification program. *Journal of Development Economics, 110,* 216–225.

Deininger, K., & Olinto, P. (1999). *Asset distribution, inequality, and growth.* The World Bank Development Research Group, Policy Research Working Paper No. 2375. https://openknowledge.worldbank.org/bitstream. Accessed on March 8, 2021.

Droller, F., & Fiszbein, M. (2021). Staple products, linkages and development: Evidence from Argentina, *The Journal of Economic History, 81*(3), 723–762.

Elis, R. (2011). *Redistribution under oligarchy: Trade, regional inequality and the origins of public schooling in Argentina, 1862–1912.* Unpublished Ph.D. Dissertation. Department of Political Science Stanford University.

Erickson, L., & Vollrath, D. (2004). *Dimensions of land inequality and economic development.* International Monetary Fund Working Paper No 04/158. https://www.elibrary.imf.org/view/journals. Accessed on February 10, 2021.

Frankema, E. (2008). *The historical evolution of inequality in Latin America. A comparative analysis, 1870–2000.* PhD Dissertation. University of Groningen.

Funari, P. P. P. (2017). Inequality, institutions, and long-term development: A perspective from Brazilian regions. In L. Bértola & J. Williamson (Eds.), *Has Latin American inequality changed direction? Looking over the long run* (pp. 113–143). Springer Open.

Galor, O., Moav, O., & Vollrath, D. (2004). *Land inequality and the origin of divergence and overtaking in the growth process: Theory and evidence.* Brown Economics Working Paper No. 2003-04. https://www.econstor.eu/bitstream/. Accessed on April 21, 2021.

Galor, O., Moav, O., & Vollrath, D. (2009). Inequality in landownership, the emergence of human-capital promoting institutions, and the great divergence. *The Review of Economic Studies, 76*(1), 143–179.

Goldin, C. (1998). America's graduation from high school: The evolution and spread of secondary schooling in the twentieth century. *The Journal of Economic History, 58*(2), 345–374.

Goñi, M. (2016). *Landed elites and education provision in England and Wales. Evidence from school boards, 1870–99.* University of Vienna Manuscript. https://www.amse-aixmarseille.fr/sites/. Accessed on April 10, 2021.

Goñi, M. (2022). Landed elites and education provision in England and Wales. Evidence from school boards, 1871–99. *Journal of Economic Growth,* 1–47.

Hagopian, F. (1996). *Traditional politics and regime change in Brazil.* Cambridge University Press.

Hartlyn, J., & Valenzuela, A. (1997). La democracia en América Latina desde 1930. In L. Bethell (Ed.), *Historia de América Latina, Política, y Sociedad desde 1930* (pp. 11–66). Cambridge University Press.

Krishna, A. (2002). Enhancing political participation in democracies: What is the role of social capital? *Comparative Political Studies*, *35*(4), 437–460.

Kuenzi, M. T. (2006). Nonformal education, political participation, and democracy: Findings from Senegal. *Political Behavior*, *28*(1), 1–31.

Lindert, P. H. (2004a). *Growing public: Social spending and economic growth since the eighteenth-century Vol. I: The story*. Cambridge University Press.

Lindert, P. H. (2004b). *Growing public: Social spending and economic growth since the eighteenth-century Vol. II: Further evidence*. Cambridge University Press.

Mariella, V. (2022). Landownership concentration and human capital accumulation in post-unification Italy. *Journal of Population Economics*, 1–70.

Nugent, J. B., & Robinson, J. A. (2010). Are factor endowments fate? *Revista de Historia Económica [Journal of Iberian and Latin American Economic History]*, *28*(1), 45–82.

Núñez, C. E. (2005a). A modern human capital stock. Spain in the 19th and 20th Centuries. In M. Jerneck, M. Mörner, G. Tortella, & S. Akerman (Eds.), *Different paths to modernity. A Nordic and Spanish perspective* (pp. 122–142). Nordic Academic Press.

Núñez, J. (2005b). Signed with an X: Methodology and data sources for analyzing the evolution of literacy in Latin America and the Caribbean 1900–1950. *Latin American Research Review*, *40*(2), 117–135.

Nunn, N. (2008). Slavery, inequality and economic development in the Americas: An examination of Engerman-Sokoloff hypothesis. In E. Helpman (Ed.), *Institutions and economic performance* (pp. 148–180). Harvard University Press.

Pennock, A. (2014). The political economy of domestic labor mobility: Specific factors, landowners, and education. *Economics & Politics*, *26*(1), 38–55.

Rajan, R. G., & Ramcharan, R. (2009). *Land and credit: A study of the political economy of banking in the United States in the early 20th century*. National Bureau of Economic Research Working Paper No 15083. https://www.nber.org/system/files/working_papers/w15083. Accessed on August 10, 2021.

Ramcharan, R. (2010). Inequality and redistribution: Evidence from US counties and states, 1890–1930. *The Review of Economics and Statistics*, *92*(4), 729–744.

Reis, J. (2005). Economic growth, human capital formation and consumption in Western Europe before 1800. In R. C. Allen, T. Bengtsson, & M. Dribe (Eds.), *Living standards in the past: New perspectives on well-being in Asia and Europe* (pp. 195–225). Oxford University Press.

Ricci, V., & Zanibelli, G. (2021). For a Multidimensional Measure of land inequality in 1930s Italy. A historical- statistical analysis. *Documentos de trabajo de la Asociación Española de Historia Económica*, *21*, 7.

Summerhill, W. (2010). *Colonial institutions, slavery, inequality, and development: Evidence from Sao Paulo, Brazil*. MPRA Working Paper, No.22162. https://mpra.ub.uni-muenchen.de/22162. Accessed on July 5, 2021.

Taylor, C. L., & Hudson, M. C. (1972). *World handbook of political and social indicators* (2nd ed.). Yale University Press.

Thiesenhusen, W. C. (1995). *Broken promises. Agrarian reform and the Latin American Campesino*. Westview Press.

Tundidor, B. (2024). Can land inequality and land reforms affect agricultural credit access? Evidence from Mexico state-level data, 1940–1960. *Economic History Research/Investigaciones de Historia Económica*, *20*(2), 18–32.

Vanhanen, T. (1997). *Prospects of democracy: A study of 172 countries*. Routledge.

Vollrath, D. (2013). Inequality and school funding in the rural United States, 1890. *Explorations in Economic History*, *50*(2), 267–284.

Wegenast, T. (2009). The legacy of landlords: Educational distribution and development in a comparative perspective. *Zeitschrift für Vergleichende Politikwissenschaft*, *3*(1), 81–107.

Wegenast, T. (2010). Cana, Café, Cacau: Agrarian structure and educational inequalities in Brazil. *Revista de Historia Económica [Journal of Iberian and Latin American History]*, *28*(1), 103–137.

Wright, G. (1986). *Old South new south: Revolutions in the southern economy since the civil war*. Basic Books.

Yarrington, D. (1997). *A coffee frontier: Land, society, and politics in Duaca, Venezuela, 1830–1936*. University of Pittsburgh Press.

Ziblatt, D. (2008). Does landholding inequality block democratization? A test of the "bread and democracy" thesis and the case of Prussia. *World Politics*, *60*(4), 610–641.

Can Land Inequality Negatively Affect Human Capital?

APPENDICES

APPENDIX A. TABLES

Table A1. Evolving of Voting Rights in Latin America.

Country	Year	Rights to Vote
Argentina	1826	Only citizens men who were married, or men citizen who were 20 years or older.
	1912	For the first time, it was not required to be an owner or know how to read and write to vote.
	1947	Women are granted the right to vote.
Brazil	1824–1875	Only "free" men (no slaves) who were ≥25 or 21 married. Must have a basic income level.
	1932	Women are granted the right to vote.
	1955	Australian Ballot was introduced*.
	1985	For the first time, it was not required to be an owner or know how to read and write to vote.
Chile	1833–1871	Only men who were ≥25 or 21 who were married. Must had basic income level and property.
	1949	Women are granted the right to vote.
	1958	Australian Ballot was introduced.
	1970	For the first time, it was not required to be an owner or know how to read and write to vote.
Mexico	1824–1833	Only men who are married or age ≥21.
Colombia	1833–1853	Only men who were ≥21 or were married men, must had basic income level and property.
	1936	For the first time, it was not required to be an owner or know how to read and write to vote.
	1954	Women are granted the right to vote.
	1988	Australian Ballot was introduced.
Costa Rica	1949	For the first time, it was not required to be an owner or know how to read and write to vote. Women are granted the right to vote.
Peru	1955	Women are granted the right to vote.
	1979	For the first time, it was not required to be an owner or know how to read and write to vote.
Uruguay	1918	For the first time, it was not required to be an owner or know how to read and write to vote.
	1932	Women are granted the right to vote.
Venezuela	1945	Women are granted the right to vote.
	1947	For the first time, it was not required to be an owner or know how to read and write to vote.

Source: Author's elaboration; Wegenast (2009), Colomer (2004), and Hartlyn and Valenzuela (1997).

Note: *Australian ballot is a voting system in which the voter's identity is not revealed; states usually provide ballots to guarantee the electoral processes.

Table A2. Management of Primary Education in Latin America, 1950s.

Country	Policy and Administration	Finance
Argentina	Each province draws up its constitution on the Republican representative model and in conformity with the principles, and guarantees of the National Constitution, to provide for the administration of justice, local government, and primary education. Within these limits, the Central Government guarantees the enjoyment and maintenance by the provinces of their institution.	Public primary education expenditure is covered by the National Budget, which lays down the proportion of general revenue to be allocated for this purpose.
Brazil	The United States of Brazil is a federal republic consisting of 20 states, a federal district with a certain degree of political and administrative autonomy, and five territories comprising regions the Federal Government administers. Education is provided under an arrangement to distribute powers between the central government and the states. The "national system" is outlined by the Constitution and governed in detail by federal statute; the "state system" is governed by each state's laws relating to primary education and the training of primary school teachers.	Because of the administrative decentralization of primary education, the country's public educational system's cost is shared by the Federal Government and the state and municipal governments in proportion to the revenue received from taxation.
Chile	Primary education is compulsory. There is a Superintendency of Public Education responsible for the inspection of national education, and its administration, under the authority of the Government. The municipalities shall hold meetings with most of their members at the time in office; they shall have such administrative attributes and dispose of such revenues as the law may determine. They shall be responsible, in particular, for (1) promoting education, agriculture, industry, and commerce; (2) administering primary schools and other educational services supported by municipal funds.	The Ministry of Education administers the funds for the maintenance and extension of State primary education. These funds are derived from the general exchequer and are disbursed in accordance with the budget approved each year by Parliament. Although municipalities were called upon by authorities to encourage primary schooling, the main burden of education is still borne by the State, which, in 1954, as in previous years, financed practically all public educational establishments.
Colombia	Freedom of education is guaranteed. The State shall exercise, however, overall supervision of institutions of learning, both public and private. Primary Education shall be free in the State schools and compulsory up to the grade determined by law.	Primary education, financed out of public funds, is the responsibility and is placed under the immediate direction and protection of the governments of the provinces (departamentos) by the ordinances of their respective assemblies; the Central government inspects it.
Costa Rica	Primary schooling is compulsory, and, with preschool and secondary education free of charge, the cost is borne by the State. State education shall be under the general direction of a higher council, constituted by	The funds for the upkeep and extension of the education system come from the national budget. At the primary school level, the State shoulders the cost not only of teachers' salaries but also of school building

(Continued)

Table A2. *(Continued)*

Country	Policy and Administration	Finance
	law, under the chairmanship of the Minister of Education.	operations, which are the responsibility of the Ministry of Public Works.
Ecuador	Primary education in official establishments shall be free; primary education in official or private establishments shall be compulsory. The State shall respect the right of parents or those representing them to give their children the kind of education they deem most appropriate. Municipalities may subsidize free private education. Such subventions shall not exceed 20% of the amount approved for education.	The State meets all expenditures involved in establishing and maintaining public schools. Municipalities are required to devote 15% of their revenue to education. Many of them allocate a larger percentage. The provincial councils assist in the construction of school buildings. Religious organizations generally finance free private schools.
Honduras	Freedom of education is guaranteed. Instruction supported by public funds shall be secular and primary education shall, in addition, be free and compulsory; municipal funds and State grants cover its cost.	The cost of all public school buildings is borne entirely by the State. Education supported by public funds is undenominational and free of charge. Primary education costs are covered by district councils, municipalities, and State grants.
Mexico	The United States of Mexico forms a representative, democratic, and federal Republic composed of States which are free and sovereign in matters of internal administration and are united in a federation along the lines set forth by the Constitution. Primary education is free and compulsory for all inhabitants of the Republic.	The Constitution provides that the Union Congress, with the object of unifying and coordinating education throughout the Republic, shall promulgate the necessary laws designed to apportion educational responsibilities between the Federation, the States, and the Municipalities and to fix the expenditure required for this public service.[a]
Nicaragua	Public education is a prior obligation of the State. The system of primary, intermediate, and professional education is under the technical supervision of the State. There are national, municipal, and private schools. All must conform to the official program of studies.	The national budget supplies the funds required for the maintenance and development of education.
Panama	Primary education is free and compulsory, and it is a function of the State which has a fundamental duty to form a sense of nationality and impart an essentially democratic pattern to society.	The State's educational program is the responsibility of the Ministry of Education and is chargeable to that Ministry's budget. Appropriations in the national budget support public primary education, and its resources include 20% of municipal revenues.

Source: Author's elaboration; World of Survey Education II, Primary Education. UNESCO 1958. Manual of Educational Statistics, first edition. UNESCO, 1961.

[a]In addition to provisions made by the public authorities, owners of agricultural estates, industries, mines, or any other kind of business situated more than two miles away from the nearest town are bound to establish and support primary schools for the benefit of the surrounding community, provided the number of children of primary school age exceeds 20. The education given in these schools is subject to the provisions of the Education Law. Consequently, the same syllabuses and teaching methods are applied in them as in State primary schools, and they come under the technical and administrative direction of the Secretariat of Public Education.

Table A3. Minimum and Maximum Holding Size, 1950–1970.

Countries	Minimum Holding Size	Maximum Holding Size
1. Argentina	1–5 ha	up to 10,000 ha and more
2. Brazil	less than 1 ha	up to 100,000 ha and more
3. Chile	less than 1 ha	up to 5,000 ha and more
4. Colombia	less than 1 ha	up to 2,500 and more
5. Costa Rica	less than 1 ha	up to 2,500 and more
6. Ecuador	less than 1 ha	up to 2,500 and more
7. Honduras	less than 1 ha	up to 2,500 and more
8. Mexico	1–5 ha	up to 10,000 and more
9. Nicaragua	less than 1 ha	up to 1,700 and more
10. Panama	less than 1 ha	up to 2,500 and more
11. USA	0.4–3.6 ha	up to 809,371 ha and more
	(1–9 acres)	(up to 2,000 acres and more)
12. Venezuela	less 0.5 ha	up to 5,000 ha and more

Source: Author's elaboration; Data from agriculture censuses of each country, 1950–1970.

Table A4. Estimates for Landgini, Illiteracy 14+, and Ratio Large Holding by Country, 1950s–1970s.

Country	Census Year	Landgini (%) (Own's estimates)	Landgini estimates by other authors			Illiteracy Rate 14+ (%) (Own's estimates)	Ratio Large Holding (%) (Own's estimates)
			Frankema (2008)	Deininger and Olinto (1999)	Taylor and Hudson (1972)		
1. Argentina	1950	80.8				12.7	29.6
	1960	80.4	81.4	85.6	86.7	8.4	31.4
	1970	86.8				7.4	32.1
2. Brazil	1950	83.7				50.6	14.5
	1960	83.4	78.7	84.1	84.5	39	10.4
	1970	83.1				33.8	9.1
3. Chile	1950	92.2				19.9	14.2
	1960	89.8	86.5			16.3	8.7
	1970	88.8				11	8.03
4. Colombia	1950					47.5	
	1960	84.2	80.5	82.9	86.4	22.5	3.5
	1970	84.2				19.1	4.3
5. Costa Rica	1950	80.5				20.6	8.8
	1960	78.7	73.9	80.6	78.2	15.6	10.4
	1970	71.4				11.5	6.9
6. Ecuador	1950	86.4	80.4	84	86.4	44.3	2.07
	1960					32.5	
	1970	77.9	77.2			25.8	2.1
7. Honduras	1950	75.7	70.6	76.5	75.7	64.8	1.7
	1960	75.7				55	1.09
	1970	77.6				43.1	1.7
8. Mexico	1950	96.3				53.2	6.06
	1960	95.3		60.7	69.4	34.2	8.06
	1970	77.3				25.8	9.59
9. Nicaragua	1950					61.6	
	1960	79.2	75.9		80.1	50.1	7.8
	1970					42.5	
10. Panama	1950	71.1				30.06	1.5
	1960	73.5	69.9	80.4	73.5	23.2	2.5
	1970	78.4				18.7	2.9
11. United States	1950	71	67.7	73.1	71	3.2	21.7
	1960	71.3				2.4	25.5
	1970	73.2				1	29.4
12. Venezuela	1950	94.5		91.7	90.9	49.01	5.6
	1960	90.2	85.7			36.7	6.4
	1970	89.1				24.07	8.6

Source: Author's elaboration; Data from each country's population and agriculture censuses, 1950–1970. Several issues of the decennial FAO, Report on the World Census of Agriculture, Rome. Taylor and Hudson (1972), Deininger and Olinto (1999), and Frankema (2008).

Table A4 and the Disaggregated Database will be explained below. To access the disaggregated database, go to: https://www.researchgate.net/profile/Barbara-Tundidor-2. Accessing this database will be useful as we analyze the new disaggregated data.

Table A4 shows the new estimates for landgini, illiteracy, the large holding ratio, and the available estimates of the most relevant authors in this field. To see the estimates for all the countries in the sample, to consult the results of the landgini, the large holding ratio, and the level of illiteracy, country by country and disaggregated for all subnational levels, access the database: https://www.researchgate.net/profile/Barbara-Tundidor-2.[37]

Thanks to resorting to the original censuses from each country, it has been possible to contribute with more new estimates for this period at national and subnational levels. At the national level (Table A4), Taylor and Hudson (1972) offer a total of 11 landginis estimates; Deininger and Olinto (1999) present a total of 10 landgini estimates. More recently, Frankema (2008) provided a complete dataset with 12 landgini estimates. This paper can offer 32 new estimates for the same period and countries thanks to the original censuses.

At the subnational level, data on land inequality for these years are also scarce. To my knowledge, only Wegenast (2010) offers a trusted landginis dataset for Brazil for this period. Brazil is the most analyzed country at the subnational level. Summerhill (2010) calculated the landginis indices for each Brazilian state for 1905, while Albertus et al. (2018) estimated a large landginis dataset for Brazil from 1995 to 2006. But apart from these valuable and laborious contributions, the data on land inequality are limited at the subnational level.

Regarding literacy data, at the national level, only Nugent and Robinson (2010) can be highlighted who calculated the literacy rate for Costa Rica, Colombia, Guatemala, and El Salvador, all for 1900, 1910, and 1930.

At the subnational level, data on literacy are even scarcer. For this reason, thanks to the compilation of the original censuses, it has been possible to build a timeline and see the evolution between and across countries.

However, before analyzing the new database, a deeper explanation of these data, the sources, and the possible complications with the use of these data are necessary. First, it must be mentioned that there has been a lot of hard and complicated archival work to collect and compile this new database on land inequality and illiteracy. All data come from the original censuses of each country. The reasons that justify the study and use of these publications are that, generally, countries offer more information in their official publications.

Nevertheless, this wealth of data also implies some complications. For example, some Latin American subnational levels changed their status for this period. It is the case of Brazil, which experiences changes in denomination and border between its states (subnational levels) during these years. In 1950, the states of Rondonia and Roraima were called Guapore and Rio Branco, respectively. Additionally, the capital, the federal district, changed its location from Rio de Janeiro to the state of Guapore. A new federal district was established independently, with its capital in Brasilia, in 1960. This decision also transformed the old federal district located in the state of Rio de Janeiro into a new state with the name of Guanabara. The state of Guanabara existed from 1960 to 1975, when it finally became part of the state of Rio de Janeiro.

Therefore, to facilitate comparability, it is necessary to emphasize that the Federal District of 1950 should be compared with the state of Guanabara in 1960 and 1970.

Colombia is another Latin American country that has experienced changes in its subnational levels. To begin with, Colombia only carried out agricultural censuses for the 1960s and 1970s. On the other hand, it did not offer data for all the departments; neither in 1960 nor 1970 were relevant agrarian statistics presented for the territories of the Amazon, La Guajira, Vichada, and Vaupes. And also, as mentioned before, some departments changed their borders during these years; this is the case of the department of Caldas. In 1960, the department of Caldas was a single department, and in 1970, two new departments originated from its territory: Quindio and Risalda. The same happens with the departments of Bolivar and Cordoba, which in 1960 were only two departments and in 1970 were combined to form a new department called Sucre. To allow comparability over time, it is, therefore, necessary to include Quindio and Risalda within the Caldas department for the entire period, even when data are available for Quindio and Risalda as independent departments. In the disaggregated public access database, the Caldas department for 1970, where Quindio and Risaldas are included, is called Antiguo Caldas. The same happens with Sucre, which is included in the departments of Bolivar and Cordoba for the entire period, although data are offered for Sucre as an independent state. In any case, the public access disaggregated database also provides the data for the independent states of Quindio, Risalda, and Sucre for 1970. Apart from these cases of Brazil and Colombia, the rest of the countries did not experience significant alterations in their subnational levels that could have affected the comparative analysis of this study, at least during these years (1950–1970).

Once the administrative changes have been clarified, we can start analyzing the new data.

Our initial focus will be on Brazil, a country with previous estimates for this period calculated by Wegenast (2010). If we access the disaggregated database and analyze Brazil, we can observe regional differences across the country. Some subnational levels with a strong landlord tradition, such as Pernambuco or Alagoas, showed higher land inequality and illiteracy than other subnational levels with more small-medium holding traditions, such as Espirito Santo, or Catalina. On the other hand, when comparing the new landgini estimates with those previously offered by Wegenast (2010), we can see how the values for each subnational level are pretty similar.

Another exciting country to analyze in a disaggregated way is Mexico. Similar to Brazil, Mexico also has regional differences. Northern states had more small-medium holding traditions than southern states, where most landowners were located and where there was more latifundia tradition (Galor et al., 2009) (See Fig. B2). However, until the 70s, there was high land inequality across the whole country; only in 70s, land inequality starts to decrease. The reason is that Mexico carried out an agrarian reform during these years.[38] Between the 1960s and 1970s, the government increased the land distribution to quell rural protests (Albertus et al., 2016), which explains the decrease in land inequality in the 1970s. It is in this decade when we can see differences between north and south: northern states such as Baja California North and South, Coahuila, Chihuahua, or Durango experience a higher decrease in land inequality and illiteracy than southern states such as Oaxaca, which in the 1970s still registered a landgini of 89.1% and an adult illiteracy rate of 45.7%.

Colombia is also a Latin American country with great regional diversity in land inequality and illiteracy levels. There is a difference between subnational levels where crops such as coffee were traditionally grown on small-medium size holdings, such as Caldas (Nugent & Robinson, 2010); and those subnational levels where the same crops were grown in latifundia systems as Cordoba, which registered a landgini of 86.1% and an adult illiteracy rate of 40.5% for the decade 1970s. Besides, as in many cases, land inequality decreased in Colombia in the 70s.[39]

Chile presents another interesting case for analysis. Similarly to Mexico and Colombia, Chile also underwent agrarian reform during these years. Although this reform did not initially significantly reduce inequality in land inequality, it ultimately contributed to reducing it.[40] Provinces such as Atacama or Antofagasta experienced sharp declines in land inequality levels and their adult and child–adult illiteracy rates during the studied period.

Finally, in this disaggregated analysis, it is necessary to mention the United States. Does the United States have regional diversity? Although, at the national level, this country does not register high values of land inequality for these years, and a large part of American agriculture has traditionally been associated with small-medium size family farms. This picture changes when we take a closer look at American subnational levels. In particular, we can observe a rich regional diversity in the levels of land inequality between the northern, eastern, and southern subnational levels (see Appendix B, Fig. B2b). The northern and eastern subnational levels registered low, very low land inequality and illiteracy rates in this period, such as Vermont, which reported a landgini of 40.5% and an adult illiteracy rate of 1.1% for the 1960s, or Iowa registered a landgini of 38.7% and an adult illiteracy rate of 0.7% for the same period. However, these levels differ from those found in the southern subnational levels, which had a strong legacy of plantation-style agriculture (Rajan & Ramcharan, 2009). They were more slightly behind in the spread of education than the northern states.[41] Examples are the subnational levels of South Carolina, Georgia, or Louisiana, which for the 1960s registered landginis of 67.8%, 62.3%, and 69.2%, respectively; and adult illiteracy rates of 5.5%, 4.5%, and 6.3%, also respectively. On the other side, these values are higher than those found in some subnational levels of countries such as Argentina. For example, Santa Cruz for the 1960s shows lower land inequality and illiteracy rate, specifically a landgini of 24.8% and an adult illiteracy rate of 5.7%. Another example is Costa Rica for the 1970s and subnational levels such as San Jose, Cartago, or Puntarenas.

This regional evidence helps us to have a complete view of land inequality and illiteracy in Latin America, the United States, and Latin America concerning the United States. Why the United States? Because it has been the country traditionally chosen as a point of reference in land distribution (Galor et al., 2009); this new disaggregated data contributes to better and more excellent knowledge about land inequality within the United States and Latin America.

Table A5. Details and Summary Statistics for Variables.

Variables	Description and sources	N	Mean	Sd	Min	Max	Model
IlliteracyRate$_{i,t}$	Share of the population cannot read and write a simple paragraph in any language of each subnational level. *Author's elaboration from the original census.*	374 173	25.9 40.6	21.6 17.2	0.7 9.3	75.4 80.01	14+ 5–10+
Landgini$_{i,t}$	Index to measure land inequality at each subnational level. *Author's elaboration from the original census.*	445 173	71.2 83.2	15.02 9.4	21.9 52.8	97.6 97.9	14+ 5–10+
Ratio Large Holding$_{i,t}$	Ratio to analyze the share of holdings with a surface larger than 100 ha about the total number of holdings for each subnational level. *Author's elaboration from the original census.*	445 173	20.6 13.6	20.9 14.6	0 0.17	96.1 69.9	14+ 5–10+
UrbanPop$_{i,t}$	The logarithm of the urban population in thousands of inhabitants of each subnational level *Author's elaboration from the original census.*	387 184	47.0 43.1	21.7 21.2	0 10.2	99.05 157.3	14+ 5–10+
Childdependency$_{i,t}$	Measures the potential need for social and economic support of the child and youth population by the working-age population. *Author's elaboration from the original census.*	336 157	4.34 4.3	0.30 0.14	3.49 3.81	4.97 4.6	14+ 5–10+
Catholics$_{i,t}$	A dummy variable indicates if, at a subnational level, 50% > of the population practice Catholicism. *Author's elaboration from the original census.*	515 214	0.72 1	0.44 0	0 1	1 1	14+ 5–10+
lDensity$_{i,t}$	The logarithm of the total population of each subnational level is divided by its total subnational level surface (km²). *Author's elaboration from the original census.*	394 182	2.4 2.4	1.5 1.6	−2.3 −2.04	8.4 8.1	14+ 5–10+
lDistance$_{i,t}$	The logarithm of the distance between the centroid of each subnational level and the capital city of every country (km). *Author's elaboration using Geographical Information System (GIS).*	492 205	6.1 6.1	1.2 1.04	2.4 3.7	8.2 7.8	14+ 5–10+
lArea$_i$	The logarithm of the total surface of each subnational level in km². *Author's elaboration from the original census.*	512 214	10.4 10.3	1.6 1.6	4.7 5.5	14.2 14.2	14+ 5–10+
Landlocked$_i$	A dummy variable indicates whether a subnational level has access to the sea. *Author's elaboration from the original census*	515 214	0.49 0.5	0.5 0.4	0 0	1 1	14+ 5–10+

Table A5. *(Continued)*

Variables	Description and sources	N	Mean	Sd	Min	Max	Model
Latitude$_i$	Absolute latitude of the centroid of each subnational level.	513	7.10	27.5	−54.7	47.03	14+
		214	−3.9	22.8	−53.1	32.6	5–10+
	Author's elaboration using Geographical Information System (GIS)						
Longitude$_i$	Absolute longitude of the centroid of each subnational level.	513	−78.7	16.02	−123	−34.8	14+
		214	−76.6	20.9	−115	−34.8	5–10+
	Author's elaboration using Geographical Information System (GIS)						

Source: Author's elaboration.

Note: Urban Population is considered the population living in cities of at least 1,000 inhabitants.

APPENDIX B. FIGURES

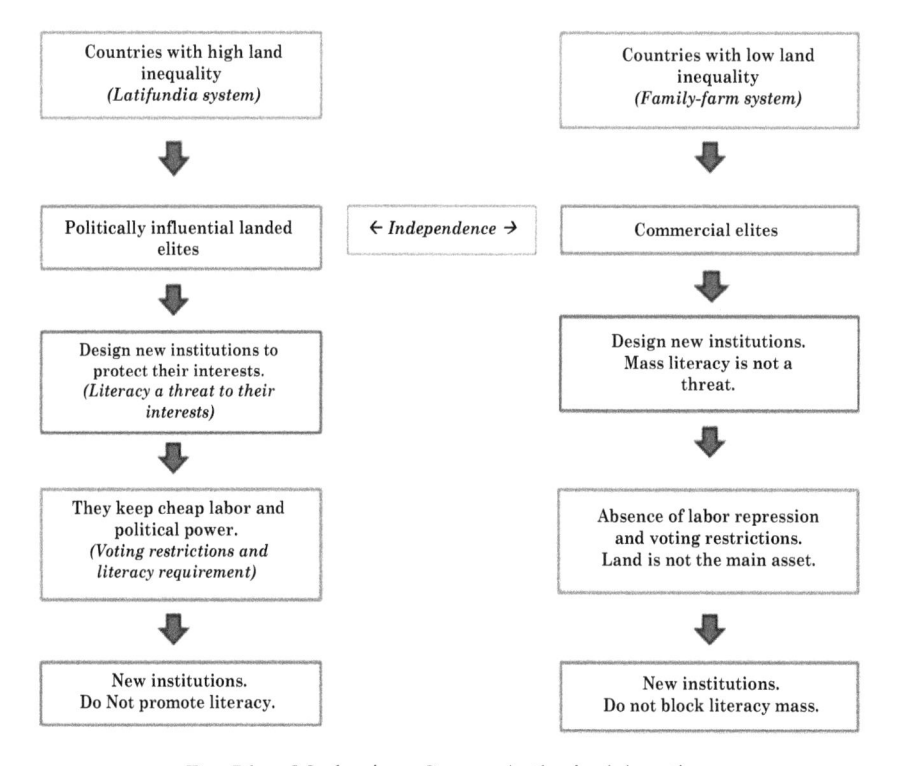

Fig. B1. Mechanism. *Source:* Author's elaboration.

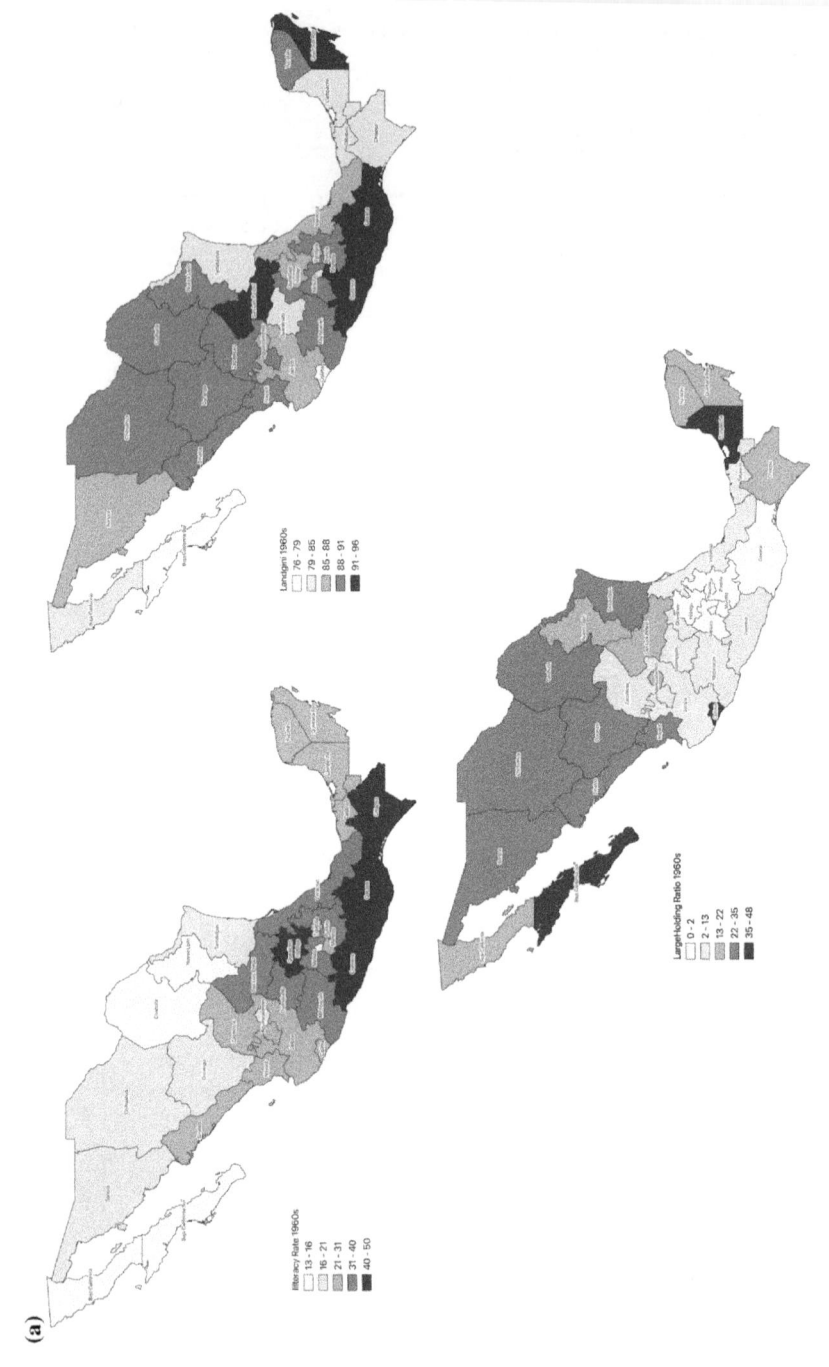

Fig. B2. (a) Illiteracy Rate, Landgini, and Ratio Large Holding for Mexico, 1960s. *Source:* Author's elaboration; Agricultural and Population Censuses from Mexico, 1960.

Fig. B2. (b) Illiteracy Rate, Landgini, and Ratio Large Holding for the USA, 1960s. *Source:* Author's elaboration; Agricultural and Population Censuses from the United States, 1960.

Fig. B?a and b show the illiteracy rate, landgini, and the large holding ratio for Mexico and United States for the 1960s. We can better appreciate the relationship between land inequality and illiteracy and how in most cases, the subnational levels with the higher land inequality also show the highest levels of illiteracy.

The southern states of Mexico, historically characterized by latifundia and landowner past, show the highest levels of landgini and illiteracy for the 1960s. Examples are Oaxaca, Guerrero, or Quintana Roo.

On the other hand, the large holding ratio offers exciting results. We can see that the percentage of large holdings in the states with higher landgini is lower than in the areas with low landgini. This result indicates that in the areas with high landgini, that is, high land inequality, a few large properties concentrate most of the land. They show a possible agrarian structure formed by a few large properties that concentrate a large part of the land versus many small properties with little concentration. It is the case of states such as Oaxaca or Puebla, where the high land inequality together with the low percentage of large holdings makes us see that a few large holdings seem to concentrate most of the land (Tundidor, 2024). These results support the argument of Cinnirella and Hornung (2016). They argue that a higher percentage of latifundia in regions with high land inequality will show a higher proportion of landowners and a higher percentage of the population subject to coercive institutions in areas with high inequality and a high large holding ratio.

These maps of the United States for the 1960s show results similar to those of Mexico. States with a latifundista past, or in the case of US states with a plantation-style past, offer higher levels of landgini and illiteracy. Examples are South Carolina, Georgia, Mississippi, and Louisiana. On the other hand, states that historically had small- to medium-sized farms, particularly in the northern and eastern states, exhibit low land inequality and illiteracy rates.

About the results shown by the large holding ratio, we can observe a behavior similar to that of Mexico. Interestingly, states with high land inequality (high landgini) show lower levels of large holdings, showing how a few large holdings seem to own most of the land.

However, it is necessary to mention several characteristics of the United States: in general, its holdings have a larger average size than those of Latin America (see Appendix A, Table A3). And as mentioned earlier in the text, in Fig. 2, Western states appear to challenge Galor's hypothesis. These states show high land inequality but low illiteracy, for example, states such as Washington, Oregon, California, and Nevada. As mentioned above, these results could be due to the importance of the agricultural sector in these states, but without landed elites who have been able to impose their criteria and privileges on the majority. Perhaps due to other powerful industries and competing elites, such as commercial and industrial. On the other hand, mountainous states such as Montana and Wyoming have been characterized by livestock farming; this economic activity can increase landgini levels due to the large farms required for it. However, this activity is less detrimental to the formation of human capital and less linked to coercive institutions than plantation-style agriculture.

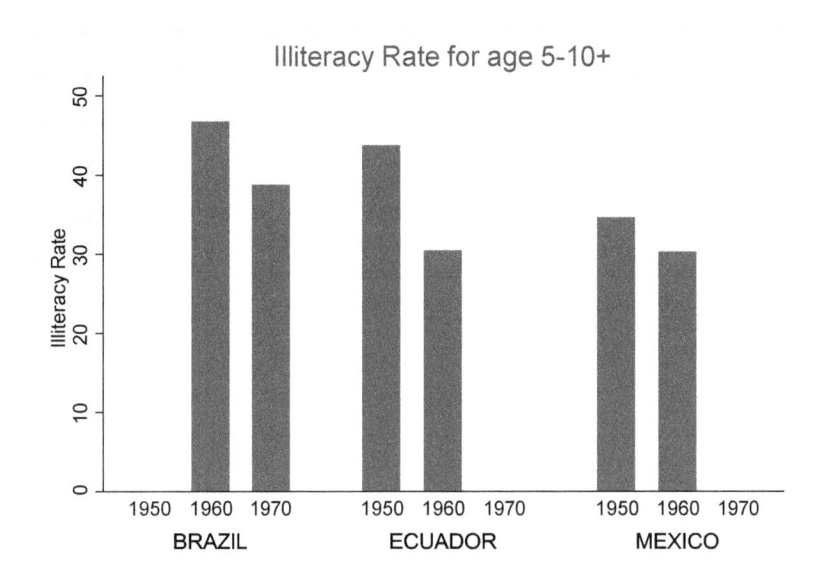

Fig. B3.   Illiteracy Rate for Ages 5–10+, 1950–1970. *Source:* Author's
elaboration; Population Censuses 1950–1970.

Some countries offer data to analyze illiteracy for the 5–10 + age group. In
these countries, we can observe that this illiteracy decreased similarly to illiteracy
for age groups 14+. Brazil, with a 46.7% percentage of child–adult illiteracy in
the 1960s, experienced a significant reduction showing a rate of 38.7% in the
1970s. Ecuador experienced the most significant decline, from an illiteracy rate of
43.7% in the 50s to 30.4% in the 60s. Mexico reduced its illiteracy for ages 5–10 +
from 34.6% to 30.2%. These countries have suffered strong landed oligarchies
and high levels of land inequality. Land inequality, despite having decreased, is
still high in most of their subnational states for this period (see Appendix A,
Table A4 and the public access disaggregated database).

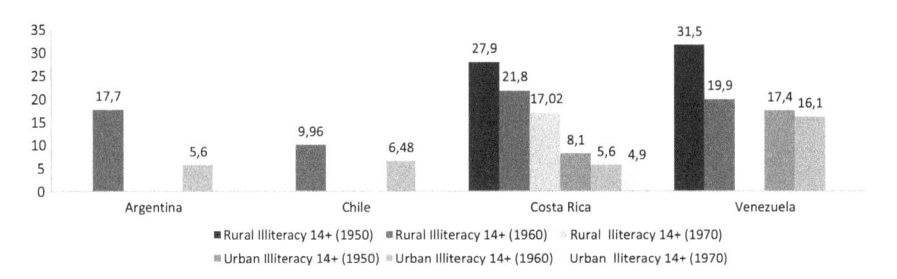

Fig. B4.   Rural and Urban Illiteracy Rate for Ages 14+, 1950–1970. *Source:*
Author's elaboration; Population Censuses 1950–1970.

Fig. B4 contains the rural and urban illiteracy rates from 1950 to 1970. In all cases, we can see how the rural illiteracy rate is higher than the urban one. In Argentina, for example, rural illiteracy reached a value of 17.7%, while urban was 5.6% in the 1960s. Chile shows a similar trend, with 9.96% rural illiteracy and 6.48% urban. In Costa Rica, rural illiteracy drops from 27.9% to 21.8% and 17.02%. In comparison, urban illiteracy registered values of 8.1% in the 1950s, 5.6% in the 1960s, and 4.9% in the 1970s, and it is noticeable that urban illiteracy is lower than rural. Venezuela shows the same behavior, with rural illiteracy greater than the urban one, with a rural illiteracy rate of 31.5% in the 1950s and 19.9% in the 1960s, and both rural and urban rates, with a decreasing trend.

FEDERAL PREEMPTION OF LOCAL GOVERNMENT TELEGRAPH FRANCHISE ENTRY BARRIERS

Aaron M. Honsowetz

Bethany College, USA

ABSTRACT

The US central government enactment of the 1866 Post Roads Act preempted state and municipal telegraph franchise entry barriers. Like present-day tele-communication companies, local franchise regulations were an entry barrier to US telegraph companies. These pre-1866 state and municipal telegraph laws were barriers of both entry and trade between states. Barriers that would of reduced the benefits of a common market if the barriers had not been preempted by the 1866 Post Roads Act. I document what laws were preempted by the 1866 Post Roads Act, explain how these laws increased entry barriers, provide evidence that pre-emption was enforced, and use two counterfactuals to calculate rough estimates of the decrease in entry costs from enforcement of the act.

Keywords: Telegraph; telecommunication law; federal preemption; entry barriers; municipal franchise; 1866 Post Roads Act

JEL Codes: H77; K21; K23; L4; L96; L98; N4; N7

1. INTRODUCTION

With the enactment of the 1866 Post Roads Act, Republicans in the 39th Congress asserted the authority of the central government by preempting local telegraph entry barriers erected by states and municipalities. Entry barriers effectively reduce the ability of competition to improve overall economic efficiency, but political entry barriers result in even larger inefficiencies from political rent seeking (Baumol et al., 1982; Gutiérrez & Philippon, 2019; Tullock, 1967). American states have been regulating telegraph companies since the founding of

Research in Economic History, volume 38
Research in Economic History, Volume 38, 127–155
ISSN: 0363-3268/doi:10.1108/S0363-326820250000038005

the first telegraph company in 1845 (Nonnenmacher, 2001).[1] While some regulations, such as laws punishing vandals caught damaging telegraph poles and wires, lowered entry costs of a telegraph company; other regulations, such as franchise requirements to conduct telegraph business, increased the entry cost of operating a telegraph company.[2]

Like other forms of telecommunication, the telegraph was susceptible to state and municipal governments using franchise requirements to erect political entry barriers.[3] Construction of conduits, poles, and wires used to provide telecommunication services are irrecoverable investments that leave telecommunication companies vulnerable to political rent extraction (Troesken, 1996, p. 8). After wires are built and investment sunk, local governments face strong incentives to extract quasi-rents from telecommunication companies. Entry barriers that explicitly grant a monopoly or de facto monopoly create a telecommunication company earning monopoly profits with larger rents for local government to extract (Lyons, 2010, pp. 407–409). Since entry barriers benefit the company protected by the barriers, a company is more likely to cooperate in sharing the rents with politicians and government in exchange for earning extraordinary profits (Nye, 2007, pp. 71, 114).

Government franchises could include stipulations, including franchise regulations, companies had to meet to receive the franchise (Joyce, 1914, p. 311). The necessity to place telegraph wires along or across public roads empowers states to require a franchise to build and operate a telegraph system (Croswell, 1895, p. 51). Most states delegated the issuing of franchises to municipal governments (Croswell, 1895, p. 109).

Franchises were used to explicitly bar telegraph competition by granting to a single telegraph company an exclusive right to operate in a state or municipality. Even if a franchise was not exclusive, requiring a franchise and complying with franchise regulations also deterred entry by increasing the sunk cost of constructing a telegraph network. Franchise regulations legally were defined as a form of compensation to government for granting the franchise, enabling states and municipalities to impose regulations beyond the general regulatory powers granted to the institutions (Joyce, 1914, p. 311). Franchise regulations issued by a state or municipality did not have to be the same for all companies. Unless forbidden by law, states and municipalities could set different franchise regulations for different companies as compensation for granting them a franchise (Gabel, 1994).

Local telegraph entry barriers reduced network benefits of competition to consumers. An additional location connected to the telegraph network increases competition at the new location and also increases competition by adding another competitive route for telegrams at all of the locations already connected to the competitor's system (Liebowitz & Margolis, 1994, p. 142; Katz & Shapiro, 1985, pp. 424–425; Shy, 2011, pp. 119, 121).[4] As the telegraph system expands, there are more locations connected to the system so each additional location increases competition at a growing number of locations. Because of network benefits from competition, the entry barriers within a state or municipality had negative spillover effects on neighboring states and municipalities. Without federal preemption to remove the entry barriers, negative spillovers are a barrier to state-to-state trade that hinders economic activity and undermines market-preserving federalism (Aranson, 1990; Hazlett, 2003; Weingast, 1992, 1995).[5]

The 1866 Post Roads Act dismantled local entry barriers by conveying federal privileges to existing and future telegraph companies, empowering them to circumnavigate state and municipal telegraph laws. The act granted the right to "construct, maintain, and operate" a telegraph line along any post road in the United States to all telegraph companies who acceded to the terms of the act (14 USC 221, 1863–1867). The federal right to operate deregulated the industry by freeing telegraph companies from the burden of securing local franchises and the local regulations attached to the franchises. To calculate the impact of the act on telegraph providers, I construct two rough estimates of the potential costs imposed on telegraph companies if local entry barriers were allowed to prevail.[6] One projects the additional pole miles of telegraph lines required to physically go around states with costly regulations. A second estimates the potential revenue losses for a competing telegraph company when it forgoes serving a city because of local entry barriers.

This is the first paper dedicated to studying how the 1866 Post Roads Act reduced entry barriers by deregulating state and municipal telegraph regulations. Works on the 1866 Post Roads Act by telegraph historians Lester G. Lindley (1971), Richard John (2010), and Joshua Wolff (2013) discuss the political history of the act and present theories on the act's effect on competition as part of their larger histories of the US telegraph system. Other Economists working on historic state and municipal regulations of the telecommunication industry studied instances during this time period where the laws were not affected by the 1866 Post Roads Act. Tomas Nonnenmacher examined the development of state regulations of the pre-1866 telegraph industry to discern the motivation of state telegraph regulations in the antebellum period (1996, 2001).[7] Other economic research on American 19th century and early 20th century municipal franchising has explored what government conditions drive public or private provision of services in industries such as gas, sewer, and water (Masten, 2010; Troesken, 1997, 2006; Troesken & Geddes, 2003).

The paper is organized as follows. Section 2 presents state and municipal laws that were local entry barriers and entry barriers for neighboring states and municipalities. Section 3 describes how the act evolved and the types of laws the 1866 Post Roads Act preempted. Section 4 calculates back-of-the-envelope estimates of the potential cost telegraph entry barriers would have imposed on telegraph entrants without the enactment of the 1866 Post Roads Act. Section 5 concludes the paper.

2. STATE AND MUNICIPAL ENTRY BARRIERS FOR TELEGRAPH COMPANIES

State and municipal regulations reduce contestability by increasing the costs of telegraph companies entering the market.[8] Not every state and municipal law increase entry costs. State laws making it a crime to purposefully destroy a telegraph line lowered the cost of maintaining telegraph networks (Nonnenmacher, 2001). But state and municipal franchising laws blocked competition and provided opportunities for politicians to extract political rents that increased entry costs for telegraph companies.

States repeatedly used franchising laws to block new entrants from competing with established telegraph companies. The franchise grant to John Watson in 1864 to construct a telegraph system in the state of Nevada forbade any other telegraph company from operating between two cities served by Watson's company (Laws of the Territory of Nevada Passed at the Third Regular Session of the Legislative Assembly Chap. LXXII 1864). In essence, the state of Nevada outlawed competition with Watson's company. Until the passage of the 1866 Post Roads Act, the only way a different telegraph company could conduct business in a city served by Watson's company was to connect that city to locations not currently served by Watson.

Nevada was not the only state trying to use franchises to block competition in the telegraph industry. The state of Florida attempted to grant a monopoly franchise to the Pensacola Telegraph Company to provide telegraph services to the city of Pensacola, Florida (Pensacola Telegraph Company v. Western Union Telegraph Company, 1877). The state of Maine awarded the American Telegraph Company the exclusive franchise to land cables upon its shores that connected Europe (Blondheim, 1994, p. 114; Wolff, 2013, p. 40).

Even when states and municipalities did not award an exclusive franchise or limit the number of franchises issued, acquiring a franchise and regulations imposed as a condition of receiving a franchise were potential entry barriers for telegraph companies. Lobbying politicians for a franchise to operate a telegraph company further increased entry costs. States without a general franchising law awarded franchises through special acts of the legislature, while states with a general franchising law granted anyone a franchise after filing the proper paperwork (John, 2010, pp. 89–90). If a company required a domestic franchise to operate within a state without a general franchise law, then it had to invest time and effort to get the political support needed to pass the act. The costs of political lobbying for a franchise to operate are not unique to telegraph companies.[9] Street railways, railroads, bridges, public ferries, water companies, gas companies, electric companies, toll roads, wharf operators, log boom companies, and banks existed in states or cities where they were required to have a franchise to operate (Joyce, 1914, pp. 41–58; Myers, 1900).

Additionally, regulations imposed as a condition of receiving a franchise were potential entry barriers for telegraph companies. Franchise regulations do not have to be the same for every company, since they are viewed as being compensation for receiving a particular franchise.[10] After the passage of the 1866 Post Roads Act, telegraph companies could avoid the cost of lobbying for a franchise and franchise regulations by incorporating in a state with a general telegraph law and using the privileges granted in the 1866 Post Roads Act to operate across the country.

3. SPILLOVER OF STATE AND MUNICIPAL ENTRY BARRIERS ON NEIGHBORING JURISDICTIONS

Neighboring state and municipal regulations were additional entry barriers for a locality. The costs of neighboring state and municipal franchises deterred entry by artificially increasing the sunk cost to connect a locality to the larger telegraph network. To send messages across distances, telegraph networks required the construction of telegraph lines between the sending and receiving destinations. If that journey required the telegraph line to cross multiple political jurisdictions, then the cost of entry barriers within those jurisdictions directly impacted the cost of entering the market to provide messages between the destinations.

Fig. 1 illustrates how high entry barriers in a political jurisdiction can spillover and increase barriers for entrants in neighboring jurisdictions. In Fig. 1, the boxes represent different state or municipal governments, and the two stars represent two locations that have demand to send and receive telegraph messages. To do this, the message has to travel across land shaded in the gray box. Assume the gray box has imposed an entry barrier, say a franchise requirement. For a new entrant to connect the destinations, it must earn a rate of return that justifies the costs of physically constructing the network plus the costs of acquiring a franchise in the shaded gray area.

The government represented by the gray box can erect entry barriers in one of three ways. First, it can simply prevent the construction of a telegraph network by refusing to grant a franchise. Second, the government can undertake regulations that increase the cost of constructing the network itself. For example, if a telegraph company is required to connect every post office by telegraph within the gray box as a condition for its franchise, it will increase the overall cost of connecting the star destinations. Third, it can impose regulations that reduce the revenue earned within the gray box. Hypothetically, the government could grant a franchise to cross the territory with no right to handle any messages destined or

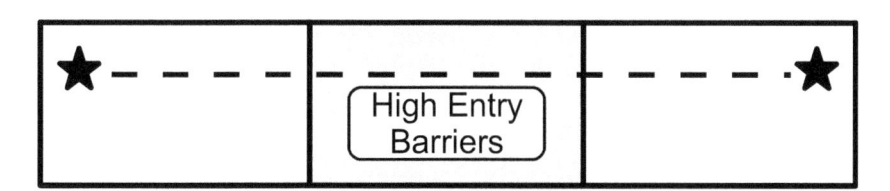

Fig. 1.   Telegraph Entry Barriers Created by Neighboring Jurisdictions.
Notes: Stars represent destinations sending and receiving telegrams. The dotted line connecting the stars is a route a telegraph company could use to construct its telegraph wires. The boxes represent a political jurisdiction, be it a US state or municipality. The shaded box contains high political entry barriers that increase a telegraph entrant's costs within it. The high entry barriers in the shaded box also serve as entry barriers for the starred destinations in the nonshaded boxes since a telegraph company must cross the shaded box to connect them.

originating from within the territory. Or, political lobbying costs and government fees for a franchise could reduce net revenue.

The costs of high entry barriers from neighboring municipal and state governments were potentially worse than the situation described in Fig. 1. The decentralized nature of the United States meant there could be multiple political jurisdictions between destinations with high entry barriers. Each additional jurisdiction increases the overall number of entry barriers for provision of telegraph service between the destinations. Each contains politicians who, either to acquire rents or benevolently transfer resources to their constituents, possess an incentive to extract network benefits from the destinations connected to the network. Theoretical analysis suggests that this increase in the number of jurisdictions who can extract tolls can result in prices between the destinations exceeding the monopoly price.[11]

4. FEDERAL PREEMPTION THROUGH THE 1866 POST ROADS ACT

When the 1866 Post Roads Act was first proposed, it was not a foregone conclusion that the bill would reduce entry barriers for all telegraph companies. Originally, the act was designed to bestow federal privileges to "construct, maintain, and operate" a telegraph line along any post road in the United States upon a single telegraph company, the National Telegraph Company (Congressional Globe 39th Congress 1st Session, p. 3075, 14 USC 221, 1863–1867, Wolff, 2013, p. 106). In Senate debates, Ohio Senator John Sherman, chair of the Senate committee that wrote the bill, expressed his belief that making the bill a general bill that applied to all telegraph companies would undermine the ability of the National Telegraph Company to raise the capital needed to successfully compete with the incumbent telegraph company, Western Union (Congressional Globe 39th Congress 1st Session, p. 3075, 3428). Senator Sherman's stated concerns about altering the bill may have had more do with how it would affect his own personal interests (Honsowetz, 2019). In a letter to financier Jay Cooke, he expressed his desire to invest in the National Telegraph Company with Cooke (John, 2010, p. 118; Sherman to Cook, 1866). Furthermore, Senator Sherman's oldest brother Charles was a director of the company (Wolff, 2013, p. 104).

It took pressure from senators like Iowa Senator James Grimes and Senator John Conness of California to get Senator Sherman to reword the bill as a general grant of federal privileges to any telegraph company organized under the laws of any state (Congressional Globe 39th Congress 1st Session, p. 3428, 3481). The change was spurred by arguments that a federal charter to a single telegraph company posed little risk to Western Union since Western Union could buy out the competitor before it constructed a single mile of telegraph line (Congressional Globe 39th Congress 1st Session, p. 3481–3489). The benefit of granting federal privileges to all telegraph companies, from Nevada Senator William Stewart's perspective, was that as long as Western Union was earning large profits, it could not buy out all competitors and avoid competition (Congressional Globe 39th

Congress 1st Session, p. 3484). Senator Stewart foresaw that investors would continue starting new telegraph companies as long as existing companies were earning high profits. Facing the possibility the bill might fail, Senator Sherman relented and modified the bill to be a general grant to all telegraph companies, including the National Telegraph Company.[12]

5. COURT INTERPRETATION OF THE 1866 POST ROADS ACT

A series of court cases clarified the reach and power of the 1866 Post Roads Act. In debate, legislators expressed concern that they were uncertain how many privileges they were actually granting to the telegraph companies. Senator Sherman argued the bill gave the right to run telegraph wires along any "post route" within the United States (Congressional Globe 39th Congress 1st Session, p. 3485). Congressman William E. Finck of Ohio interpreted the bill as a federal grant to use eminent domain to acquire land for telegraph lines (Congressional Globe 39th Congress 1st Session, p. 3745). Senator Thomas Hendricks of Indiana described the bill as the federal government authorizing a telegraph company organized in one state to operate within a different state and criticized how it presumed some sort of federal power because a road happened to be designated a "post road" (Congressional Globe 39th Congress 1st Session, pp. 3488–3489).

What did the bill actually mean? An early question addressed in the Supreme Court of Nevada was whether a telegraph company had to formally accede to the terms of the act to receive its benefits (Western Union Telegraph Co. Appellant v. Atlantic and Pacific State Telegraph Co., Respondent, 1869).[13] The court ruled a company could not benefit from any of the privileges of the act without written proof it had properly filed its agreement to the terms.

The courts also resolved whether or not the act granted free access to right of way along post roads. An 1874 federal circuit court ruled that the act did not convey telegraph companies the right to condemn private property to use as telegraph right of ways without compensation (Atlantic and Pacific Telegraph Company v. Chicago Rock Island and Pacific Railroad Company, 1874; Lindley, 1971, p. 217). Land owners had to be compensated either directly through purchase or by condemnation procedures "in accordance with" state laws.[14] Nor was the act a federal grant for out of state telegraph companies to use state condemnation proceedings to acquire telegraph right of ways (Western Union Telegraph Company v. Pennsylvania Railroad Company, 1904).[15]

As revealed from court cases, the act did grant telegraph companies the ability to "construct, maintain, and operate" a telegraph network along any post road on land a company acquired (14 USC 221, 1863–1867). This grant, ruled the Nevada State Supreme Court, empowered telegraph companies to operate within a state without a franchise granted by the state, even if the state had granted an exclusive franchise to a different telegraph company (Western Union Telegraph Co. Appellant v. Atlantic and Pacific State Telegraph Co., Respondent, 1869). The US Supreme Court concurred with this interpretation when it ruled on

Pensacola Telegraph Company v. Western Union Telegraph Company in 1878 (1877).

The precedent from *Pensacola Telegraph Company v. Western Union Telegraph Company* inspired courts to grant landholders the right to breach exclusive contracts with a telegraph company. An exclusive contract with a telegraph company is a promise by the landholder not to permit any other telegraph company to construct a telegraph line upon the landholder's land. The Federal Circuit Court of Indiana ruled *Pensacola Telegraph Company v. Western Union Telegraph Company* implies that any contract, be it private or public (government franchise), could not be used to prevent someone who acceded to the terms of the 1866 Post Roads Act from constructing, maintaining, and operating a telegraph line (Western Union Telegraph Co. v. American Union Telegraph Company et al., 1879). The practical result was that courts refused to uphold an exclusive contract when a land owner breached it by authorizing a different telegraph company that had acceded to the 1866 Post Roads Act to erect telegraph facilities upon the land owner's property.

6. CONSTRAINT OF STATE AND MUNICIPAL ENTRY BARRIERS BY FEDERAL PREEMPTION

The courts' interpretation of the 1866 Post Roads Act destroyed the ability of municipalities and states to exclude telegraph companies from operating within their territory. A requirement to hold a corporate charter from the state to operate within it or a requirement to secure a franchise from a state or a municipality to operate within their territory enabled states and municipalities to exclude telegraph companies (Scott & Jarnagin, 1868, pp. 7–8). In some cases, government franchises explicitly granted an exclusive right to provide particular telegraph services or the exclusive right to provide all telegraph services in a geographical area.[16]

The 1866 Post Roads Act did not grant a federal franchise per se. The act protected telegraph companies from costly franchises by allowing telegraph companies to select the most favorable state franchise (Joyce & Joyce, 1907, p. 53).[17] The act provided privileges to a telegraph company registered in any state of the United States. This meant a telegraph company still had to incorporate in a state and acquire a state franchise. But once a company had done so, the company did not need any additional franchises to operate elsewhere within the United States.

Losing the ability to require a local telegraph franchise limited the ability of states and municipalities to regulate the telegraph industry. Prior to the 1866 Post Roads Act, states and municipalities were able to implement regulations as a condition of being awarded a telegraph franchise. If a telegraph company violated regulations that were a condition for receiving the franchise, the franchise could potentially be revoked and the company forced to halt operations (Joyce & Joyce, 1907, p. 379).

States and municipalities could use franchise regulations to impose different costs on different telegraph companies and were not required to have a general law granting a telegraph franchise to all companies that met its conditions. Franchises could be negotiated on a case by case basis, with each case containing its own set of regulations. Theoretically, one company might be able to operate only in six counties with no price regulation while another company might operate statewide and be required to have its prices approved by a local price board.[18] With the federal grant to operate from the 1866 Post Roads Act, telegraph companies no longer needed to consent to local regulations in order to acquire a franchise from every state or municipality where they operated.

The 1866 Post Roads Act did not exempt telegraph companies from all state and municipal regulations. States and municipalities could still use their police powers (Cook, 1920, p. 77; Jones, 1916, p. 63). Police powers enabled states and municipalities to impose regulations on the height or placement of telegraph poles, to order the removal of poles/wires deemed to be a nuisance, or to require that telegraph lines be laid underground (Jones, 1916, pp. 63–64). Unlike franchise regulations, police powers were general regulations that applied to all telegraph companies operating in a municipality or a state. The 1866 Post Roads Act did not prevent states from conveying some privileges that were only received by domestic telegraph companies. Many states only allowed telegraph companies registered in the state to use eminent domain to acquire right of way (Jones, 1916, p. 175).[19]

7. EVIDENCE OF ENFORCEMENT OF THE 1866 POST ROADS ACT

In contrast to the experience with recent Federal attempts at preemption, local governments were largely unsuccessful at evading the 1866 Post Roads Act. Contemporary local governments continue to defy the federal government's efforts to use the 1996 Telecommunication Act and the 1992 Cable Act to preempt local telecommunication franchise requirements (Hazlett, 2007). Local governments find technical ways to comply with the letter of the laws without complying with their spirit. These acts prohibited municipalities from granting an exclusive franchise to a cable company, but they did not state how long a municipality had to take to process a company's application (Lyons, 2010, pp. 408–409). Verizon reported that out of the 113 franchise applications waiting for approval in March 2005, only 10 had been approved by March 2006 (Lyons, 2010, p. 409). In response to municipal delay tactics, the Federal Communications Commission (FCC) issued new guidelines in 2007 that capped the time municipalities had to approve a new franchise at 60 days for companies already holding right of way access and 6 months for companies yet to secure right of way access (Lyons, 2010, p. 410).

State and municipal efforts to circumvent the 1866 Post Roads Act were hindered by the courts' ability to grant telegraph companies the right to operate a telegraph network. If a state or municipality tried to enforce either an exclusive franchise for a single company or require a state or municipal franchise, courts would instruct telegraph companies to ignore these since they were granted the right to "construct, maintain, and operate" a telegraph network by the federal government (14 USC 221, 1863–1867, Cook, 1920, pp. 67, 69, 76; Joyce & Joyce, 1907, pp. 126–127; Western Union Telegraph Company v. City of Richmond, 1909). Florida provided the Pensacola Telegraph Company an exclusive franchise within its corporate charter to serve the City of Pensacola, Florida (Pensacola Telegraph Company v. Western Union Telegraph Company, 1877). When Western Union, which had acceded to the terms of the 1866 Post Roads Act, began construction of its own telegraph line to Pensacola in 1874, the Pensacola Telegraph Company sought an injunction to prevent its completion and operation. Upon appeal to the United States Supreme Court, the court ruled Western Union had a federal right from the 1866 Post Roads Act to operate the telegraph line and refused to grant an injunction.

Courts granted telegraph companies permission to build and operate when states or municipalities used bureaucratic procedures or regulations to avoid complying with the 1866 Post Roads Act (Cook, 1920, p. 69). The Town of Essex attempted to exclude the New England Telegraph Company from continuing to operate within the town by refusing to grant the company a construction permit to repair its telegraph lines (Cook, 1920, p. 69; New England Telegraph Co. of Massachusetts v. Town of Essex, 1913; Town of Essex v. New England Telegraph Co. of Massachusetts, 1916). Federal courts ruled that the attempt to use the construction permitting process to exclude a telegraph company violated the right to "construct, maintain, and operate" a telegraph line granted in the 1866 Post Roads Act and permitted the company to repair their telegraph lines (14 USC 221, 1863–1867). A county in Georgia attempted to exclude Postal Telegraph-Commercial Cable from operating along a road by ordering the removal of its poles that were in the center of a road after the county widened it (Carver v. The State, 1912). A Georgia court of appeals ruled that the 1866 Post Roads Act protected the company's right to operate telegraph lines alongside the road, and that it was within the company's rights to relocate its poles alongside the road when the county refused to designate a new location for the poles.

Telegraph company employees were protected from state laws that were declared in violation of the 1866 Post Roads Act. If states or municipalities arrested telegraph employees for breaking laws that violated the 1866 Post Roads Act then courts would halt prosecution and secure the employees release from prison (Cook, 1920, pp. 67, 180). In 1891, a foreman of Postal Telegraph-Commercial Cable was arrested for constructing a telegraph line along a post road in Colleton County, South Carolina (*Ex parte* Conway, 1891). A Federal Circuit Court ordered the county to drop charges and release the foreman because Postal Telegraph-Commercial Cable was granted the right to construct telegraph lines along post roads by the 1866 Post Roads Act. In a similar case, a county in Georgia was ordered by the Georgia Court of Appeals to release a Postal Telegraph-Commercial Cable employee who relocated a telegraph line the court deemed was protected by the 1866 Post Roads Act instead of removing it as demanded by the county (Carver v. The State, 1912).

8. WESTERN UNION FAILED TO USE 1866 POST ROADS ACT TO ELIMINATE ALL COMPETITION

Some might argue the 1866 Post Roads Act further empowered Western Union to reduce the threat of competition. One concern is that Western Union used the act to enter the territory of other regional telegraph monopolies to drive them out of business. That concern is unfounded since all the regional monopolies had already consolidated with Western Union prior to the act's proposal and passage (Honsowetz, 2019; Nonnenmacher, 2006).[20]

Additionally, the remaining non-Western Union allied "large" telegraph companies operated telegraph networks that paralleled Western Union's pre-existing system (Reid, 1879, pp. 447, 590–595).[21] The Eastern Telegraph Company connected Philadelphia to New York City via a series of towns in New Jersey. The Insulated Lines Telegraph Company operated a line from Boston to Washington DC. The Franklin Telegraph Company built a second competing route from Boston to Washington DC. That said, the inability of the Franklin Telegraph Company to get franchise access to cities, especially New York City, later drove it to merge with The Insulated Lines Telegraph Company who already had franchise access.

A second concern is that the 1866 Post Roads Act might have strengthened Western Union's ability to systematically engage in predatory pricing against future competition. The 1866 Post Roads Act granted Western Union's competitors the ability to operate in all municipalities without any franchise regulations. The act hence prevents Western Union from using markets protected from competition by municipal franchise from funding a predatory pricing scheme.[22]

9. ESTIMATING COST FROM REGULATIONS

As shown in Fig. 1, the cost of connecting two destinations by telegraph was affected by state and municipal entry barriers between the destinations. To estimate the potential cost created by the entry barriers, I constructed two counterfactuals. The first one estimates how many additional pole miles it would take to geographically circumnavigate an area with high entry barriers in 1889 and 1911. The second estimates the potential revenue loss if a telegraph company was denied the opportunity to provide telegraph service to cities along a route in 1904 and 1908.

10. COST OF CIRCUMVENTING GEOGRAPHICALLY ONEROUS REGULATIONS

In this section, I provide estimates of how many additional miles of telegraph poles would be needed to go around a state with high entry barriers.

Fig. 2 shows two routes to connect the starred destinations. The direct route crosses the territory of a government with high entry barriers, indicated with a shaded box. The barriers in the shaded box may be high enough that the most

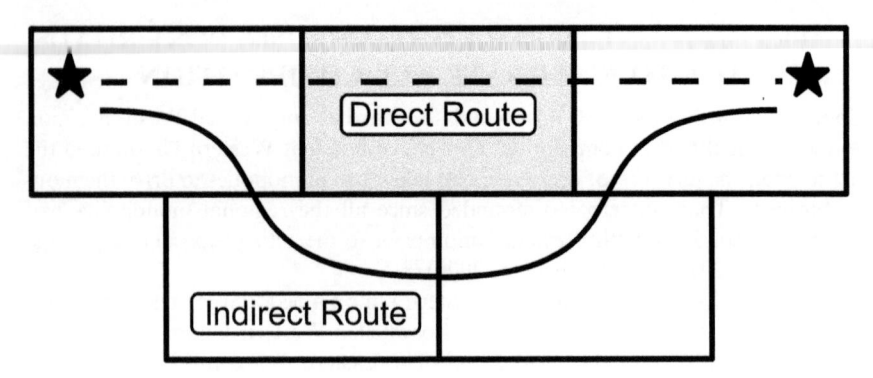

Fig. 2.   Circumnavigating Telegraph Entry Barriers. *Notes:* Stars represent
destinations sending and receiving telegrams. The dotted and solid lines are two
different routes a telegraph company could use to construct its telegraph wires. The
boxes represent a political jurisdiction, be it a US state or municipality. If costs from
franchising regulations within the shaded box were high enough, a telegraph company
might elect to use an indirect route to connect destinations. An extreme example of
cost for a telegraph company is when a political jurisdiction grants an exclusive
franchise to a different telegraph company.

economical route for a telegraph company is to construct a longer indirect route
that avoids crossing the jurisdiction.

Circumventing regulation is in this way a realistic hypothetical. States and
municipalities sometimes granted exclusive contracts to single telegraph companies. Atlantic and Pacific Telegraph desired to cross the state of Nevada to
connect California (Western Union Telegraph Co., Appellant, v. Atlantic and
Pacific State Telegraph Co., Respondent 1869). Their plan to cross the state was
delayed because the state of Nevada had granted an exclusive franchise to
Western Union to serve California.[23] Atlantic and Pacific Telegraph challenged
the legality of the franchise in the Nevada State Supreme Court. While the court
ruled that a company who acceded to the terms of the 1866 Post Roads Act could
operate anywhere within the state, it also ruled a telegraph company that did not
accede to the terms of the act was barred from infringing on Western Union's
exclusive franchise. This ruling implies that prior to the 1866 Post Roads Act, the
only way to reach California after the state granted an exclusive franchise was to
secure a route around the state of Nevada.[24]

To estimate the cost of going around the state of Nevada, I estimate how
many additional miles of telegraph poles would have been needed to connect San
Francisco with Denver, Colorado, and Omaha, Nebraska, in 1911 and 1889.
Alternative routes are constructed by finding the shortest route along the US rail
network using 19th century GIS rail maps assembled by Jeremy Atack (2013,
2014a, 2014b).[25] Building along railway rights of ways was the cheapest means of
constructing a telegraph network (Griswold et al., 1930; Nonnenmacher, 1996;
Western Union 1934; Wolff, 2013, pp. 204, 247). Railroad contract costs were

relatively low because a single contract acquired hundreds of miles of right of way. Shorter telegraph poles could be used along railroads versus along roads since there were fewer instances where people and vehicles needed to go underneath the wires. Transportation costs for telegraph construction were lower along railways because material could be rolled directly off railcars for construction.

Fig. 3 illustrates the shortest routes along railways between Denver, Colorado, and San Francisco, California, in 1889. Fig. 4 illustrates the shortest routes along railways between Omaha, Nebraska, and San Francisco, California, in 1911. In both cases not surprisingly, the route through Nevada was shorter than the routes around Nevada.

Table 1 estimates the pole mileage increase incurred by telegraph companies connecting Denver and Omaha to San Francisco if they were excluded from Nevada. As the rail network expanded between 1889 and 1911, the difference in mileage for circumnavigating Nevada increased from Denver and Omaha. The results in Table 1 understate the severity of a telegraph company being excluded from operating across Nevada in the 1860s and 1870s. The first American transcontinental railroad connected San Francisco with the Eastern portion of the United States in 1869 by traversing Nevada. An alternative route was not available for telegraph companies until the completion of the second

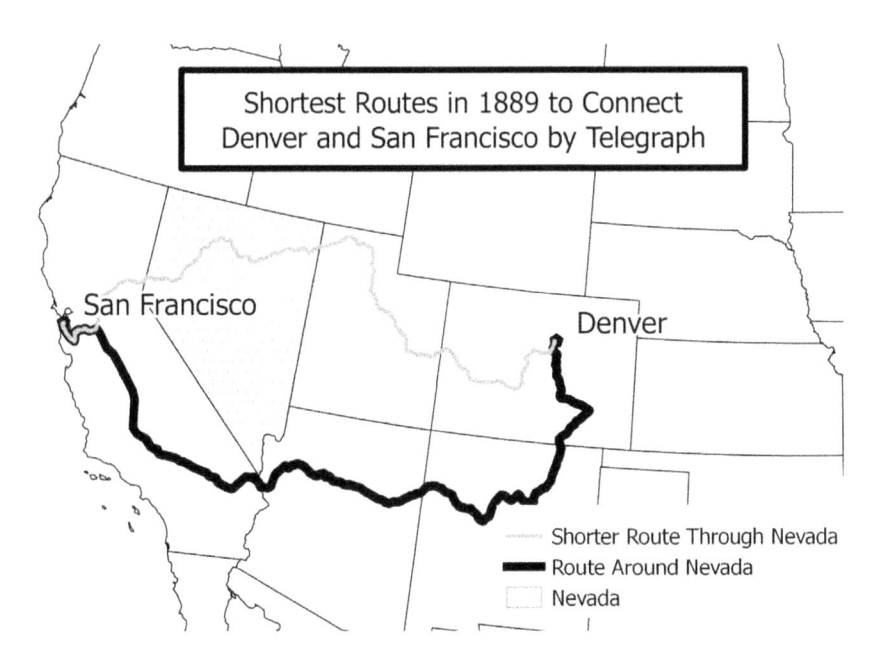

Fig. 3.   Shortest Routes in 1889 to Connect Denver and San Francisco by Telegraph. *Notes:* Distances are calculated by using GIS maps of the US railroad network assembled by Jeremy Atack (2014b). Telegraph lines are assumed to be built along railroads to take advantage of lower construction and maintenance costs. Map layer provided by Commission for Environmental Cooperation (2010).

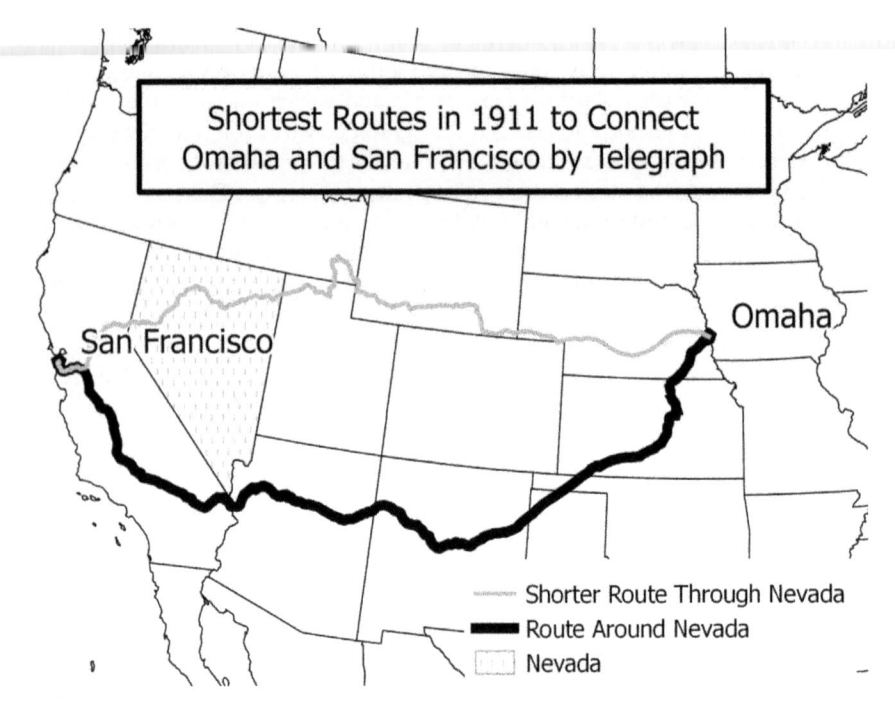

Fig. 4.　Shortest Routes in 1911 to Connect Omaha and San Francisco by Telegraph. *Notes:* Distances are calculated by using GIS maps of the US railroad network assembled by Jeremy Atack (2014A, 2014b). Telegraph lines are assumed to be built along railroads to take advantage of lower construction and maintenance costs. Map layer provided by Commission for Environmental Cooperation (2010).

Table 1. Miles of Pole Lines to Connect Telegraph Lines to San Francisco With and Without Permission to Cross Nevada.

City	Year	Distance to San Francisco Crossing Nevada	Distance to San Francisco Excluded from Nevada	Difference
Denver	1911	1,481	1,655	174
	1889	1,583	1,739	156
Omaha	1911	1,983	2,082	99
	1889	2,128	2,190	62

Notes: Distances are calculated by using GIS maps of the US railroad network assembled by Jeremy Atack (2014a, 2014b). Telegraph lines are assumed to be built along railroads to take advantage of lower construction and maintenance costs. All distances are in miles.

transcontinental railroad that bypassed Nevada in 1881. That meant that without the 1866 Post Roads Act, an exclusive franchise from the state of Nevada was in essence an exclusive franchise to connect the West Coast to the rest of the United States until 1881.

11. POTENTIAL REVENUE LOST FROM EXCLUSION BY MUNICIPALITIES

In this section, I provide estimates of the potential revenue loss faced by entrants when municipalities erect entry barriers. One way a telegraph company could offset part of the sunk cost of constructing a telegraph network between two destinations was to serve other locations along the route. If states or municipalities had granted local monopolies, in the intervening jurisdictions, potential entrants could be discouraged from proceeding. In Fig. 5, a telegraph company desires to connect the two destinations indicated by the stars. Between the two destinations in the gray rectangle is a square municipality that has erected high entry barriers, such as an exclusive franchise to a different telegraph company, making it uneconomical for an entrant to provide telegraph services to the square municipality. Since this municipal entry barrier decreases the potential revenue available to cover the cost of connecting the star destinations, it also is as an entry barrier for connecting the star destinations.

Granting exclusive municipal franchises was not unheard of in the telegraph industry. The state of Florida attempted to grant an exclusive franchise to a single company to serve the city of Pensacola (Pensacola Telegraph Company v. Western Union Telegraph Company, 1877).[26] The state of California granted the California State Telegraph Company an exclusive franchise to operate a telegraph line between a series of cities (California State Telegraph Co. v. Alta Telegraph Co. 1863; Reid, 1879, p. 500). The Alta Telegraph Company violated this franchise by paralleling the California State Telegraph Company's lines. The California State Supreme court imposed an injunction that ordered the Alta Telegraph Company to cease operating its telegraph offices paralleling the California State Telegraph Company's telegraph lines.

Using internal Western Union data from the early 20th century, I construct estimates presented in Tables 3–6 of the total potential receipts Western Union's largest late 19th century competitor, Postal Telegraph, would have forgone had it

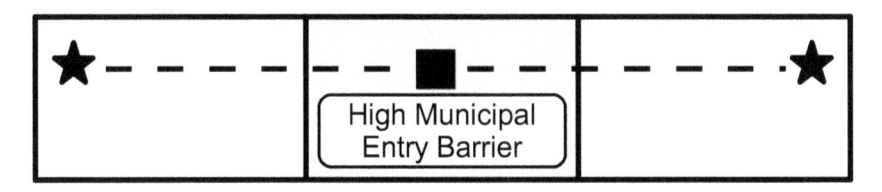

Fig. 5. High Municipal Telegraph Entry Barrier. *Notes:* Stars represent destinations sending and receiving telegrams. The dotted line is a route a telegraph company could use to construct its telegraph wires. The solid black square in the gray box represents a municipality a telegraph company is barred from serving while connecting to the star destinations. The inability to provide service to the square municipality prevents the telegraph company from using the net earnings from the square municipality to contribute to covering the sunk cost of constructing the telegraph line serving the star destinations.

been excluded from serving some of the cities along its network. Western Union maintained a series of statistical notebooks to provide information to Western Union executives. Some of the statistical notebooks are preserved in the Western Union Archive at the Smithsonian's Lemelson Center for the Study of Invention and Innovation (Western Union, 1901–1908).

One notebook contains the receipts Western Union earned at its 17 highest earning offices for the year 1904 and its 45 highest earning offices for October 1908.[27] The 17 highest grossing offices accounted for 42% of Western Union's receipts in 1904, and the 45 highest receipt grossing offices accounted for roughly 59% of Western Union's receipts in October 1908.[28] In the same notebook, Western Union calculated that 68.9% of their receipts from New York City and Chicago were from messages destined for locations also served by Postal Telegraph-Commercial Cable (Western Union, 1901–1908). My Postal Telegraph-Commercial Cable receipt estimates assume this percentage is true for all cities served by Postal Telegraph-Commercial Cable and Western Union.

I calculate two estimates for the potential receipts lost if excluded from each marketplace: one assuming Postal Telegraph-Commercial Cable captured 15% revenue in the market place and another assuming it captured 25%.[29] The US Census estimated that Postal Telegraph-Commercial Cable captured at most 25% of the US telegraph market revenue (United States Census Bureau, 1975, p. 779). Supporting the possibility that Postal Telegraph-Commercial Cable might have earned 25% of all telegraph revenue is a US Senate report that noted Postal Telegraph-Commercial Cable handled around 26% of all messages and Western Union the remaining 74% in 1908 (Senate Document, 1909, p. 55).[30] The more conservative figure of 15% comes from an Interstate Commerce Committee case where it was reported Postal Telegraph-Commercial Cable earned 15% of US telegraph revenue in 1918 (Hochfelder, 2012, p. 165; Interstate Commerce Commission, 1918, p. 735).

Tables 3–6 identify two destinations served by Postal Telegraph-Commercial Cable and some of the cities along the routes between them. The cities and routes were identified from the Postal Telegraph-Commercial Cable (1904, 1906) tariff books held at the New York Public Library. Each book contains a list of all locations served by Postal Telegraph-Commercial Cable and a map of the company's telegraph network.

Table 2 and Table 3 are constructed from annual Western Union receipts for 1904. Table 2 uses the 15% estimates to calculate receipts along the northern route between New York City and San Francisco.[31] If Postal Telegraph-Commercial Cable was excluded from Buffalo, Cleveland, and Chicago, it would be equivalent to losing almost 70% of the receipts earned in New York City and San Francisco. Table 3 uses the 25% estimate to calculate the receipts along the route between New York City and Washington DC. If Postal Telegraph-Commercial Cable was barred from serving Philadelphia and Baltimore, the loss in receipts would equal almost 25% of the receipts collected in New York City and Washington, DC.

Tables 4 and 5 are constructed with receipts for the month of October in 1908. Table 4 uses the 25% estimates to calculate receipts along the route between Cincinnati and New Orleans. Losing the receipts from Louisville and Nashville would be the equivalent of losing 34% of the receipts earned between Cincinnati

Table 2. Postal Telegraph-Commercial Cable Estimated 1904 Annual Receipts New York City to San Francisco-Northern Route.

Terminus of Route	Estimate of Postal Telegraph Receipts at Terminus ($)	Cities Along Route	Estimated Receipts of Cities Along Route ($)	Estimated Receipts of Cities Along Route Relative to Aggregate Terminus Cities (%)
New York	286,234.27	Buffalo	22,794.88	6.6
city to San		Cleveland	23,203.78	6.8
Francisco	57,043.73	Chicago	192,957.73	56.2
Aggregated	343,278.00		238,956.40	69.6

Notes: Route is based on route used by Postal Telegraph-Commercial Cable from its 1904 Tariff Book. Postal Telegraph had two routes between New York and San Francisco. This table is based on the northern route. Receipts for Postal Telegraph-Commercial Cable are estimated from Western Union receipts in Appendix 1 using the assumption it captured 15% of receipts in the telegraph market. See Appendix 3 for full details of how the table was calculated and Appendix 4 for complete list of projected Postal Telegraph-Commercial Cable city receipts.

Table 3. Postal Telegraph-Commercial Cable Estimated 1904 Annual Receipts New York City to Washington DC

Terminus of Route	Estimate of Postal Telegraph Receipts at Terminus ($)	Cities Along Route	Estimated Receipts of Cities Along Route ($)	Estimated Receipts of Cities Along Route Relative to Aggregate Terminus Cities (%)
New York	540,664.73	Philadelphia	100,068.29	17.1
city to		Baltimore	45,968.70	7.8
Washington, DC	45,937.93			
Aggregated	586,602.66		146,036.99	24.9

Notes: Route is based on route used by Postal Telegraph-Commercial Cable from its 1904 Tariff Book. Receipts for Postal Telegraph-Commercial Cable are estimated from Western Union receipts in Appendix 1 using the assumption it captured 25% of receipts in the telegraph market. See Appendix 3 for full details of how the table was calculated and Appendix 4 for complete list of projected Postal Telegraph-Commercial Cable city receipts.

and New Orleans. Table 5 uses the 15% estimates to calculate receipts along the southern route between New York City and San Francisco.[32] Pittsburgh, Indianapolis, St. Louis, and Kansas City were adjacent to the route. If Postal Telegraph-Commercial Cable was prevented from serving these cities, the decline in receipts would be almost 40% of the total receipts from New York City and San Francisco.

The estimates underestimate the damage Postal Telegraph-Commercial Cable would suffer if municipal franchising excluded it from particular cities. The estimates presented in Tables 3–6 and Appendices 4 and 5 likely underestimate the share of revenue Postal Telegraph-Commercial Cable earned in large cities. For much of its history, Postal Telegraph-Commercial Cable did not compete for the entire US

Table 4. Postal Telegraph-Commercial Cable Estimated October 1908 October Receipts Cincinnati to New Orleans.

Terminus of Route	Estimate of Postal Telegraph Receipts at Terminus ($)	Cities Along Route	Estimated Receipts of Cities Along Route ($)	Estimated Receipts of Cities Along Route Relative to Aggregate Terminus Cities (%)
Cincinnati to New Orleans	8,881.67	Louisville	4,124.67	23.5
		Nashville	1,928.33	10.9
	8,741.67			
Aggregated	17,623.33		6,071.00	34.4

Notes: Route is based on route used by Postal Telegraph-Commercial Cable from its 1906 Tariff Book. Receipts for Postal Telegraph-Commercial Cable are estimated from Western Union receipts in Appendix 2 using the assumption it captured 25% of receipts in the telegraph market. See Appendix 3 for full details of how the table was calculated and Appendix 5 for complete list of projected Postal Telegraph-Commercial Cable city receipts.

Table 5. Postal Telegraph-Commercial Cable Estimated October 1908 October Receipts New York City to San Francisco-Southern Route.

Terminus of Route	Estimate of Postal Telegraph Receipts at Terminus ($)	Cities along Route	Estimated Receipts of Cities Along Route ($)	Estimated Receipts of Cities Along Route Relative to Aggregate Terminus Cities (%)
New York city to San Francisco	40,091.82	Pittsburg	4,078.24	8.6
		Indianapolis	2,116.94	4.5
	7,313.65	St. Louis	7,329.71	15.5
		Kansas city	5,242.76	11.1
Aggregated	47,405.47		18,767.65	39.6

Notes: Route is based on route used by Postal Telegraph-Commercial Cable from its 1906 Tariff Book. Postal Telegraph had two routes between New York and San Francisco. This table is based on the southern route. Receipts for Postal Telegraph-Commercial Cable are estimated from Western Union receipts in Appendix 2 using the assumption it captured 15% of receipts in the telegraph market. See Appendix 3 for full details of how the table was calculated and Appendix 5 for complete list of projected Postal Telegraph-Commercial Cable city receipts.

telegraph market. Instead, it concentrated on serving the larger commercial cities (Hochfelder, 2012, p. 39). So for Postal Telegraph-Commercial Cable to have captured 15%–25% of the overall revenue for the US telegraph market, it needed to capture an even larger percentage of the revenue earned in large commercial cities. Total reductions in receipts in Tables 3–6 are further underestimated because the estimates do not account for the expected decline of messages sent on Postal Telegraph-Commercial Cable telegraph lines from cities it continued to serve. Customers are less likely to use Postal Telegraph-Commercial Cable's network to send a telegram if it did not have an office at the final destination.

Table 6. Postal Telegraph-Commercial Cable Estimated 1908 October Receipts New York City to San Francisco-Northern Route.

Terminus of Route	Estimate of Postal Telegraph Receipts at Terminus ($)	Cities Along Route	Estimated Receipts of Cities Along Route ($)	Estimated Receipts of Cities Along Route Relative to Aggregate Terminus Cities (%)
New York city to San Francisco	40,091.82	Buffalo	3,018.18	6.4
		Cleveland	3,103.24	6.6
	7,313.65	Chicago	26,436.88	55.8
Aggregated	47,405.47		32,558.29	68.7

Notes: Route is based on route used by Postal Telegraph-Commercial Cable from its 1906 Tariff Book. Postal Telegraph had two routes between New York and San Francisco. This table is based on the northern route. Receipts for Postal Telegraph-Commercial Cable are estimated from Western Union receipts in Appendix 2 using the assumption it captured 15% of receipts in the telegraph market. See Appendix 3 for full details of how the table was calculated and Appendix 5 for complete list of projected Postal Telegraph-Commercial Cable city receipts.

12. CONCLUSION

The 1866 Post Roads Act exemplifies politicians' use of the central government to eliminate entry barriers erected by local governments. Telegraph entry barriers enacted by states and municipalities not only affected entry into their local markets but were also trade barriers that increased entry barriers for neighboring markets. Trade barriers by local governments reduce the economic gains of a common market and undermine market-preserving federalism (Hazlett, 2003; Weingast, 1992, 1995).

The 1866 Post Roads Act largely withstood efforts by states and municipalities to evade preemption by the central authority. Unlike federal preemption of the cable industry in the late 20th century, courts were empowered by the act to remove entry obstructions erected by local governments, ensuring telegraph companies were able to operate. Without the protection of the 1866 Post Roads Act, new telegraph companies would have been deterred by upfront expenditures that then would be sunk. Estimates assembled using early 20th century records specify the potential reduction in telegraph revenue caused by municipal entry barriers that would have been available to offset the sunk cost of telegraph construction. Projections of alternative telegraph routes to circumnavigate state entry barriers reveal the additional pole miles it would take to circumnavigate odious state entry barriers.

Devoid of central government protection, telecommunication companies will face local entry barriers. States and municipalities erected telegraph entry barriers prior to the 1866 Post Roads Act. They attempted to erect telegraph entry barriers after the passage of the act and imposed entry barriers upon early telephone companies not protected by the act (Gabel, 1994; John, 2010, pp. 278–279). States and municipalities continue to impose entry barriers on telephone, cable, and broadband companies in the late 20th century into the 21st century (Hazlett, 2007; Lyons, 2010). The 1866 Post Roads Act is a successful model on how the central government can safeguard the benefits of telecommunication competition from local governments.

NOTES

1. Tables tracking nonfranchise state telegraph regulations and their enactments can be found in Nommenmacher's (1996, 2001) "Law, Emerging Technology and Market Structure: The Development of the Telegraph Industry: 1838–1868," and "State Promotion and Regulation of the Telegraph Industry, 1845–1860."

2. A franchise is permission to operate a business, such as a telegraph company, within a geographical area, possibly for a limited period of time.

3. For examples, see: Telegraph: (This paper); Telephone Companies: David Gabel (1994) and Richard Gabel (1969); Cable TV Companies: Hazlett (1985–1986, 1986, 2007), Posner (1972), and Samon (2004); Cellular Companies: Hazlett (2003) and Shonafelt (2012).

4. Network industries' economic efficiency improved when it faced competition in the late-20th century (Shy, 2001, pp. 7–8).

5. Weingast states that under market preserving federalism, "the lower government are prevented from using their regulatory authority to erect trade barriers against the goods and services from other political units" (1992, p.10–11). Weingast cites Aranson as providing the best "statement of the economic effects of federalism." Aranson's most conservative definition of the boundary for the legit use of federal preemption of states is based on Chief Justice Marshall's inspection doctrine set forth in his opinion in Gibbons V. Ogden (1990, pp. 68–69). The federal government cannot preempt state inspection requirements because the inspection prepares products to be traded across state lines and does not restrict a common market. The federal government can preempt laws that interfere with engaging in commerce itself, such as state-granted monopoly, by "facilitate(ing) free trade" (p. 72).

6. See Honsowetz (2018) for empirical evidence supporting that after the passage of the 1866 Post Roads Act, Western Union faced multiple new entrants who repeatedly challenged Western Union for serving the US Telegraph Market.

7. David Gabel (1994) researched the effect municipal franchise regulations had on competition in the telephone industry, which was not preempted by the 1866 Post Roads Act since federal courts determined the 1866 Post Roads Act only applied to telegraph companies (City of Richmond v. Southern Bell, 1899; John, 2010, p. 278).

8. See Baumol, Panzar, and Willig's *Contestable Markets and the Theory of Industry Structure* (1982).

9. Troesken wrote that the franchise bidding process in the water industry from 1850 to 1899 was susceptible to political corruption (2006, pp. 263–264). Milo Maltbie, an advocate for reforming New York City's franchise process, was concerned that all franchises were susceptible to political corruption (1900, pp. 197–201).

10. See Gabel's (1994) work on the negative impact of franchise regulation on competition in the telephone industry to observe the potential of franchise regulations becoming an entry barrier for telegraph competition. State laws governing the telephone industry paralleled the telegraph industry since courts regularly interpreted state and municipal laws created for telegraph companies to also apply to telephone companies (Joyce & Joyce, 1907, p. 14). The exception was that the US Supreme Court ruled telephone industry was not granted any privileges by the 1866 Post Roads Act, so any entry barriers experienced by telephone companies would have likely also been applied to telegraph companies if the act had not been enacted (City of Richmond v. Southern Bell Telephone & Telegraph Co., 1899).

11. If the entry barriers in the political jurisdiction resulted in a telegraph network that required multiple telegraph companies to handle a telegram between destinations, then prices could exceed the monopoly price and quality could be less than a monopolist (Economides & Lehr, 1994; Nonnenmacher, 2006). A similar outcome can be observed in models of government tolling of trade routes along rivers (Gardner et al., 2002) or along roads (Karni & Chakrabarti, 1997).

12. The bill passed with 16 votes for, and 13 votes against, with 20 votes absent. The bill would have failed if two senators had elected to vote against the 1866 Post Roads Act instead of for the act (Congressional Globe 39th Congress, p. 3490).

13. The court based its ruling on Sec. 4. of the act "And be it further enacted, That before any telegraph company shall exercise any of the powers or privileges conferred by this act, such company shall file their written acceptance with the Postmaster-General of the restrictions and obligations required by this act." (14 U.S. Statute at Large 221 1863–1867).

14. This interpretation of the act was later upheld in 1878 by the US Supreme Court (Pensacola Telegraph Company v. Western Union Telegraph Company, 1877).

15. The exception being the state of California where state courts ruled a foreign telegraph company that acceded to the 1866 Post Roads Act could condemn right of way under California state laws (Cook, 1920, pp. 34, 47).

16. Examples: The state of California granted an exclusive right to the California Telegraph Company to serve a series of cities, including San Francisco and Sacramento, along a specific route (California State Telegraph Co. v. Alta Telegraph Co. 1863; Scott & Jarnagin, 1868, pp. 10–11). The state of Nevada granted a franchise to John Watson that stated no other competitor within Nevada could operate between two cites Watson served as long as Watson's telegraph company connected Humboldt County to San Francisco (Laws of the Territory of Nevada Passed at the Third Regular Session of the Legislative Assembly Chap. LXXII 1864; Western Union Telegraph Co. Appellant v. Atlantic and Pacific State Telegraph Co., Respondent 1869). The state of Maine granted the American Telegraph Company an exclusive franchise to land cables to handle telegraph messages destined to and from Europe (Blondheim, 1994, p. 114; Wolff, 2013, p. 40). Note that by 1866, Western Union had acquired the franchises owned by the California Telegraph Company, John Watson, and the American Telegraph Company (Reid, 1886, pp. 209, 503).

17. Although Simon G. Croswell considered the 1866 Post Roads Act a grant of a federal franchise in his book, *A Treatise on the Law Relating to Electricity* (1895), as did Archibald H. McMillian in his book, *Telephone Law* (1908, p. 47).

18. Examples of different requirements for different franchise holders can be found in the telephone industry, which faced similar state regulations as telegraph companies but did not qualify to benefit from any of the provisions in the 1866 Post Roads Act (City of Richmond v. Southern Bell Telephone & Telegraph Co. 1899; Cook, 1920, p. 78; Gabel, 1994).

19. A few of the states in 1920 that only allowed domestic telegraph companies to use eminent domain to acquire land included: Colorado, Ohio, Illinois, Pennsylvania, and Vermont (Union Pacific Railroad Company v. Colorado Postal Telegraph-Cable Company, 1902; Western Union Telegraph Company v. Pennsylvania Railroad Company 1904; Western Union Telegraph Company of Illinois, Appellant, v. The Louisville and Nashville Railroad Company et al. Appellees 1915; Cook, 1920, pp. 34–46).

20. Telegraph companies had consolidated to acquire market power and possibly more importantly, lower various transaction costs involved from interchanging telegram messages (Nonnenmacher, 1996, 2006). Interchange telegrams had a higher risk of a message being lost, and the lack of clear legal accountability prevented many customers from getting full refunds for lost messages. The extra costs to interchanging gave a single telegraph company a competitive edge over a network comprised of telegraph companies interchanging among themselves.

21. Large is a relative term; while their limited networks competed directly against Western Union, their scale of operations were many orders of magnitudes smaller than Western Union's.

22. That said, one might argue that an entrant looking to challenge Western Union needed to enter enough regional markets to prevent Western Union from generating the funds needed for a predatory pricing strategy from the regions without an active competitor.

23. The state statue for the franchise Nevada awarded Western Union an exclusive franchise to connect the state to particular cities in California and once that was completed, further awarded Western Union an exclusive franchise on all cities it connected in Nevada (Laws of the Territory of Nevada Passed at the Third Regular Session of the Legislative Assembly Chap. LXXII 1864). The Nevada Supreme Court described the franchise as being exclusive for the entire state in its ruling in the case Western Union Telegraph Co., Appellant, v. Atlantic and Pacific State Telegraph Co., Respondent (1869).

24. The US Telegraph Company built a competing telegraph line across the state of Nevada prior to the 1866 Post Roads Act (Reid, 1879, p. 521; Thompson, 1947, p. 404; Wolff, 2013, p. 86). It was able to cross Nevada in spite of Nevada's exclusive franchise granted to Western Union because the federal government granted the US Telegraph Company a federal franchise to connect particular territories west of the Mississippi River in the "Idaho Act" (Statues at Large, Chapter 220, 38th Congress first Session; Thompson, 1947, p. 404; Wolff, 2013, p. 76). The US Telegraph Company merged with Western Union in 1866 (Reid, 1879, p. 525).

25. To learn more about Jeremy Atack's GIS maps of the US railroad network see his article "On the Use of Geographic Information Systems in Economic History: The American Transportation Revolution Revisited" (2013).

26. This was an attempt because Florida granted the exclusive franchise after the passage of the 1866 Post Roads Act, so Western Union used the 1866 Post Roads Act to enter the market.

27. The complete list of offices and their earnings can be found in Appendix 1 and Appendix 2.

28. To estimate total monthly receipts for Western Union in October 1908, I divide the total 1908 fiscal year revenue for messages by 12.

29. Appendix 3 formally documents the steps I use to estimate Postal Telegraph-Commercial Cable's revenue in each city in which it competes with Western Union. Appendix 4 and Appendix 5 contain the estimates of revenue earned in each city by Postal Telegraph-Commercial Cable.

30. The report stated that Postal Telegraph-Commercial Cable handled 22,130,000 messages in 1908 and Western Union handled 62,371,287. This excludes messages sent on leased wires and messages handled for railroad companies.

31. Postal Telegraph-Commercial Cable also had a southern route that connected the two cities.

32. Postal Telegraph-Commercial Cable also had a northern route that connected the two cities.

REFERENCES

Aranson, P. H. (1990). Federalism: Doctrine against balance. In *Liberty Fund, INC. Symposium on Freedom and Federalism*, April 19 to 20, Arlington, VA. Unpublished Paper, special collections at the University of Rochester River Campus Libraries, Print.

Atack, J. (2013). On the use of geographic information systems in economic history: The American transportation revolution revisited. *The Journal of Economic History*, *73*(2), 313–338.

Atack, J. (2014a, December). Historical geographic information systems (GIS) database of U.S. Railroads for 1911. https://my.vanderbilt.edu/jeremyatack/data-downloads/

Atack, J. (2014b, December). Historical geographic information systems (GIS) database of U.S. Railroads for 1889. https://my.vanderbilt.edu/jeremyatack/data-downloads/

Atlantic and Pacific Telegraph Company v. Chicago Rock Island and Pacific Railroad Company. (1874, July). 2 Fed.Cas-12, Cass No. 632.

Baumol, W. J., Panzar, J. C., & Willig, R. D. (1982). *Contestable markets and the theory of industry structure*. Harcourt Brace Jovanovich, Inc.

Blondheim, M. (1994). *News over the wires*. Harvard University Press.

California State Telegraph Co. v. Alta Telegraph Co. (1863, July). 22 Cal. 398.

Carver v. The State. (1912). 11 Ga. App. 22.

City of Richmond v. Southern Bell Telephone and Telegraph Co. (1899, May 22). 19 S. Ct. 778, 43 L. Ed. 1162.

Commission for Environmental Cooperation (2010). North American Atlas.

Congressional Globe 39th Congress 1st Session. (1866). pp. 3075, 3077, 3428-3429, 3481-3489, 3745, and 3747. https://catalog.loc.gov/vwebv/search?searchCode=LCCN&searchArg=12036437&searchType=1&permalink=y. https://www.congress.gov/browse/39th-congress

Cook, W. W. (1920). *A treatise on Telegraph law*. Wm. Siegrist, Inc.

Croswell, S. G. (1895). *A treatise on the law relating to electricity*. Little, Brown, and Company.

Economides, N., & Lehr, W. (1994). The quality of complex systems and industry structure. In W. Lehr (Ed.), *Quality and reliability of telecommunications infrastructure*. Lawrence Erlbaum.

Ex parte Conway. (1891). 48 Fed. 77. https://case-law.vlex.com/vid/ex-parte-conway-893744666

Gabel, R. (1969). The early competitive era in telephone communication, 1893-1920. In C. C. Havighurst (Ed.), *Law and contemporary problems* (pp. 340–359). Spring. https://scholarship.law.duke.edu/lcp/vol34/iss2/8/

Gabel, D. (1994). Competition in a network industry: The telephone industry, 1894-1910. *The Journal of Economic History*, *54*(3), 543–572.

Gardner, R., Gaston, N., & Masson, R. T. (2002, August). Tolling the Rhine in 1254: Complementary monopoly revisited. Technical report, workshop in political theory and policy analysis. Indiana University.

Griswold, A. H., Gantt, R. A., Allsopp, C. B., Scovill, L. R., Kern, H. L., Strickland, C. H., & Leigh, W. E. (1930, May 20). *Memorandum of conference on railroad contracts held in Mr. Griswold's Office*, May 20, 1930. Western Union Telegraph Company Records 1820-1995 at The Smithsonian Lemelson Center for the Study of Invention & Innovation.

Gutiérrez, G. & Philippon, T. (2019, June). The failure of free entry. NBER Working Paper No. 26001. https://www.nber.org/papers/w26001

Hazlett, T. W. (1985-1986). Private monopoly and public interest: An economic analysis of the cable television franchise. *Pennsylvania Law Review*, 1335–1409.

Hazlett, T. W. (1986, April). Competition vs Franchise monopoly in cable television. *Contemporary Policy Issues*, *4*(2), 80–97.

Hazlett, T. W. (2003). Is federal preemption efficient in cellular phone regulation? *Federal Communications Law Journal*, *56*(1), 5.

Hazlett, T. W. (2007). Cable TV franchises as barriers to video competition. *Virginia Journal of Law and Technology*, *12*(2), 1–82.

Hochfelder, D. (2012). *The telegraph in America, 1832-1920*. The John Hopkins University Press.

Honsowetz, A. (2018). Federal preemption and competition in the post 1866 United States telegraph market. https://papers.ssrn.com/sol3/papers.cfm?abstract_id=2499856

Honsowetz, A. (2019). Pro-consumer legislation supported by elites: The curious case of the 1866 Post Roads Act. *Public Choice Analyses of American Economic History*, *3*, 88–102.

Interstate Commerce Commission. (1918). 'Private wire contracts,' case 5421. In *Interstate commerce commission reports* (Vol. 50). Government Publication Office.

John, R. (2010). *Network nation: Inventing American telecommunications*. The Belknap Press of Harvard University Press.

Jones, W. (1916). *A treatise of the law of telegraph and telephone companies: Including electric law* (2nd ed.). Vernon Law Book Company.

Joyce, J. A. (1914). *A treatise on franchises*. The Banks Law Publishing Company.

Joyce, J. A., & Joyce, H. C. (1907). *A treatise on electric law comprising the law governing all electric corporations uses and appliances also all relative public and private rights* (2nd ed., Vol. 1). The Banks Law Publishing Co.

Karni, E., & Chakrabarti, S. K. (1997). Political structure, taxes and trade. *Journal of Public Economics*, *64*, 241–258.

Katz, M. L., & Shapiro, C. (1985). Network externalities, competition and compatibility. *The American Economic Review*, *75*(3), 424–440.

Liebowitz, S. J., & Margolis, S. E. (1994). Network externality: An uncommon tragedy. *The Journal of Economic Perspectives*, *8*(2), 133–150.

Lindley, L. G. (1971). *The constitution faces technology: The relationship of the national government to the telegraph, 1866-1884*. Diss. Rice U.

Lyons, D. A. (2010). Technology convergence and federalism: Who should decide the future of telecommunications regulation? *University of Michigan Journal of Law Reform*, *43*(2), 383-434.

Maltbie, M. R. (1900). A century of franchise history. In *The history of public franchises in New York city (Boroughs of Manhattan and the Bronx)* (pp. 194–206). Reform Club Committee on City Affairs.

Masten, S. E. (2010). Public utility ownership in 19th-century America: The "Aberrant" case of water. *Journal of Law, Economics, and Organization*, *27*(3), 604–654.

McMillian, A. H. (1908). *Telephone law: The organization and operation of telephone companies*. McGraw Publishing Company.

Myers, G. (1900). *The history of public franchises in New York city (Boroughs of Manhattan and the Bronx)*. Reform Club Committee on City Affairs.

New England Telegraph Co. of Massachusetts v. Town of Essex. (1913). 206 Fed. 926.

Nonnenmacher, T. W. (1996). *Law, emerging technology and market structure: The development of the telegraph industry: 1838-1868*. Diss. U of Illinois at Urbana-Champaign.

Nonnenmacher, T. W. (2001). State promotion and regulation of the telegraph industry, 1845-1860. *The Journal of Economic History*, *61*(1), 19–36.

Nonnenmacher, T. W. (2006). Network quality in the early telegraph industry. *Research in Economic History*, *23*, 61–82.

Nye, J. V. C. (2007). *War, wine and taxes: The political economy of Anglo-French trade*. Princeton University Press.

Pensacola Telegraph Company v. Western Union Telegraph Company. (1877, March). 96 U.S. 1; 24 L. Ed. 708 Supreme Court of the United States.

Posner, R. A. (1972). The appropriate scope of regulation in the cable television industry. *Bell Journal of Economics and Management Science*, *3*(1), 98–129.

Postal Telegraph-Cable Company. (1904, January). *Postal telegraph cable company list of offices*. James Kempster Print.

Postal Telegraph-Cable Company. (1906, January). *Postal telegraph cable company list of offices*. James Kempster Print.

Reid, J. D. (1879). *The telegraph in America* (1st ed.). Weed, Parsons and Company.

Reid, J. D. (1886). *The telegraph in America and Morse Memorial* (2nd ed.). John Polhemus Publisher.

Samon, J. E. (2004). When "Yes" means no: The subjugation of competition and consumer choice by exclusive municipal cable franchises. *Seton Hall Law Review*, *34*(2), 7.

Scott, W. L., & Jarnagin, M. P. (1868). *A treatise upon the law of telegraphs; with an appendix, containing the general statutory provisions of England, Canada, the United States, and the States of the Union, upon the subject of telegraphs*. Little, Brown, and Company.

Senate Document. (1909, February 16). *Investigation of Western Union and Postal Telegraph-cable companies*. No. 725 Vol. 14, 60th Congress 2nd Session. https://books.google.com/books?id=RmHSoAEACAAJ&dq=Investigation+of+Western+Union+and+Postal+Telegraphcable+companies&hl=en&newbks=1&newbks_redir=0&sa=X&ved=2ahUKEwiE2bXLlZKJAxXkF1kFHQukMiQQ6AF6BAgMEAE

Sherman, J. to Cooke, J. (1866, July 30). *Jay Cooke papers at the historical society of Pennsylvania*.

Shonafelt, M. W. (2012). Whose streets? California public utilities code section 7901 in the wireless age. *Hastings Communication and Entertainment Law Journal*, *35*, 371.

Shy, O. (2001). *The economics of network industries*. Cambridge University Press.

Shy, O. (2011). A short survey of network economics. *Review of Industrial Organizations*, *38*, 119–149.

Thompson, R. L. (1947). *Wiring a continent: The history of the telegraph industry in the United States 1832-1866*. Princeton University Press.

Town of Essex v. New England Telegraph Company of Massachusetts. (1916, December). 239 U.S. 313 Supreme Court of the United States.

Troesken, W. (1996). *Why regulate utilities?: The New institutional economics and Chicago gas industry, 1849-1924*. University of Michigan Press.

Troesken, W. (1997). The sources of public ownership: Historical evidence from the gas industry. *Journal of Law, Economics, and Organization*, *13*(1), 1–25.

Troesken, W. (2006). Regime change and corruption: A history of public utility regulation. In E. L. Glaeser & C. Goldin (Eds.), *Corruption and reform: Lessons from America's economic history* (pp. 259–281). University of Chicago Press.

Troesken, W., & Geddes, R. (2003). Municipalizing American waterworks, 1897-1915. *Journal of Law, Economics, and Organization*, *19*(2), 373–400.

Tullock, G. (1967). The welfare costs of tariffs, monopolies, and theft. *Western Economic Journal*, *5*(3), 224–232.

Union Pacific Railroad Company v. Colorado Postal Telegraph-Cable Company (1902). 30 Co. 133.

United States Census Bureau. (1975). Chapter R: Communications. In *Historical statistics of the United States, colonial times to 1970, Bicentennial Edition, Part 2*. U.S. Government Printing Office.

Weingast, B. R. (1992). The economic role of political institutions. Institute for Policy Reform Working Paper Series. https://ageconsearch.umn.edu/record/294809?v=pdf

Weingast, B. R. (1995). The economic role of political institutions: Market preserving federalism and economic development. *Journal of Law, Economics, and Organization, 11*(1), 1–31.

Western Union Telegraph Co., Appellant, v. Atlantic and Pacific State Telegraph Co., Respondent. (1869, April). 5 Nev. 102. Supreme Court of Nevada.

Western Union Telegraph Company. (1901–1908). *Statistical notebook 1901-1908.* Western Union Telegraph Company Records 1820-1995 at The Smithsonian Lemelson Center for the Study of Invention & Innovation.

Western Union Telegraph Company. (1934). *The Western Union telegraph company's general agreements with railroads.* The Smithsonian Lemelson Center for the Study of Invention & Innovation.

Western Union Telegraph Company of Illinois, Appellant, v. The Louisville and Nashville Railroad Company et al. Appellees. (1915). 270 Ill. 399.

Western Union Telegraph Company v. City of Richmond. (1909). 178 Fed. 310.

Western Union Telegraph Company v. Pennsylvania Railroad Company. (1904, December). 195 U.S. 594; 25 L. Ed. 332, Supreme Court of the United States.

Western Union Telegraph Co. v. American Union Telegraph Co. et al. (1879, July). 29 F. Cas 790. Federal Circuit Court, D. Indiana.

Wolff, J. D. (2013). *Western Union and the creation of the American corporate order, 1845-1893.* Cambridge University Press.

APPENDIX 1
WESTERN UNION 1904 TELEGRAPH RECEIPTS BY CITY

City	Dollar Value	Percent of Total Receipts
Baltimore	$200,154	1%
Boston	$469,830	2.3%
Buffalo	$187,476	0.9%
Chicago	$1,586,977	7.9%
Cincinnati	$304,084	1.5%
Cleveland	$190,839	1%
Denver	$181,572	0.9%
Kansas city	$303,274	1.5%
Los Angeles	$213,528	1.1%
Minneapolis	$220,826	1.1%
New York city	$296,983	1.5%
New Orleans	$2,354,128	11.8%
Philadelphia	$435,711	2.2%
Pittsburgh	$261,896	1.3%
San Francisco	$469,155	2.3%
St. Louis	$604,603	3%
Washington DC	$200,020	1%
Rest of country	$11,538,178	57.6%

Notes: Data are from the Western Union Telegraph Company (1901–1908). The cities listed are the 17 largest Western Union offices in terms of receipts. Records are unclear if receipts are for the 1904 Western Union fiscal year or calendar year.

APPENDIX 2
FORTY-FIVE LARGEST WESTERN UNION OFFICES BY OCTOBER 1908 OFFICE RECEIPTS

Rank	City, State	Receipts
1	New York, NY	$227,187
2	Chicago, IL	$149,809
3	Boston, MA	$44,098
4	St. Louis, MO	$41,535
5	San Francisco, CA	$41,444
6	Philadelphia, PA	$38,079
7	Kansas city, MO	$29,709
8	Cincinnati, OH	$26,645
9	New Orleans, LA	$26,225
10	Pittsburgh, PA	$23,110
11	Minneapolis, MN	$23,009
12	Los Angeles, CA	$21,343
13	Washington, DC	$19,638
14	Cleveland, OH	$17,585
15	Denver, CO	$17,367
16	Buffalo, NY	$17,103
17	Baltimore, MD	$16,325
18	Detroit, MI	$15,631
19	Seattle, WA	$15,298
20	Milwaukee, WI	$13,548
21	Omaha, NE	$12,588
22	Louisville, KY	$12,428
23	Portland, OR	$12,167
24	Indianapolis, IN	$11,996
25	Atlanta, GA	$11,131
26	St. Paul, MN	$10,979
27	Dallas, TX	$9,725
28	Duluth, MN	$9,705
29	Memphis, TN	$8,631
30	Columbus, OH	$7,920
31	Houston, TX	$7,797
32	Fort Worth, TX	$7,416
33	Spokane, WA	$7,407
34	Salt Lake City, UT	$7,080
35	Savannah, GA	$6,910
36	Rochester, NY	$6,387
37	Nashville, TN	$5,785
38	Toledo, OH	$5,759

(Continued)

Rank	City, State	Receipts
39	Jacksonville, FL	$5,730
40	San Antonio, TX	$5,529
41	Richmond, VA	$5,455
42	Goldfield, NV	$5,364
43	Galveston, TX	$5,276
44	Birmingham, AL	$5,044
45	Newark, NJ	$5,042

Notes: Data are from the Western Union Telegraph Company (1901–1908). Receipts listed in the table are for all telegraph offices earning $5,000 or more in receipts for the month of October in 1908.

APPENDIX 3
FORMULA FOR ESTIMATING POSTAL TELEGRAPH-COMMERCIAL CABLE CITY RECEIPTS

Let $I = \{i_1, \ldots, i_n\}$ denote different locations served by Postal Telegraph-Commercial Cable (Postal) and Western Union. Receipts used are listed in Appendices 1 and 2. Western Union estimated 68.9% of its receipts in cities served by Postal were to locations also served by Western Union is used in Eq. (2) (Western Union 1901–1908).

1. W_i = Western Union receipts at location i
2. $C_i = W_i*68.9\%$ = Western Union receipts at location i to location served by Postal

Let S_i denote the share of the total receipts earned by Western Union where S_i is $0 \leq S_i \leq 1$. Let $1-S_i$ denote the share of the receipts earned by Postal.

3. $T_i = C_i * \left(\frac{1}{S_i}\right)$ = Total estimated competitive receipts for Postal and Western Union
4. $P_i = T_i*(1-S_i)$ = Postal estimated receipts at location i

APPENDIX 4
POSTAL TELEGRAPH-COMMERCIAL CABLE ANNUAL RECEIPTS ESTIMATES BY CITY IN 1904

City	With 15% of Market	With 25% of Market
Baltimore	$24,336.37	$45,968.70
Boston	$57,125.80	$107,904.29
Buffalo	$22,794.88	$43,056.99
Chicago	$192,957.73	$364,475.72
Cincinnati	$36,973.04	$69,837.96
Cleveland	$23,203.78	$43,829.36
Denver	$22,077.02	$41,701.04
Kansas city	$36,874.55	$69,651.93
Los Angeles	$25,962.49	$49,040.26
Minneapolis	$26,849.84	$50,716.37
New Orleans	$36,109.64	$68,207.10
New York city	$286,234.27	$540,664.73
Philadelphia	$52,977.33	$100,068.29
Pittsburgh	$31,843.47	$60,148.78
San Francisco	$57,043.73	$107,749.27
St. Louis	$73.512.61	$138,857.16
Washington DC	$24,320.08	$45,937.93

Notes: Data are from the Western Union Telegraph Company (1901–1908). The cities listed are the 17 largest Western Union offices in terms of receipts. Records are unclear if receipts are for the 1904 Western Union fiscal year or calendar year. Estimates are based on the methodology set forth in Appendix 3. With 15% of the market means 15% of the market Western Union estimated it competed with Postal Telegraph-Commercial Cable.

APPENDIX 5
POSTAL TELEGRAPH-COMMERCIAL CABLE RECEIPTS ESTIMATES BY CITY IN OCTOBER 1908

City, State	With 15% of Market	With 25% of Market
Atlanta, GA	$1,964.29	$3,710.33
Baltimore, MD	$2,880.88	$5,441.67
Birmingham, AL	$890.12	$1,681.33
Boston, MA	$7,782.00	$14,699.33
Buffalo, NY	$3,018.18	$5,701.00
Chicago, IL	$26,436.88	$49,936.33
Cincinnati, OH	$4,702.06	$8,881.67

(Continued)

City, State	With 15% of Market	With 25% of Market
Cleveland, OH	$3,103.24	$5,861.67
Columbus, OH	$1,397.65	$2,640.00
Denver, CO	$3,064.76	$3,241.67
Detroit, MI	$2,758.41	$5,210.33
Duluth, MN	$1,712.65	$3,235.00
Fort Worth, TX	$1,308.71	$2,472.00
Galveston, TX	$931.06	$1,758.67
Houston, TX	$1,375.94	$2,599.00
Indianapolis, IN	$2,116.94	$3,998.67
Jacksonville, FL	$1,011.18	$1,910.00
Kansas city, MO	$5,242.76	$9,903.00
Los Angeles, CA	$3,766.41	$7,114.33
Louisville, KY	$2,193.18	$4,142.67
Memphis, TN	$1,523.12	$2,877.00
Milwaukee, WI	$2,390.82	$4,516.00
Minneapolis, MN	$4,060.41	$7,669.67
Nashville, TN	$1,020.88	$1,928.33
New Orleans, LA	$4,627.94	$8,741.67
New York city, NY	$40,091.82	$75,729.00
Newark, NJ	$889.76	$1,680.67
Omaha, NE	$2,221.41	$4,196.00
Philadelphia, PA	$6,719.82	$12,693.00
Pittsburgh, PA	$4,078.24	$7,703.33
Portland, OR	$2,147.12	$4,055.67
Richmond, VA	$962.65	$1,181.33
Rochester, NY	$1,127.12	$2,219.00
Salt Lake City, UT	$1,249.41	$2,360.00
San Antonio, TX	$975.71	$1,843.00
San Francisco, CA	$7,313.65	$13,814.67
Savannah, GA	$1,219.41	$2,303.33
Seattle, WA	$2,699.65	$5,099.33
Spokane, WA	$1,307.12	$2,469.00
St. Louis, MO	$7,329.71	$13,659.67
St. Paul, MN	$1,937.47	$3,659.67
Toledo, OH	$1,016.29	$1,919.67
Washington, DC	$3,465.53	$6,546.00

Notes: Data are from the Western Union Telegraph Company (1901–1908). Receipts listed in the table are for all telegraph offices earning $5,000 or more in receipts for the month of October in 1908 that was also served by Postal Telegraph-Commercial Cable.

THE ANATOMY OF A POLICY FAILURE: NIXON'S ATTEMPT TO CONTROL INFLATION

Burton A. Abrams and James L. Butkiewicz

University of Delaware, USA

ABSTRACT

Richard Nixon and his advisors were aware of the inherent economic problems of wage–price controls: suppressed inflation, shortages, biases, avoidance, cheating, etc. Nixon's secret White House tapes reveal that Nixon disliked controls, never expecting them to extinguish inflation but only agreed to them to deflect attention from devaluation of the dollar. The political popularity of his controls changed his view of them, even producing a second freeze on retail prices in 1973. Importantly, the tapes reveal that Nixon pushed for inflationary monetary policies long after his 1972 reelection. Federal Reserve Chair, Arthur Burns, seemingly capitulated to Nixon's pressures by restraining interest rate increases in Federal Open Market Committee meetings. Politics won out over economics. Nixon and his advisors avoided addressing the reason for increasing inflation – the monetary expansion that Nixon pressured Arthur Burns to pursue in support of his 1972 re-election – an expansion that continued long after the election. This tragic policy failure was avoidable had the administration focused on controlling the true cause of the inflation.

Keywords: Inflation; wage–price controls; monetary policy; political business cycle; Nixon's White House tapes

JEL codes: E52; E58; E64; G28; H11; N1

1. INTRODUCTION

The 1970s proved to be the worst decade for US inflation in the 20th century. During the decade, many explanations were offered for the government's

Research in Economic History, Volume 38, 157–180
Copyright © 2025 Burton A. Abrams and James L. Butkiewicz
Published under exclusive licence by Emerald Publishing Limited
ISSN: 0363-3268/doi:10.1108/S0363-326820250000038006

inability to extinguish inflation; oil price increases, budget deficits, the Vietnam War, labor union strikes, meat shortages, monopoly power of large firms and unions, inflationary expectations, etc. Near the end of the decade, President Jimmy Carter in a nationally televised address exclaimed:

> Inflation is obviously a serious problem. What is the solution? I do not have all the answers. Nobody does. Perhaps there is no complete or adequate answer. But I want to let you know that fighting inflation will be a central preoccupation of mine during the months ahead and I want to arouse the nation to join me in this effort.[1]

Inflation worsened and Carter failed in his reelection bid in 1980.

Missing from the litany of the government's explanations for the decade of inflation is what we believe to be the single most important factor, excessively expansionary monetary policy. Numerous studies now support the monetary explanation for inflation in the 1970s (see, e.g., Barsky & Killian, 2001; Bernanke & Mihov, 1998; Clarida et al., 2000; Nelson, 2022; Orphanides, 2003; Romer & Romer, 2002). Previous investigation of the Nixon tapes revealed how Richard Nixon pressured Arthur Burns, Chairman of the Federal Reserve, to keep interest rates low and the money supply growing robustly despite warnings from Burns himself and Milton Friedman, the leading economist for a monetary explanation for inflation (Abrams, 2006; Abrams & Butkiewicz, 2012, 2017).

To enhance his reelection chances and to allegedly fight inflation, Nixon initiated the most intrusive peacetime price controls in US history. Starting on August 15, 1971, Phase I imposed a 90-day freeze on wages and prices. Phases II, III and IV plus a second price freeze followed. A new bureaucracy was formed: A Cost of Living Council, a Pay Board, a Price Commission and a Committee on Interest and Dividends. The various positions and personnel are listed in Table 1. On April 30, 1974, after nearly 3 years of operation, the Cost of Living Council was disbanded, effectively ending price controls except for those on energy that persisted for another year and a half. To say that Nixon's price control experiment ended in failure would be an understatement.

Previous work on Nixon's wage and price controls using his secret White House tapes ended with his announcement of the 90-day freeze on wages and prices (Abrams & Butkiewicz, 2017). Much more of the story is revealed on subsequent recordings. The tapes provide firsthand observation of backroom dealings and positions taken by Nixon and his advisors. We have reviewed relevant conversations and have uncovered confirmation of previous reports by others and some startling new aspects of the experiment in price controls.

Nixon never expected his price controls would solve the inflation problem. His disdain for controls changed abruptly when they proved politically popular. This paved the way for a second freeze, this time just on retail prices, despite objections from his economic advisors. The tapes also reveal new information on behind the scenes political machinations: an "inspired" leak of information to favored news sources and a plot to politicize the Bureau of Labor Statistics through reorganization with party loyalists. Form won out over substance: "just say it's working [price controls]," Nixon tells economic advisor Herbert Stein before his press conference; Nixon tells a senator who is being pressured by

Table 1. Nixon's Wage and Price Controls.

Phases:

Phase I. August 15, 1971. 90-day freeze on wages and prices (freeze 1)

Phase II. November 14, 1971. Pay Board's instructions were to bring down inflation to 2–3% by the end of 1972, set ceiling for pay raises at 5.5% for largest corporations and unions.

Phase III. January 11, 1973. Pay board dissolved. Voluntary controls on wages and prices.

Freeze 2. June 13, 1973, 60-day freeze of retail prices (freeze 2)

Phase IV. August 13, 1973.

April 30, 1974, cost of living Council abolished; authority for wage and price controls expired.

Organizations and players:

Cost of Living Council. Chairman John Connally, director Donald Rumsfeld. Charged with overseeing the goals of the economic stabilization program.

Pay Board. Chairman Judge George H. Boldt. Fifteen members, five each from the public, business and labor. Subject to majority voting rule.

Price Commission. Chairman C. Jackson Grayson. Seven members "representative of the general public." Chair appointed by president. Subject to majority voting rule. Oversaw price increases in the regulated sector.

The Committee on Interest and Dividends. Chair of the board of Governors to serve as Chair (Arthur Burns). Instructions: to obtain voluntary restraints on interest rates and dividends.

constituents for interest rate controls to "Give them the gobbly gook that we're doing something." Abandoning his economic common sense in favor of political gain, Nixon inquires why a new price freeze on food can't be initiated.

The tapes confirm the irreconcilable differences between special interest groups on the Pay Board making it totally ineffective. Importantly, Nixon's most senior staff demonstrated a misunderstanding of inflation and, with few exceptions, those members of the administration who knew better avoided identifying monetary policy as the primary source of the inflation. Nixon, looking ahead to the 1974 mid-term elections, continued to push for expansionary monetary policy after his 1972 reelection.

Romer and Romer (2002) suggest politics may have played a role in the Federal Reserve's inability to extinguish inflation, but that the evidence is limited. The tapes produce new evidence of the importance of politics in explaining the monetary policy failure. Nixon made it known to his advisors that he didn't want a tight monetary policy to derail the economic boom. Of his advisors only George Shultz and Herbert Stein dared raise the possibility, quickly dropped, that the inflation was being fueled by a too expansionary monetary policy. Nixon's other advisors were either unconvinced or ignorant of the money-inflation linkage or feared raising the issue given their knowledge of Nixon's insistence on easy money. In any event, Arthur Burns, Chair of the Federal Reserve, seemingly capitulated to pressure from Nixon to restrain interest rate increases needed to fight inflationary pressures. All told, this set the stage for continued inflation throughout the decade. In the sections that follow, we review the conversations that highlight the machinations and misunderstandings and errors of commission and omission that contributed to the policy failure to control inflation and we reinforce the case for the monetary explanation for inflation during the 1970s.

Only President Nixon and the tape installer, Alexander Butterfield, were aware that conversations in the White House were being taped. Although Nixon had full knowledge of the taping, his conversations were seemingly unrestrained. His vocal criticisms of staff and opponents, his antisemitic remarks, his plots at dirty trickery, his unpresidential vulgarisms and, of course, his role in the Watergate break in suggest that he himself forgot or certainly never expected the tapes to be heard publicly.

The recent passing of George Shultz (February 6, 2021) and Donald Rumsfeld (June 30, 2021) reminds us that nearly all the key players on the tapes are gone. But the tapes remain, giving us insight into what really happened, how and why the wage and price controls failed, and important lessons for the future. The following are summaries and quotes from key taped conversations that followed the imposition of the 1971 wage and price freeze.

Section 6.2 chronicles conversations during the 90-day freeze. Section 6.3 reviews Phase II conversations. Conversations about Phase III and its failures are discussed in Section 6.4. Section 6.5 covers conversations during Freeze II until the end of taped conversations. Section 6.6 concludes.

2. CONVERSATIONS DURING PHASE I: A 90-DAY FREEZE ON WAGES AND PRICES (AUGUST 15, 1971, TO NOVEMBER 15, 1971)

White House Tapes, Conversation 008-016 (August 16, 1971) The day after the imposition of the freeze.

Richard Nixon holds a telephone conversation with his speechwriter William Safire. Nixon has received advanced word that the latest GNP numbers are surprisingly good, better than what he had hoped. He seeks Safire's help in leaking the good news to friendly media a day earlier than the official release. As the official release was scheduled for Friday, a Thursday release would allow friendly media a head start in "hopping and thinking" on the favorable news before the weekend. Nixon calls his early release strategy an "inspired leak," but such a leak runs the risk of illegal insider trading.

Nixon tells Safire about the unexpected good GNP number.

Nixon: "Well, they've just done the revised figure, and it's 30.8."[2]

Safire: "Boy, oh, boy."

Nixon: ". . .Here's what I have in mind: First of all, it is not to be released until [*unclear*]. It isn't to be released until Friday. And I learned the figure yesterday, and I said to him [George Shultz, Director of the Office of Management and Budget and later Secretary of the Treasury], now look here, they ought to release it. They can't sit on a figure this long. . .Second point – I agree on this point. I don't think we ought to try to get her out and trumpet it, you know, and this and that and the other thing, because I think it speaks for itself quite loudly. On the other hand, it is one of those things where any individual who can be absolutely trusted that we know on the economic side, should sort of pick it up. It will not go unnoticed. Now, the other thing is that it's particularly important that it get in the news magazines, see – "

Safire: "Right."

Nixon: "–now coming out Friday and so forth. And I think a little leakage to the two news magazines on Thursday, you know, might start them hopping and thinking and so forth."

Safire: "OK. Right, I – "

Nixon: "Oh, and *US News*. Oh, [White House Chief of Staff] Bob Haldeman is sitting here, and he says *US News* closes, of course, Thursday or Friday. So, what I'd like for you to do is to jump up over there and have a talk with George [Shultz]."

Safire: "Right."

Nixon: "And do some thinking about how it ought to be, how we can get it out best and get the biggest well, you know, I mean, it should not be, I think the way to do it when you've got, I mean, when the news is really good, is not to brag too much about it."

Safire: "Well, in other words, to handle it with some subtlety but make sure [*unclear*] –"

Nixon: "Some subtleties that will hypo it, you see, because this isn't sensational, but it's very good. I mean, when you go – you remember that was the number we were hoping we'd get in the first instance, was 30…. And it might be – now the only problem that I was even thinking with one like this, the inspired leak thing, the difficulty with that is that we've got other kinds of figures of this sort that we do not want to [*chuckles*] use inspired leaks on, you know what I mean?"

Safire: "Right."

Nixon: "So, I don't know if that's it. But I do think that the little conversation with regard to getting it around – when you get the solid figure to people that…you know the types of people I'm talking about, there's *US News*, there's *Time*, there's *Newsweek*. You might talk to [White House news consultant John A.] Scali and see what – well, for example, now there's one I know you can get a good ride on, you know, they've that fellow [Louis] Rukeyser."[3]

Safire: "Right, ABC."

Nixon: "ABC, who's our friend."

Safire: "Right."

Nixon: "He'll write it like hell, but if he just gets it the day, you know, if you tell him Thursday in advance, he'll get ready and put out a good little story on it."

White House Tapes, Conversation 9-99 (September 20, 1971). Nearly 5 weeks into the wage and price freeze.

Nixon complains to Charles Colson (Director of the Office of Public Liaison) that he believes false data are being released by the Bureau of Labor Statistics (BLS). Nixon notes that 19 of the 21 BLS staff are Jewish and the Commissioner of BLS, Geoffrey Moore, is weak and easily manipulated by his staff. Particularly irritating to Nixon is a headline in *The Star* [Washington Star newspaper], "Prices Edge Up Despite Freeze."

Colson and Nixon work on a plan to place a loyalist below BLS Commissioner Geoffrey Moore – a loyalist who will see that the *correct* numbers [emphasis added] are released by the BLS.

Colson: "Harold Pastor's assistant is one of the ones we want to bring over [to BLS]. He's totally political. He's done miracles with the figures out of [the Department of] Commerce. You don't see any bad figures out of Commerce anymore. He knows how to do it."

Nixon: "That's right."

Later, Nixon: "Reorganization in BLS is the most important thing we can do."

Colson: "We've got to challenge the bastards."

Nixon: "Not only challenge them but where you've got to make a judgement call whether the point is up or down. Sometimes if it's at 0.6 of a percent and you make a call to round it up or below. Well, god dammit just round it below."

Just a few months later, the Administration's reorganization of the Bureau of Labor Statistics moved two of Nixon's targets, Harold Goldstein, Assistant Commissioner of the BLS, and Chief Economist Peter Henle, out of meaningful jobs.[4] Nixon does indeed get rid of Moore in January 1973 by requiring all top appointees to submit resignation letters. Moore's is one that Nixon accepts.

White House Tapes, Conversation 9-122 (September 22, 1971)

Nixon notes that Leonard Woodcock, President of the United Auto Workers, and George Meany, President of the AFL-CIO, and representatives on the Pay Board, have been vocal in complaining about the rise in corporate profits. Nixon asks George Shultz if they need to treat them with "kid gloves" to keep them from resigning from the Board. Shultz responds in the negative saying if Meany and Woodcock want to keep their union members employed and happy, they need to be working for profitable companies. Shultz indicates he will see that Meany and Woodcock get the message.

White House Tapes, Conversation 584-3 (October 5, 1971) – Five weeks remaining on the wage and price freeze.

Nixon meets with John Connally (Secretary of the Treasury), Shultz, Paul McCracken (outgoing Chair of the Council of Economic Advisers) and Herbert Stein (incoming Chair of the Council of Economic Advisers) to discuss plans for Phase II. The primary goal of Phase II is to bring the inflation rate down to between 2–3% by the end of 1972. The consensus is that wage contracts previously agreed to may make this unachievable. They discuss possible strategies to finesse the problem including getting labor to "rollback" previously agreed to wage increases or get labor to delay wage increases until after the election, now over 1 year away. Nixon, rather naively, asks why businesses couldn't start lowering prices.

Substantial thought and discussion went into the timing, content and length of Nixon's initial announcement of Phase II. Nixon said his televised time should be under 15 minutes. For maximum impact, it was decided the announcement would be made in "prime time." Care was taken to make sure the announcement did not conflict with any televised baseball game. Nixon said the details of Phase II would be left to Connally to explain the next day. Nixon would emphasize that Phase II is merely a continuation of the already successful Phase I and that he would call on all Americans for their continued help in supporting Phase II. As we show below, labor had a different agenda.

White House Tapes, Conversation 581-11 (September 30, 1971)

Nixon received the preliminary report on the Boards and Commissions that would transition the economy from the Freeze into the "thaw." The report calls for a Cost of Living Council overseeing the Boards and Commissions. The proposal calls for a Price/Cost/Profits Board, a Pay Board and a Rent Board. The Pay Board in this preliminary report would remain essentially unchanged in name and substance. Shultz explains that it will be a tripartite board including equal numbers of public, labor and business representatives. Interestingly, Shultz, in a prescient moment, goes on to say why he thinks the Pay Board will fail; labor will make unrealistic demands and the business and public representatives will object and labor will walk off the board.

The intricacies and difficulties in even assigning names to the boards lead Nixon to exclaim that all of this will have to be explained to the public by Connally. Later, an exasperated Nixon exclaims... "This whole damn thing contradicts our basic philosophy." He then states "We're leading a monster...but it could be worse if we don't do this..." Nixon envisions the Democrat-dominated Congress setting up a more permanent price regulation scheme.

When discussing interest rate controls, Shultz recommends putting Arthur Burns in charge. "Why?" asks Nixon. Shultz replies... "Because to keep interest rates down he'll have to increase the money supply." The men laugh. Both Nixon and Shultz have been pressuring Burns to keep interest rates low and to boost the money supply. John Connally, Chair of the proposed Cost of Living Council, had been designated to oversee interest rates. Arthur Burns now gets the position.

White House Tapes, Conversation 10-121 (October 7, 1971)

Nixon and Burns confer on the telephone. Burns congratulates Nixon on reaching a plan for Phase II. Nixon asks Burns if he is comfortable with heading the Committee on Interest and Dividends. Burns mentions he thought about passing this position off to Maurice Stans, then US Secretary of Commerce. Nixon strongly opposes this saying a Stans committee did not have the "moral authority" of a Burns committee. Nixon points out that the position is "pure jawboning" anyway. Nixon mentions that even conservative Senator John McClellan came to tell Nixon something had to be done about interest rates. Nixon tells McClellan to tell those pressuring him (McClellan) for interest rate controls... "Give them the gobbly gook that we're doing something."

White House Tapes, Conversation 287-21 (October 11, 1971)

Nixon, Shultz and Donald Rumsfeld (Counselor to the President and soon-to-be Director of the Cost of Living Council) discuss issues relating to the upcoming Phase II. Nixon tells the incoming Director of the Cost of Living Council to "deregulate as fast as you can" if the inflation rate is held down to below 4% and the unemployment rate falls to 5%. "As fast as you get it regulated, deregulate it. Make people think we're doing everything we can but do as little as possible."

Nixon explains his concern that wage and price controls could become a business "crutch" and so he wants to deregulate as soon as possible.

> *Nixon*: "...If everybody in the country wanted wage and price controls therefore we should give it to them...I never thought that because I know they wouldn't work...but we were triggered into it by that damn international problem....we're getting some political benefit out of it [controls]...the economic issue is not nearly as potent against us as it was. Wouldn't you agree?"[5]

> Rumsfeld agrees.

> *Nixon*: "People think we're trying. We can ride that for a while but in the final analysis, what counts is what works.... For a while now we've got to create the impression that we're all working together."

Butkiewicz and Ohlmacher (2021) detail the important role of the "international problem" in triggering wage–price controls to deflect attention away from the end of dollar convertibility into gold.

White House Tapes, Conversation 303-9 (October 26, 1971)

Nixon, Connally and Shultz focus discussions on international exchange rates. The 90-day freeze on prices and wages has been in place for over 70 days and no concern for inflation is raised. In fact, Nixon states his now well-known preference for inflation over unemployment. He relates what happened as a result of a too tight monetary policy in 1960 (leading to a Nixon election defeat).

> *Nixon*: "We're not going to let this happen again this year, John [Connally]."

This reinforces the view that Nixon cared little about fighting inflation and that the wage and price controls were established for the benefit of public relations.

White House Tapes, Conversation 13-22 (October 27, 1971)

Nixon discusses the Pay Board with Shultz. He would like to get an agreement on the Pay Board to defer wage increases to avoid what the public would see as "a total cave-in to Meany."

The end of the 90-day freeze is a little over 2 weeks away. The freeze has held up labor's previously negotiated wage increases. Meany and other labor leaders plan to enforce those contracts when the freeze ends. These increases will be substantially in excess of the guidelines set by Phase II.

White House Tapes, Conversation 618-32 (November 15, 1971) – 90-day wage and price freeze ends.

Nixon has a short meeting with a photographer and the key heads of Phase II organizations: Judge George H. Boldt (Chairman of the Pay Board), C. Jackson Grayson (Chairman of the Price Commission), and Donald Rumsfeld (Director of the Cost of Living Council). Judge Boldt expresses his optimism for canceling retroactive pay increases that are scheduled to take place. While he admits to the sanctity of contracts, he asserts that the public policy to fight inflation should take precedent. Rumsfeld says if wages for autoworkers are not held back, General Motors plans to push the wage increase right on to the prices of its automobiles. Boldt's optimism proves to be unfounded.

3. CONVERSATIONS DURING PHASE II: THE PAY BOARD'S INSTRUCTIONS WERE TO BRING DOWN INFLATION TO BETWEEN TWO AND THREE PERCENT BY THE END OF 1972 AND TO SET A CEILING FOR PAY RAISES AT 5.5% FOR THE LARGEST CORPORATIONS AND UNIONS

White House Tapes, Conversation 15-58 (November 20, 1971). Five days into Phase II.

Nixon and Shultz discuss their concerns about possible Pay Board resignations. Shultz describes Meany as "irascible" and "unstable." They discuss the goal of trying to isolate Meany. They also voice concern that the public members of the Board might walk off as well. If labor walks off, they discuss continuing the Board with just the public members (no business or labor). Shultz prefers to reimpose the freeze if the Board falls apart.

Nixon: "People like the freeze."

Shultz: "It isn't a question of whether or not we are at war with Meany and company. It's only a question of how to wage the war."

Nixon: "Absolutely, absolutely."

Nixon notes the necessity for a contingency plan if the Pay Board falls apart. The Board has only been operating for 5 days and it already shows signs of falling apart.[6]

White House Tapes, Conversation 15-63 (November 20, 1971)

Nixon discusses the Pay Board with John Connally. Meany and Lane Kirkland, another AFL-CIO labor union leader, have received pay raises for themselves well beyond the guidelines set by Phase II.

Nixon: "Get this Pay Board to cite Meany and the AFL-CIO for giving him and Lane Kirkland these enormous increases in violation of the guideline."

Nixon: "If labor walks out. . .why not another freeze?"

Connally agrees, and he, Shultz, and Nixon all now agree on another freeze if the Board falls apart.

White House Tapes, Conversation 15-76 (November 21, 1971)

Nixon notes that "Everybody's got to make a sacrifice" and that Meany's wage increase is not in "the spirit of things."

In an ironic twist, Shultz quotes Lord Acton's "power tends to corrupt and absolute power corrupts absolutely." Although intended for Meany, it could well apply to other political actors as well.

White House Tapes, Conversation 15-80 (November 21, 1971)

Woes with the Pay Board continue.

Nixon: "We can't get along with them [Meany and organized labor], but the question is can we do anything without them?"

Coal and dockworkers are threatening strikes, and Nixon discusses imposing Taft-Hartley, an act that gives the President the authority to intervene in strikes that threaten or create a national emergency.

Nixon: "Must not appear to be caving-in to Meany."

Shultz: "Both Senate and House committees voted for wage retroactivity."

Nixon: "So that will take us off the hook here."

Retroactivity refers to allowing wage contracts signed prior to price controls. Labor demanded that these previously agreed-to increases in wages be permitted even if they exceeded the wage guidelines. The Democrat-controlled House and the Senate will now get the blame for any inflation attributed to these wage increases.

Nixon: "We've got to be practical about things like the coal and dock [wage] settlement. Frankly, we got to just grin and bear it about those."

Coal workers would receive a 17.5% increase in their wages while the guideline called for a 5.5% ceiling on raises.

White House Tapes, Conversation 622-012 (November 22, 1971)

Nixon and H. R. Haldeman discuss Meany's 28% pay raise despite the guideline of 5.5%. Nixon cautions against sanctioning Meany at the Pay Board for fear he might walk off. Nonetheless, they tentatively decide that should Meany resign from the Pay Board, both the Labor and Business parts of the Pay Board should be disbanded. Under this scenario, the public component of the Pay Board would remain.

White House Tapes, Conversation 622-015 (November 22, 1971)

Nixon and John Ehrlichman (White House Domestic Affairs Advisor) discuss the continuing problem with Meany on the Pay Board. Ehrlichman gives a very positive view of the economy: "Everything in the way of market demand seems to be there. It's consumer pull. Loans, installment credit, consumption, retail purchases, housing starts, building permits, all those kind of things in the consumption area."

Nixon and Haldeman discuss the ongoing problem with Arthur Burns.

Nixon: "I'm really sick of Arthur, his business of beating around. Let him speak up on the money supply."

Haldeman: "The problem with Burns is... he is in a job and at a point in his life that he wants history to record he was the central banker that stopped inflation...It's damn sad."

While the economy is heating up, Nixon continues to pressure Arthur Burns to keep interest rates low and the money supply growing (Abrams, 2006; Abrams & Butkiewicz, 2012). Both Haldeman and Nixon believe Burns is obstructing Nixon's reelection campaign by holding back on monetary policy. If Burns wanted history to record that he was the central banker who stopped inflation, he failed miserably.

White House Tapes, Conversation 650-9 (January 18, 1972). Two months into Phase II.

Nixon, Burns, and Connally discuss various aspects of Phase II, the Pay Board and the Price Commission. The men identify a litany of reasons why the Pay Board will fail: exceptions (for strategic workers such as coal miners and aerospace workers), evasion (by business and small farmers), and circumvention (e.g., reclassification of employees to give raises by "promotion").

Burns pushes for Arthur Goldberg [then a private lawyer and former Ambassador to the United Nations under Lyndon Johnson] to replace Judge George H. Boldt as Chairman of the Pay Board. Burns states: "Judge Boldt is one of the finest human beings... but he has no administrative abilities or understanding and no leadership." Connally says Boldt has "an impossible job." Burns' recommendation supporting Arthur Goldberg, a Democrat, goes nowhere.

The men discuss that Nixon should maintain "distance" from the Board and Commission, despite giving them his recommendations. Connally emphasizes they are "autonomous." Nixon can always claim that it was the Pay Board's recommendation for any excessive wage increases, not his.

Connally notes: "They're apparently knowledgeable people."

The "autonomy" of the Pay Board's decisions gives Nixon plausible deniability for inflationary pay increases. Nixon makes it clear what he thinks about wage and price controls: "I'm not keen on controls ... we have to have them from a public relations standpoint."

Nixon indicates he only wants to control major enterprises and leave the small and medium sized enterprises and businesses that comprise 75% of the number of businesses exempt from reporting requirements. He indicates they still do have a "moral responsibility" to control prices.

Nixon gives an interesting assessment of small and medium-sized businesses compared to big businesses, "Main Street versus Wall Street." Main Street businesses are the "base for our support." They are "our kind of folks" (patriotic, religious, etc.).

Nixon: "The small businessman kind of believes in things, in the country, state, church and God."

The big businessmen, on the other hand according to Nixon, cares only about satisfying their boards of directors and keeping their jobs. Leaving small and medium sized businesses outside of the reporting requirements (and essentially outside of price regulations) is practical and serves to benefit a group that serves as Nixon's base of support.

Burns raises a warning about the early pay board decisions: "They are making some extravagant wage recommendations." Regarding business profit margins, Burns says they are dangerously low.

White House Tapes, Conversation 650-12 (January 18, 1972)

Nixon asks Shultz if he is as discouraged as Arthur Burns about the Pay Board. Shultz says it isn't realistic for Arthur to think the Board will be able to knock everyone's increase in wages down to 5%. He says that Arthur thought the Board was a failure in approving a 10% wage increase to the construction industry. Shultz's view was that it was a success – knocking the wage increase to 10% from the original demand of 19%. Shultz says, nonetheless, that the Board is "a shaky enough situation" and that Judge Boldt is "not a particularly good administrator." From the business side, Shultz says General Electric representative Virgil B. Day is a "wild card" and the union people "conduct a kind of guerilla warfare." Shultz tells Nixon he should plan for the eventuality that the Board breaks down.

The evidence is that wage increases are running high even with Pay Board oversight. There is a strong underlying inflationary pressure developing and this will be revealed after the price and wage controls are eventually ended.

White House Tapes, Conversation 670-5 (February 14, 1972). Three months into Phase II.

Nixon, Ehrlichman, and Shultz discuss the economic situation. Nixon mentions he has read the Louis P. Harris poll about the controls program. Shultz discusses the result.

> *Shultz*: "The danger in the situation, it seems to me is, the poll seems to say, the public doesn't feel *garbled* it's [controls] working very well."

> *Nixon*: "Exactly. ... prices aren't going down low enough."

Shultz worries that the public may lack confidence in the wage and price controls. The men interpret the poll as the public wanting a stronger regulatory response. But a stronger response, especially with regards to labor, carries potentially heavy political costs. The Teamsters' deferred wage increase ends in April and the Teamsters and Longshoremen have indicated they will demand fully the wage agreement put in place before the price controls. This increase will be substantially higher than the Pay Board's standard but preventing the wage increase risks a strike that would cripple the transportation system. Nixon notes he certainly does not want such a strike going into the final months of his 1972 reelection campaign.

The political problems in dealing with the Pay Board and the Price Commission is revealed when Nixon tells Shultz:

> *Nixon*: "Connally totally disagrees with Arthur [Burns] that the Pay Board ought to be tougher than the Price Board [*sic*]... Connally said 'Arthur can say that but how the hell can anyone who has to be elected say that'... You might do it [be tougher on wages than prices] but you damn well can't say it."

Connally is revealed to be a price hawk and Burns a pay hawk. Shultz and Nixon are politically pragmatic. Both agree that the Longshoremen and Teamster pay increase must go through in order to avoid risking a costly transportation strike.

White House Tapes, Conversation 676-12 (March 1, 1972)

John Connally meets with the President and reports that there is a general feeling that things are going to be better, and both agreed that the economy is better than they thought. Most administration officials failed to connect increasingly rapid monetary growth to increasing inflation. Connally reported positively that during the first 5 weeks of 1972, M1 grew at about 10.5% annually, and M2 was up 13.5%. In an earlier *Newsweek* column (May 3, 1971), Milton Friedman warned of increased inflation due to increased money growth, a warning rarely heard within the White House.

White House Tapes, Conversation 21-126 (March 21, 1972)

Burns' appointment as chair of the Committee on Interest and Dividends created a serious conflict of interest for the Chair of the Federal Reserve Board. Fighting inflation required slower money growth and higher interest rates.

However, the prospect of increased interest rates infuriated Nixon. Shultz reports that Burns is abroad saying he wants to get interest rates up.

Nixon: "Burns saying that is a jackass damn thing."

Shultz: "It's a terrible thing."

A few minutes later,

Nixon: "The interest rate thing is totally opposed to our policy....Arthur is in charge of the damn committee to keep interest rates down ... and here he's letting them go up. ... You can't have the chief controller advocate interest rates go up."

White House Tapes, Conversation 324-43 (March 21, 1972)
Nixon discusses the economic situation and the Pay Board with Haldeman, Connally, Rumsfeld and Colson. The CPI will be released the next day and food prices have pushed the average out of "the target range." Labor is still a problem for the Pay Board and the men discuss the possibility of reducing the Board from 15 members down to seven. One labor and one business representative would join the five members representing the public.
White House Tapes, Conversation 326-1 (March 22, 1972)
AFL-CIO President George Meany resigns from the Pay Board on this date claiming the Board is anti-labor and pro-business. Three other labor leaders resign, as do four of the business members. Meany's resignation was triggered by the Board's trimming the Longshoremen's wage increase to 14.9% from 20.9%.[7]
Nixon meets with Ehrlichman, Haldeman, Connally, Shultz, Stein, Rumsfeld and Colson to discuss Meany's resignation and how to respond.

Nixon: "We want a very strong public statement at 4 o'clock and a written statement too...If he's not going to work, we've got to kick him in the ass....He's asked for it and he's going to get it."

After discussion, cooler heads prevail, and it is decided the President's response should be "measured" and not emotional.
Herbert Stein, chair of the Council of Economic Advisors, enters. Nixon discusses with him Stein's speech on wage and price controls scheduled for the next day.

Nixon: "Simply say the wage and price control system is working."

Stein: "We will meet our goal of two and a half to three percent [inflation rate]."

The two discuss food prices, which have been rising faster than other prices.

Nixon: "Could we just put a freeze on food prices?"

Stein explains why he thinks it is a bad idea. Stein worries about the instability a food price freeze might cause. The presidential election is now less than 8 months away.

While food price inflation increased from 3% to 4.3% in 1972, overall inflation fell from 4.3% to 3.3%. However, Burns' loose monetary policy beginning in 1970 had set the stage for increased inflation during the next several years. Fig. 1 displays the CPI rate of inflation and money growth lagged 2 years. While the energy and food supply shocks exacerbated inflation in late 1973 and 1974, the link between monetary growth and inflation is clear. This is the evidence that Milton Friedman had consistently provided to support his claim that inflation is always a monetary phenomenon. Although the money-inflation connection has weakened in recent years, the relationship at that time was strong and widely recognized.

White House Tapes, Conversation 794-2 (October 9, 1972)

Nixon meets with the Quadriad comprised of Burns, Shultz, Stein, and new OMB Director Cap Weinberger. Donald Rumsfeld also attends the meeting. During this meeting, Burns opines that an incomes policy, not reduced monetary growth, was necessary to reduce inflation.[8]

> Burns: "Do you think you can escape a new inflationary spiral next year without a tough Pay Board? Without a Pay Board knocking down the wage

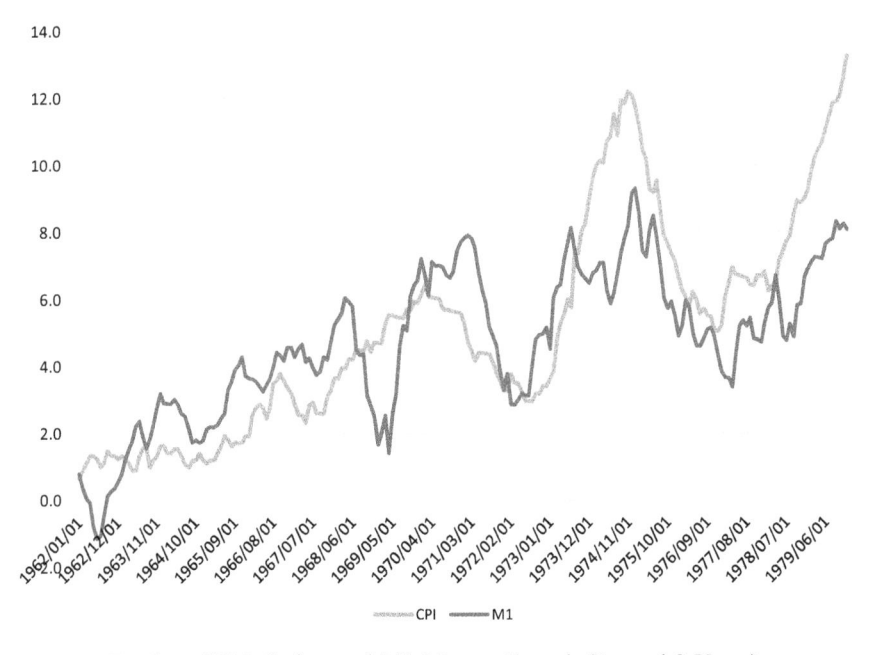

Fig. 1.   CPI Inflation and M1 Money Growth (Lagged 2 Years).

guideline from 5½ to 4, possibly 4½? And having a Price Commission
behaving in such a fashion that the Pay Board could get by, politically and
psychologically? I don't think you can."

Later in the same meeting, Donald Rumsfeld incorrectly blames continuous
inflation on the one-time price level effects of government regulations. He complains that bills passed fail to look at costs and listed government programs
increasing costs as a cause of inflation.

4. CONVERSATIONS DURING PHASE III. NIXON HAS BEEN REELECTED AND CONTROLS ARE NOW VOLUNTARY

White House Tapes, Conversation 849-1 (February 5, 1973)

Phase III begins on January 11, 1973. In February, Nixon meets with Shultz,
Stein, Roy Ash, newly appointed director of the Office of Management and
Budget, and John Ehrlichman. Stein and Shultz raise the issue of monetary
growth, with Shultz reporting that Monetarist economists have said rapid
monetary growth would increase the rate of inflation. Nixon raises the fear of a
credit crunch and how circumstances are similar to the 1969–1970 downturn.
Shultz notes that real economic growth exceeds capacity growth, so real growth
can be expected to slow. After further discussion of economic issues, Shultz
directly addresses monetary policy. He states that monetary growth has been too
high, and that Burns is conscious of this. Saying that they did not want to take
chances prior to the election, Burns had held off on raising the discount rate and
other actions. Shultz continues that tighter money now would increase interest
rates in the short run and that Burns, worried about his scheduled testimony,
wants to show that he is tough on inflation.

Nixon focuses on Burns' pending testimony. He worries that Burns will make
harmful predictions and that he needs to know how much was riding on his
testimony. Although the issue of excessive money growth was raised, the President never engages with the topic, and the issue is not addressed during the
remainder of the meeting. Money growth remains at its high level for several
more months.

In a Federal Open Market Committee meeting (March 19–20, 1973), Burns
carries forward Nixon's concern about a too-tight monetary policy be stating that
"time has come for a pause in the process of tightening." He warns that the
FOMC is in danger of carrying restraint too far and causing a recession in late
1973 or in 1974 and that it is time for a brief pause. The fed funds upper target
range was increased by a modest ¼%.

The rate of inflation falls in 1972, reaching a low of 2.9% in August, but
gradually increases through the rest of the year. The inflation rate increases
steadily throughout 1973, peaking at 8.9% in December, and averaging 6.2% for

the year, with food price inflation rising to 14.5%. Nixon's advisors reported shortly after the beginning of Phase III that inflation was falling.

White House Tapes, Conversation 413-17 (February 23, 1973)

Haldeman reports to Nixon that a Harris poll finds the public thinks the new Phase III is not strong enough, and they don't have full public confidence in Phase III. Haldeman concludes that the President doesn't want a big bureaucracy, and Haldeman doesn't know how else to do it.

White House Tapes, Conversation 420-11 (March 16, 1973)

Ehrlichman tells Nixon that Phase III is a flop. He sees it crumbling everywhere.

White House Tapes, Conversation 887-26 (March 22, 1973)

Shultz warns Nixon and Ehrlichman that Phase III is failing.

Shultz: "I think that we're in trouble with Phase III, and that we've got to think about it very hard, and we come up with something."

Nixon replies that he will have to take a political standpoint, while Ehrlichman states that they have a public relations (PR) problem.

White House Tapes, Conversation 896-6 (April 15, 1973)

Ehrlichman again focuses on improved PR as the way to promote the success of Phase III.

White House Tapes, Conversation 900-28 continued on 901-1 (April 18, 1973)

In a subsequent meeting with the Quadriad, and Ehrlichman, Burns asks to be relieved as chair of the Committee on Interest and Dividends.[9] Burns states that it takes time and energy, that it affects the prestige of the Fed, and that the Fed is pulled into a political process. Nixon wants Burns to stay on and will reconsider when things cool off.

Nixon reiterates his belief that Federal Reserve Policy needs to be expansionary to help in the next election.

Nixon: "For God's sakes the Fed has screwed us in every election. ... Let's be sure they won't do it this year. ... In 1972 the Fed came through like gangbusters."

Nixon later warns that he did not want the cost of ending inflation to be the ending of the ongoing boom in real growth, comparing the current state of the economy to its 1971 condition:

Nixon: "I remember, however, in 1971 August, when we adopted the August 15 policy ... we had a recession and inflation. Now, at this time, we have a boom and inflation. The point is that we do not want to take action now which would fail to deal with the inflation, and which would stop the boom. In other words, what we would have again is the worst of both worlds, a recession and still inflation."[10]

However, due to the lagged effects of policy, reducing monetary growth would slow the economy before slowing inflation. Nixon also states that his understanding is that there is not much agreement in the group as to what to do.

Roy Ash replies that he felt that there was not much that could be done to substantially change the fundamentals. Herb Stein agrees with Ash and opines that he didn't think anybody thought that the recent rates of inflation were going to continue. Nixon then notes that everyone agrees that the Fed is restrained but not "too damned restrained, right Arthur?" Monetary growth remains high through June.

Later in the meeting, Burns warns: "Our predictions have not been good, Mr. President. Let's just recognize that."

In a sense, Stein prediction that the recent rate of inflation wouldn't persist was correct. The rate of inflation accelerated in the ensuing months.

Herb Stein asks if Nixon plans to lead people in the direction of a return to a free market, Burns expresses his doubt in market forces in favor of the administered-price view, saying that there was no free market. "What's the use of kidding ourselves?" He continues saying that large firms, unions and farmers' organizations do what they want. The head of the Federal Reserve states that only an incomes policy, not responsible monetary policy, could control inflation.

Nixon wants to believe that the rate of inflation will come down and asked if Burns agrees.

Nixon: ". . . But folks, it's going to get better. And you've just got to tell 'em that. And, and, it just can't stay at this level. It can't do that anymore . . . You don't see 10% for the next three or four months, do you?"

Burns: "No, I don't."

The lengthy discussion turns to requiring pre-notification of price increases, anticipatory price increases, profits, energy prices and the possible effect of pre-notification on wage settlements.

Nixon concludes: "My own view is, my own view is, after hearing all this, my own view is that, that there is nothing that we should do that's really going to help, not really. That it's all marginal, on controlling inflation. . . . We do have the usual psychological problem, where we have to do something to deal with that."[11]

Earlier Nixon notes that they are fighting the "battle of the budget" due to inflation concerns. Later Nixon again stresses the importance of continuing the boom:

Nixon: "Let us do nothing in order to curb the inflation that we destroy the boom. . . . If something will work to curb the inflation. . .then let's do it."

Nixon does not want the Fed to be too restrained, so the option of reducing monetary growth is not discussed.

White House Tapes, Conversation 905-10 (April 26, 1973)

Several days later, discussing policy options such as a freeze or price rollback with Ehrlichman and Shultz, Nixon again concludes: "But when you come right down to it, George, there isn't a damn thing that will work. That's, that's my view of it."

Nixon then asks Ehrlichman's view, who suggests PR and finding a "Merchandizing Manager" for Phase III.

Nixon knows that monetary restraint would help fight the inflation problem but that would curb the economic boom and only restrain inflation later. In previous taped conversations, Nixon clearly acknowledges his knowledge of the lags associated with monetary policy.

White House Tapes, Conversation 909-3 (May 2, 1973)

During a meeting of the President, Vice-President Spiro Agnew and members of the economic team, Shultz says that monetary and fiscal conditions would not now be tightened. Rather, they would try to hold the line that was set and not tighten beyond that. Monetary growth rates remain elevated, but the monetary aggregate growth rates would begin to decrease in July. During the meeting, Burns worries about an investment boom, suggesting a variable investment tax credit as a countercyclical weapon, but he does not mention monetary growth or interest rates. As the meeting was ending, Nixon observed that the economy was booming with inflation. He restates that they need to handle the boom and restrain inflation without causing a recession. He does not want to have inflation and no boom, observing, "at least people are working."

White House Tapes, Conversation 933-3 (June 6, 1973)

Inflation, especially of food prices, is becoming a serious problem. A 2% increase in wholesale prices in May forces Nixon to explore possible actions. Nixon meets with new Chief of Staff Alexander Haig and they discuss the possibility of a 60-day freeze of prices. Haig reports that Connally would break with Nixon if Nixon didn't take dramatic economic action. Connally wants a freeze on food exports but Haig disagrees.

White House Tapes, Conversation 933-8 (June 6, 1973)

In a subsequent meeting with Nixon and Haig, new Counselor for Domestic Affairs Melvin Laird tells the President that some action now is necessary. Nixon worries that Congress will enact a 90-day freeze. Nixon believes this will not work but that he needs to preempt Congress. Laird agrees that it is better to preempt.

White House Tapes, Conversation 934-5 (June 7, 1973)

Meeting the next morning, Haig tells Nixon: "I personally think we should do a freeze." Haig says that the economists (Shultz, Stein, and John T. Dunlop, Director of the Cost of Living Council) are doctrinaire, as they apparently oppose a freeze, although Nixon wants Dunlop to manage the system to prepare for the next phase, saying Dunlop is not as doctrinaire as the others. Haig advises that a "big play" would put Nixon in a leadership position.[12] Nixon feels that a 60-day freeze would provide time to develop a good following program.

White House Tapes, Conversation 39-141 (June 7, 1973)

Speaking the same evening with Connally, Nixon says that they have a political problem due to the 2% increase in wholesale prices, and they need to make a dramatic move. Connally suggest a return to stricter Phase II controls or imposition of a second freeze, and says that a freeze would be easier. Nixon says he is considering a 60-day freeze. Connally recommends mandatory controls following the freeze, saying that inflation is not going to stop. He concludes that they do not have a free society or prices set by competitive forces. Connally espouses the administered price theory, failing to understand the true monetary cause of inflation.

White House Tapes, Conversation 935-4 (June 11, 1973)

Meeting with Haig to discuss options for the next phase of controls, Nixon says that going back to a system like Phase II would cause shortages and black markets.

White House Tapes, Conversation 935-7 (June 11, 1973)

Nixon meets with Haig, Connally, Shultz, Stein and John Dunlop to discuss plans for a second price freeze and the post-freeze controls. During the meeting, Nixon expresses his dislike of controls.

Early in this meeting, Nixon says to his economic team that there is a deep philosophical split among them due to sensitivity to political realities. One of the main issues discussed during the meeting is inflation of food prices. Bad weather and Russian grain purchases had exacerbated the increase in prices. However, during many of the conversations, inflation is attributed to supply shocks to food and fuel, ignoring the effect of aggregate demand and monetary policy. Nixon concludes that the food price increase is beyond his control and voices his dislike of controls.

> *Nixon*: "It hasn't been anybody's fault, doggone it. ... The situation is beyond our control. Let's face it. God just didn't help us...I don't want to have controls at all ... What we ought to do is get rid of all the wage and price controls. I'd love that."

Then he adds that they had to be concerned about Congress.

White House Tapes, Conversation 937-13 (June 12, 1973)

Meeting with Ash the day before the announcement of Freeze II, Nixon says that he wants as narrow of a freeze as possible, with no interest, rent, profits or wages frozen. He again takes a supply shock view, blaming food as the culprit. Ash voices his support for a freeze, saying it is bad economics but good politics. Nixon feels the food inflation has run its course and hopes to get out of the controls business if the situation improves.

White House Tapes, Conversation 938-3 (June 12, 1973)

Nixon meets with Haig, Shultz, Ash, Stein, Connally and Dunlop. The President says that he wants the post-freeze program to be close to Phase III, and that Phase III had gone quite well. He feels it had done more than the country realized. He also wanted a strong PR campaign during the freeze to get the country's attention and make people aware that they were dealing with the problem.

Nixon was clearly confounded about inflation. He wanted inflation to be controlled without ending the boom, and he wanted Phase IV to be like Phase III, even though the voluntary controls of Phase III failed.

5. CONVERSATIONS DURING FREEZE II, A FREEZE OF RETAIL PRICES ONLY

On June 13, Nixon announces a maximum 60-day retail price freeze. This includes food prices, but excludes wages, rents and farm prices.

White House Tapes, Conversation 945-3 (June 19, 1973)

Nixon and Haig discuss the length of the freeze. Shultz apparently wants a 30-day freeze, but Nixon disagrees: "I think the freeze is going to be 60 days." Nixon then adds that George is doctrinaire, and that Burns is a pain in the ass and wrong most of the time. Haig agrees that Shultz, Stein and Dunlop were doctrinaire, and this was not good, as you need to get the other side of the picture. The influence of Nixon's economists has been diminished, as political actions dominate economic concerns, even though the President himself didn't like controls.

White House Tapes, Conversation 948-12 (July 11, 1973)

Connally tells the President that the 60-day freeze is not going to be disastrous. Everyone is for the package and the program is a good program. Nixon again expresses his dislike of controls, saying the goal must be to get out of controls as soon as possible.

Taping ends.

6. CONCLUDING REMARKS

When Alexander Butterfield revealed the existence of the taping system during the Watergate hearings, Nixon had the taping system shut down on the same day, Monday, July 16, 1973, so an inside view of the end of the freeze and Phase IV decisions is not possible.

The wage and price controls that were used to fight inflation proved to be a monumental failure. The tapes reveal that Nixon and all his close advisors, except George Shultz, failed to understand the root cause of the inflation, a continuously excessive monetary policy. Even Arthur Burns believed monetary policy alone couldn't tame the inflation and advocated controls. Political form won out over economic substance. "Just say its working," Nixon told Herbert Stein to announce regarding the controls. John Ehrlichman advised the president that better public relations were needed and that they needed to find a "merchandizing manager." Nixon repeatedly expressed his disdain for controls and his belief that they wouldn't work. Yet, he embraced them at least in part for fear that the Democrat-dominated congress would seize the initiative on controls, make them permanent, and make Nixon look weak.

Nixon and his staff often focused on sectoral price increases, saying if only prices hadn't risen for food or energy their inflation goals would have been met.

Of course, during any inflation some prices will rise faster than the average. Along with energy prices, food price inflation and beef shortages were the primary concern during the first months of 1973. Nixon and most of his staff viewed the food and beef situation as a supply shock, due to Russian grain purchases and a poor harvest. A subsequent study of the 1973 food price inflation (Eckstein & Heien, 1978) found the primary cause to be domestic monetary policy.

The food-price freeze, except for beef, ended after only 35 days, on July 18. The price freeze ended as scheduled on August 12, with a ceiling on beef prices in effect to September 12. Phase IV began on August 13. However, Phase IV was stricter than Phase III for areas under control (Rockoff, 1984). There was sector-by-sector decontrol, which distorted relative prices, and by the end of Phase IV, only 12% of the CPI was under control (Blinder & Newton, 1981). Rockoff (1984) concludes that Nixon's controls imparted no permanent economic benefit on prices.

An econometric analysis of the entire controls experience by Blinder and Newton (1981), estimating two different models, find that the peak reduction of inflation occurred in February 1974, with the reduction being between −3.1% and −4.2%. One of their models finds that inflation catch up was complete by December 1975 – controls had no lasting effect on the price level. The second model finds a permanent effect of −2.4% by December 1975. However, both models find controls increased the variance of inflation, concluding that increased variance of inflation imposes the greatest social costs, making this "the most serious condemnation of controls" (p. 21).

The Federal Reserve's policymaking body, the Federal Open Market Committee, met monthly. In January through March 1973, they recommended slower monetary growth for an abatement of inflationary pressures. However, in April, they recommended moderate growth of monetary aggregates, and monetary growth rates increased. In May and June, they again recommended slower growth of the money supplies. After June 1973, money growth began a short-lived decline, as seen in Fig. 1.

Speaking on the phone with Charles Colson during the original wage-price freeze (*White House Tapes, Conversation 8-84*, September 10, 1971), Nixon promised: "We're making a commitment to the American people and the Congress that we were going to set up a system that would avoid another runaway inflation."

Why did the wage-price policies fail? Merely imposing controls without addressing underlying causes of inflation only provides a temporary cosmetic effect. Eliminating controls cause prices to rise to their market equilibrium levels. The Nixon administration made the mistake that Milton Friedman said would occur with wage and price controls. Thinking controls would limit inflation, monetary policy became more expansionary, rather than appropriately contractionary. While Shultz and Stein in one meeting did connect inflation to monetary growth, other members of the administration espoused fallacious theories of inflation, and even Shultz and Stein failed to see the coming acceleration of inflation. Nixon focused on fiscal, rather than monetary discipline. Only in his last year in office did Nixon agree to slower monetary growth to control inflation (Matusow, 1998). As seen in Fig. 1, money growth began a short-term decline in

June 1973. The economic peak came a few months later in November, followed by a recession. Inflation averaged 11% in 1974.

Money growth rates increased in the spring of 1975, followed by increased inflation in the first months of 1977. Paul Volcker finally tamed inflation, but at the cost of high unemployment. As Arthur Burns told the Federal Open Market Committee, inflation had never been reduced without causing a recession.[13] Hopefully, the lasting lesson of Nixon's wage–price controls is that not only do controls not work, but also that politicians will likely succumb to the temptation to pursue expansionary policies, exacerbating the economic damage from wage and price controls.

ACKNOWLEDGMENT

We thank Stacie Beck, David Black, Farley Grubb, Saul Hoffman, and an anonymous referee for helpful comments and suggestions.

NOTES

1. October 14, 1978. http://www.pbs.org/wbgh/americanexperience/features/primary-resources/carter-anti-inflation/
2. The figure refers to an estimated $30.8 billion increase in nominal Gross National Product.
3. Louis Rukeyser was the creator and host of the popular television program Wall Street Week that aired on Friday nights on PBS.
4. New York Times. (1971, October 10). F5. Washington Post. (1988, September 11). "Bush associate, under Nixon, surveyed Jews in BLS."
5. Abrams and Butkiewicz (2017) and Butkiewicz and Ohlmacher (2021) discuss Nixon's handling of the "damn international problem" and that it was the reason for Nixon's August 15, 1971 New Economic Policy.
6. Rocco Siciliano (2002) served as a business member on the Pay Board and provides a firsthand account of the Board's dysfunctionality.
7. New York Times. (1972, March 17). p. 1.
8. Burns discussed his meeting in his secret diary (Burns, 2010, pp. 79–80). He noted his statement regarding wage guidelines but said nothing about monetary policy.
9. Burns' request is met with garbled, but clearly astonished and laughing background comments from the other meeting participants.
10. A recession ended and an expansion began in November 1970, per the National Bureau of Economic Research's business cycle dates (https://www.nber.org/research/data/us-business-cycle-expansions-and-contractions). To Nixon, the slow decline of the unemployment rate is likely the reason he felt the economy remained in a recession.
11. In an earlier meeting Haldeman raised the inflation problem and Nixon replied that there was nothing that could be done about it except a freeze (Oval 876-5, 3/12/73).
12. A football fan, Nixon loved the "big play" analogy for momentous political acts such as his trip to China and the August 15, 1971 "Nixon shock." Thomas (2016) writes, "he loved the idea of the 'big play' that would surprise his enemies." p. 208.
13. Federal Open Market Committee. (1973, March 19–20). Memorandum of discussion (p. 108).

REFERENCES

Abrams, B. A. (2006). How Richard Nixon pressured Arthur Burns: Evidence from the Nixon tapes. *The Journal of Economic Perspectives, 20*, 177–188.

Abrams, B. A., & Butkiewicz, J. L. (2012). The political business cycle: Evidence from the Nixon tapes. *Journal of Money, Credit, and Banking, 44*, 385–399.

Abrams, B. A., & Butkiewicz, J. L. (2017). The political economy of wage and price controls: Evidence from the Nixon tapes. *Public Choice, 170*, 63–78.

Barsky, R. B., & Killian, L. (2001) Do we really know that oil caused the great stagflation? A monetary alternative. In B. S. Bernanke & K. Rogoff (Eds.), *NBER macroeconomics annual* (Vol. 16, pp. 137–183). The MIT Press.

Bernanke, B. S., & Mihov, I. (1998). Measuring monetary policy. *Quarterly Journal of Economics, 113*(3), 869–902.

Blinder, A. A., & Newton, W. J. (1981). The 1971-1974 controls program and the price level: An econometric post-mortem. *Journal of Monetary Economics, 8*, 1–23.

Burns, A. F. (2010/1972). *Inside the Nixon administration: The secret diaries of Arthur Burns* (R. H. Ferrell, Ed.). The University Press of Kansas.

Butkiewicz, J. L., & Ohlmacher, S. (2021). Ending Bretton Woods: Evidence from the Nixon Tapes. *The Economic History Review, 74*(4), 922–945.

Clarida, R., Gali, J., & Gertler, M. (2000). Monetary policy rules and macroeconomic stability: Evidence and some theory. *Quarterly Journal of Economics, 115*(1), 147–180.

Eckstein, A., & Heien, D. (1978). The 1973 food price inflation. *American Journal of Agricultural Economics, 60*, 186–196.

Federal Open Market Committee. (1973, March 19–20). *Memorandum of discussion* (p. 108).

Friedman, M. (1971, May 3). *Money explodes* (p. 81). Newsweek. https://www.proquest.com/docview/1866773834/fulltext/178DA96B629B4729PQ/86?accountid=10457&sourcetype=Magazines

Matusow, A. J. (1998). *Nixon's economy: Booms, busts, dollars, and votes.* University Press of Kansas.

National Bureau of Economic Research. (2021). https://www.nber.org/research/data/us-business-cycle-expansions-and-contractions

Nelson, E. (2022). *How did it happen? The great inflation of the 1970s and lessons for today.* Economics and finance discussion series 2022-037. Board of Governors of the Federal Reserve System. https://doi.org/10.17016/FEDS.2022.037

New York Times. (October 10, 1971). The reluctant statisticians: Some are reorganized out of their jobs (p. F5). https://www.proquest.com/hnpnewyorktimes/docview/119265909/2BB4A1C67A64164PQ/1?accountid=10457&sourcetype=Historical%20Newspapers

New York Times. (1972, March 17). Pay board reduces raise for coast dock workers (p. 1). https://www.proquest.com/hnpnewyorktimes/docview/119423546/F3AC13C6BA3B49C4PQ/1?accountid=10457&sourcetype=Historical%20Newspapers

Orphanides, A. (2003). The quest for prosperity without inflation. *Journal of Monetary Economics, 50*, 633–663.

Jimmy Carter, J. (1978, November 15). "Anti-Inflation Program." 24 October 1978. *Vital Speeches of the Day, XLV*(3), 66–69. The American Experience.

Rockoff, H. (1984). *Drastic measures: A history of wage and price controls in the United States.* Cambridge University Press.

Romer, C. D., & Romer, D. H. (2002). The evolution of economic understanding and post-war stabilization policy. In Federal reserve bank of Kansas City (Ed.), *Rethinking stabilization policy* (pp. 11–78). Federal reserve Bank of Kansas City.

Siciliano, R. (2002, May-June). The Nixon pay board – A public administration disaster. *Public Administration Review, 62*(3), 368–373.

Thomas, E. (2016). *Being Nixon: A man divided.* Random House.

Washington Post. (1988, September 11). Bush associate, under Nixon, surveyed Jews in BLS. https://www.proquest.com/docview/139406806/C88038CBAE6F4811PQ/1?accountid=10457&sourcetype=Historical%20Newspapers

White House Tapes. Richard Nixon Presidential Library and Museum, Yorba Linda, California. https://www.nixonlibrary.gov/white-house-tapes; https://prde.upress.virginia.edu/content/nixon